THE INNOVATION ILLUSION

THE

HOW SO LITTLE IS CREATED BY

INNOVATION

SO MANY WORKING SO HARD

ILLUSION

FREDRIK ERIXON
AND BJÖRN WEIGEL

YALE UNIVERSITY PRESS
NEW HAVEN AND LONDON

For information about this and other Yale University Press publications, please contact:
U.S. Office: sales.press@yale.edu   yalebooks.com
Europe Office: sales@yaleup.co.uk   yalebooks.co.uk

Typeset in Adobe Caslon Pro by IDSUK (DataConnection) Ltd
Printed in Great Britain by TJ International Ltd, Padstow, Cornwall

Library of Congress Cataloging-in-Publication Data

A catalogue record for this book is available from the British Library.

10 9 8 7 6 5 4 3 2 1

CONTENTS

PREFACE

Oddly, it was not until we began to pen this preface that it occurred to us that we have written the economic history of our own lifetime. *The Innovation Illusion* starts in the early 1970s, which also happens to be the time when both of us were born. Not that we knew much about innovation and economics then, but our journey to adolescence – in a remote place in northern Sweden once described, unfairly, as the part of the country where the sun never shines – was one of rising expectations. That period had its own economic problems, but people around us still felt the future to be a friend and that the younger generations were going to live far richer lives.

And why not? Everything seemed to work pretty fine. Schools in remote villages like ours were, unlike today, actually quite good. Libraries nested everywhere. Whatever sport you were interested in, there were public pools and centers open for most, if not all, preferences. The economy hummed along, despite mounting macroeconomic problems. Productivity growth was still fine. Real wages went up. Unemployment was low, at least in the beginning, and most young men and women who wanted to leave their parental homes could get a job and an apartment, or even own a small house. Across the world, Sweden was still seen as a utopia, and who would not like to live there?

In fact, it turned out that many Swedes did not like it. Like other parts of Europe, the country was at the tail end of the long growth cycle that started a few years after the end of World War II. Sweden had been lucky. Neutrality had shielded the country from major war damage, and all its skilled and innovative industrial companies could enjoy remarkable export growth in the following decades while the rest of Europe was still rebuilding and spending large amounts on capital, machinery and infrastructure goods. But Sweden was fraying at the edges – and its economic system was gradually consuming rather than cultivating human talent. Our parents' boomer generation entered an economy in which aspirations for human development were unleashed. The economy we got to know, however, was gradually shrinking the universe for individuals and their desire to pursue a different life than the one they were born into.

With one political party continuously in government for 32 years, the arrogance of power was wearing away people's sense of freedom. It curtailed the openness to ideas, dissent, and people who did not want their lives to be plain vanilla. Taxes had become almost oppressive. The filmmaker Ingmar Bergman left the country to become a tax fugitive in West Germany. The writer Astrid Lindgren drew the ire of the high and mighty for complaining that her marginal tax rate was 102 percent (meaning that she had to pay more in tax than she got in income for every new penny earned). Sweden was not far from introducing a hard version of a Yugoslavia-style workers' fund, which gradually would have transferred the ownership of listed companies into union-controlled funds.

We did not observe it then, but Sweden at the time was a planning machine. It was a hybrid economy, combining bits and pieces of capitalism and socialism from a smorgasbord of economic ideologies. Swedish planning, it was said, worked wonders for people, business, and the government. Prosperity required economic planning – and hordes of managers. But the heavy hand of government gradually stymied experimentation and economic initiative. Sweden was supposed to be different from other countries, but that presumption, along with the country's general faith in its exceptionalism, proved dead wrong. Swedes were neither smarter nor better than others, and once the long postwar growth boom had ended the soufflé did not rise anymore. The only way Sweden could maintain its competitiveness was to make its citizens poorer through recurring devaluations.

We grew up, became adolescent, and increasingly the secluded and managerialist nanny culture seemed to itch like a skin rash. But then came globalization – and, boy, what liberation that was for the country and us. It felt as if we had left the ice age and discovered a world with flora and fauna. The Cold War suddenly ended. Sweden sparked life into some of its ossified sectors and fossilized monopolies.

Politics changed. The economy changed. More importantly, people changed. Aspirations were unleashed again and, for us, it meant they could break free from Sweden's territorial borders, and enjoy the fruits of new global freedoms. The internet multiplied everything, not least the corporate esprit. Businesses suddenly showed a desire to become something other than the crony-based and bureaucratic operations they had developed into over several decades.

Twenty years later, after a financial crisis and the Great Recession, we are not just older but also bothered by how many of those past economic aspirations got lost along the way. Globalization has petered out, at least for now. The managerialist economy took a holiday, but unfortunately only for a while. It returned, somewhat rejuvenated – but still as an organization of man, society, and the economy that shelters excessive bureaucracy and numbs characteristics of a vibrant and innovative economy: eccentricity, ingenuity, and entrepreneurship. Perhaps it is just us, but does it not feel as if you need a social disorder these days to break free from the economic culture in order to pursue really innovative change?

Sweden is not the odd one out, but part of a Western phenomenon, embraced by the corporate as well as the political sector. Bureaucracy bulges everywhere – and along with it, its vices of defensiveness and putting comfort first. Today, the West is anxious about the world, fearful of the future, and nostalgic about the past. Its politics has expanded from redistribution to retribution, and the populist revolt behind that shift blames foreigners, multinationals, and politicians for having changed society beyond recognition. Poor economic expectations and rising income inequality have fueled the suspicion that the "elite" has prospered at the expense of workers, and – unfortunately – there is some truth in that view. The rentier economy that has evolved over the past decades has gradually depressed the economy. With low productivity and economic growth, a business sector that hides from competition, and political leaders that pursue excessive and highly complex regulations, economic opportunity gets lost.

There is a larger drama behind that change. The Western economic principle is no longer capitalism, at least not in the way we used to think about it. In its current version, capitalism no longer carries many promises of human development and improved economic expectations. Its future feels cloistered, as if it is playing the blues in an air-conditioned room, if you remember the nightmare from the film of *The Blues Brothers*. It no longer champions that go-getting spirit and optimism about the future that defined its past. The rentier economy instead weakens the conditions for economic experimentation, entrepreneurship and contestable competition. In such an economy, expectations about fast and furious innovation are, at best, illusions. At worst they cause a political reaction that reinforces the barriers to a dynamic economy.

The future of capitalism is not apocalyptic, but it is not spawning economic and human development in the way it used to, or in the way it could. This book is not intended as a contribution to the long series of economic horror stories, but it delivers an uncomfortable message. The current woes of the economy have been in the making for a long time. They started around the time we were born. Now capitalism needs intensive care. But that is hopefully not its end. After all, the book is about our economic lifetime – and, if we are lucky, we are not even halfway through it yet.

ACKNOWLEDGMENTS

We are in debt to many people. Like every other book, *The Innovation Illusion* builds on previous work and experiences we have gained in different capacities. Several colleagues and clients have in the past two decades helped us to shape much of our understanding of the economy and building businesses. They are too many to mention, but they all deserve our gratitude.

In this book, we draw heavily on a vast amount of excellent research in economics, business administration, and public policy. While our own research for this book has spanned more areas than we first imagined, we have often found that we have been drawn to some special communities of scholars. The work by Luigi Zingales, Raghuram Rajan (before he left to head the Reserve Bank of India), Chad Syversen and their colleagues at the University of Chicago Booth School of Business has been a source of knowledge and inspiration, especially their research on finance, corporate governance, and productivity. Edmund Phelps and his colleagues at Columbia University's Center on Capitalism and Society have provided us with thought-provoking research and opinions in the territory of economics and culture. The McKinsey Global Institute and the Boston Consulting Group have business thinkers that inspired us with insights into business administration and corporate value creation. W. Chan Kim, Renée Mauborgne, and James C. Collins expanded our understanding of uncertainty and business performance. Trade economists like Richard Baldwin, Jagdish Bhagwati, Gene Grossman, and Anthony Venables have helped to shape much of our core thinking about companies and globalization. Recent work by Pol Antràs and others on trade, contracts, and industrial organization have also encouraged our thinking. In Europe, economists at the London School Economics and the OECD have been valuable sources for our work, not the least on trade, wages, inequality, and productivity. There is plenty of interesting research on digital innovation and how it is reshaping some markets and economies. Erik Brynjolfsson and Andrew McAfee and their colleagues at the MIT Sloan School of Management and the MIT Center for Digital Business deserve a particular mention. Likewise, Robert Gordon's work on productivity and American prosperity – in some ways the antithesis to Brynjolfsson and McAfee's work – has given us an extraordinary number of insights.

Throughout the work on this book we have been reminded of the significance of many classical or political economists in the nineteenth and twentieth centuries. There are few roads to understanding business and the economy that do not stop by Karl Marx, Joseph Schumpeter, and Friedrich Hayek. One can dispute their politics, but their insights into the economy are instructive for a contemporary student in that field. Similarly, when we have reread works by scholars like John Kenneth Galbraith, Alexander Gerschenkron, and Susan Strange, to name just three, we have been struck by their insights. Much of the work on corporate governance, business development and strategy that we have covered has felt like a bland version of the original thought, which often came from Peter Drucker, Michael Porter, Henry Minzberg, Philip Kotler, and Igor Ansoff. There are several thinkers today that can be put in the same category. If you get bored by all those who just repeat the conventional wisdom about the economy and how it evolves, pick any work from these economic thinkers and you will immediately fire up: David Autor, Tyler Cowen, Deirdre McCloskey, Malcolm Gladwell, David Graeber, Deepak Lal, Joel Mokyr, Matt Ridley, Richard Sennett, Robert Solow, Lawrence Summers, and Peter Thiel. Their works have contributed to our thinking for this book. Likewise, there are many successful investors and entrepreneurs whose thinking about innovation and business creation have inspired us. Innovation happens through entrepreneurship and it is impossible to grasp innovation without understanding the business motivations behind it. In reality, books like ours cannot substitute for studies of successful entrepreneurs like Warren Buffett, Steve Jobs, Jeff Bezos, Elon Musk, and Sam Walton, and the business environment they and others created in their respective firms.

More people than we can mention have generously taken the time to talk through particular issues with us or showed us the power of new technology and innovative business ideas. We are particularly grateful to a group of friends who have read, commented and in other ways helped us with various versions of the manuscript. Kurt Geiger, Guy de Jonquières,

Mats Langensjö, Janerik Larsson, Philippe Legrain, Nicklas Lundblad, Johan Norberg, Jorge Sà, Razeen Sally, Karl Wennberg, and Carl-Johan Westholm have all helped to make our ideas and the manuscript much better. Three anonymous reviewers of our initial synopsis also helped to chart the direction of our argument.

Yale University Press and Taiba Batool, our editor, deserve a special mention. We are very grateful that they accepted our proposal to write this book. Yale University Press was our first priority when we started to look for a publisher, and we are still surprised that they readily accepted a proposal that clearly erred on the contrarian side of the argument over innovation and capitalism. Taiba Batool has acted beyond the call of duty and made this book so much better than we could have done without her guidance. Ann Bone did an excellent job in cleaning the manuscript from bad grammar, inconsistencies, and errors.

Our work colleagues have been patient with us during the years that this book has been work in progress. We are fortunate to have colleagues who not just share our desire for contrarian thinking, but also understand that writing a book cannot be combined with normal work and office life. In the first period of our work, Maria Salfi provided us with excellent research assistance.

The final thanks go to our families – Tove, Arthur and Albert (Fredrik's family) and Anna-Karin, Oliver, Alexander and Cordelia (Björn's family). They have all been extraordinarily supportive and accepted that we have spent evenings, weekends and, last summer, weeks with each other rather than with them.

Fredrik Erixon and Björn Weigel
Brussels/Stockholm, June 2016

1

INTRODUCTION

That so few now dare to be eccentric, marks the chief danger of the
time.

John Stuart Mill, *On Liberty*

Is capitalism really what we think it is?

Modern capitalism is like a painted ceiling in a cloistered cathedral, depicting the illusion of a clear blue sky. Corporate and political leaders in the West project an image of capitalism as a borderless space, restless for change and impatient for innovation. The reality, though, is that capitalism is trembling under the weight of bureaucratic and conformist corporations with few instincts left for radical innovation. Just as in John Stuart Mill's quest for liberty and individuality, there is too little eccentricity in our economy, with far too few who refuse, as Mill put it, to "bend the knee to custom."[1]

While many boast about their aptitude for innovation, the actions of investors, managers and legislators suggest that capitalism has become dull and hidebound. Companies chase efficiency gains and progressively make goods and services a bit better and cheaper. However, their ambition to build business on the back of innovation seldom moves beyond a "me too" adaptation of products, and their focus has largely shifted from frontier innovation to incremental development. Rising prosperity in most quarters of the world means there are more people chasing new and brilliant ideas, and that more money than ever is spent on scientific research. But innovation is about output, not input – not visions but results. And that takes us to one of the Western world's key economic problems today: there is too little breakthrough innovation, not too much, and the capitalist system that used to procure eccentricity and embrace ingenuity all too often produces mediocrity.[2]

The paradox, though, is that it does not feel like this. Dazzled by all the new technology, many feel like passengers on an unstoppable train that can only accelerate. And that is not an altogether sanguine future, portending only positive expectations about how life will change. People worry about not measuring up to new technology. Many already find it taxing to conform to 24/7 online demands, to keep up with a constant email flow, social media, and ever growing demands to improve efficiency.

People in the West are increasingly unhappy with their jobs. The Conference Board, an economics consultancy, suggests that dissatisfaction with work in the United States has been growing for several decades and that a majority of the workforce is now dissatisfied rather than satisfied with their jobs.[3] Academic research confirms that that job satisfaction in the US has been on a downward trend since the 1970s.[4] This trend challenges the usual perceptions about what drives job satisfaction, such as pay or job security. While they are important, surveys suggest that job satisfaction, in the United States at least, is also linked to economic dynamism, productivity growth, and economic opportunity. Although workers are materially better off today than they were in the 1960s, and have safer working environments, many are afforded fewer economic opportunities and consequently have lower aspirations.

Research by the pollster Gallup confirms the observation. More than half of workers in North America and Western Europe are "not engaged" at work, with about one-fifth being "actively disengaged," making them not just unproductive but sources of workplace negativity. Alarmingly, no more than one in seven workers in Europe are "psychologically committed to their jobs," and therefore they are unlikely "to be making positive contributions to their organizations."[5] Reduced engagement has many sources, but one is the widening gap between the expectations of work efficiency, which are growing, and falling hopes for an improved life and higher payment as a consequence of being more efficient. Many people in the West feel they are working longer, harder, and faster – but that they are running to stand still. If the pace of today's economy is already out of control, they may ask, where will it all end?

The feeling is understandable, because everything seems to be accelerating and new technology has a great impact on the way we live our lives. Many things that can go digital now do and we are invariably surprised by how many goods and services actually make that journey into the cyber economy. Less than ten years ago, the mobile phone was by and large a device used to perform the same service as when Alexander Graham Bell made that historic first telephone call in 1876. Smartphones were on the market; busy members of the corporate class carried BlackBerry clip cases on their belts. However, 80 percent of the time mobile phones were still used to make or receive calls, or to send or receive text messages.[6]

Today the smartphone is the social secretary of modern society, connecting us to the app economy, helping to access news, pay bills, warm up the car, order food, book train tickets and gym classes, or connect with friends and family. People across the world use smartphones and tablets to improve work efficiency and to organize their lives. These devices are reshaping the way some markets work, especially media and games. In 2020, 4 billion people, or 80 percent of the adult population, are expected to own and use a smartphone. The world, to borrow from *The Economist* magazine, will be a "planet of phones."[7]

Advances in technology are not just confined to the mobile sector. Many discoveries and innovations coming out of science labs are astonishing. Isaac Asimov in 1964 predicted a world of robots, and cars with "robot brains"; this no longer seems like science fiction.[8] Driverless cars can now be seen on American roads – and the flying car may soon become a reality. Commercial and affordable space flights can be a reality in the next decade. Our generation, born in the 1970s, may live to see the first human mission to Mars.

Medical devices are also experiencing a revolution. Advanced surgery can now be done by robots, observed and managed remotely by a surgeon. A patient can be monitored with the assistance of a mobile phone. There is already enough technology to fill a do-it-yourself style warehouse for healthcare diagnostic gadgets. If you want to control your general health conditions, you can purchase a Jawbone bracelet. If you suffer from rheumatoid arthritis, you can implant SetPoint's nerve stimulator and download the tablet app to manage it. If you are worried about colon cancer, you no longer have to wait for an appointment with a cancer specialist: you can use PillCam's digestive track sensor to screen for it. If all these technologies are already available today, imagine what innovations the world will relish once the development of nanotechnology, artificial intelligence (AI), biomedicine, robotics, and digitalized information has gathered pace. It is clear that we are not in Kansas anymore.

Electronic devices will soon be able to communicate with each other and perform everyday services in real time, without our command or even knowledge. Data, like money, never sleeps. When it reaches the "second half of the chessboard,"[9] to use a phrase from techno futurists, the exponential growth of computer capacity can disrupt life, technology, and markets far faster than in the past. Experts quarrel about the exact date, but in a few decades they say we will reach the point of technological singularity. That is when artificial intelligence will outsmart human intelligence. Robots will then not just beat us at chess but recursively improve themselves and constantly develop their own skills in a way that humans can no longer control. Artificial intelligence will represent an intelligence that the best human brains of this world cannot even fathom. "Man is something that shall be overcome," declared Friedrich Nietzsche, and that pledge now seems closer to reality than ever before.[10]

Technological singularity is therefore the point of no return for the human species, at least if you believe some technology dystopias. Artificial intelligence, at this point, will surpass our wildest imagination and robots will render us obsolete. Equipped with advanced cognitive skills they will perform very complex tasks – and not just routinized or highly patterned ones. Perhaps the robot vacuum cleaner will not just dust the house but also finish the crossword puzzle you could not solve and help your children with their homework. Better at solving problems, no doubt, but a far more challenging prospect for humans is that robots will also be more creative and innovative, perhaps even better lovers.[11] Inventor Clive Sinclair argues that "once you start to make machines that are rivalling and surpassing humans with intelligence, it's going to be very difficult for us to survive." In other words, resistance is futile and, for Sinclair, AI dominance "is just an inevitability." Steve Wozniak, one of Apple's founders, is equally gloomy and suggests that humans "will be the family pets," or possibly the "ants that get stepped on" in the New Machine Age.[12] Today, Americans fear robots more than death.[13]

It is not surprising that people are both fascinated and frightened. For many of us, this is not just a weird sci-fi future, but – just like life in Thomas Hobbes's state of nature – one that appears "solitary, poor, nasty, brutish, and short." Some brilliant minds suggest that artificial intelligence is a far bigger threat to humanity than nuclear war and bioterrorism. An American tech thinker suggests we have already stepped into a world when technological progress behaves like Lord Voldemort, leader of the racist Death Eaters in the *Harry Potter* books.[14] Robots and machine intelligence will not only substitute for highly skilled labor, they will obliterate the comforting notion that education always makes labor competitive and employable, regardless of the pace of technological change. Work as we know it will be a thing of the past. Demand for human labor will sink to an all-time low.

Some think this world will be deeply unequal, materially as well as psychologically. In the emerging technofeudal society, all the economic benefits will go to the top, or those who own the robots. Demoted to the economic netherworld, labor will be poor and have nothing but leisure time. One of the greatest future challenges for humankind, argue some tech philosophers, is how to avoid a completely sedentary lifestyle. How will humans be stimulated, challenged, or provoked when the machines have put us all at risk of being turned into obese, lonely and numb vassals? High on vacuous soap entertainment and blinded by social media, many in this world may long for software to recode humans into robots.

The planning machine

But is this really a convincing vision of our future? We believe not. As in the past, innovation will by and large make societies better and more prosperous. While we take a pessimistic view of innovation today, our pessimism is about the falling level of dynamism in our economy, not technology itself. Dystopian visions of technology and what it will do to societies are a genre that is as old as technological change itself, and modern history is littered with thinkers who made patently false claims about the future of technology. Many technology futurists – pessimists as well as optimists – get technology and innovation wrong because they have a misguided, almost machine-like idea of how the economy works. They think of technology and the economy in a way that resembles the planned economy, where economic renewal happens just because better technology emerges. However, just because one input of the economy (technology) gets changed, it does not follow that economic behavior will improve.

Consider the case of Stafford Beer, an international management consultant, cybernetic genius, and creator of Cybersyn.[15] In a way, Beer's story is not much different from that of other business consultants working to improve economic organizations with the help of powerful computers, advanced algebra, and big data. Like other experts on cybernetics, an interdisciplinary field of research about control and communication, Beer's philosophy of economic management drew on psychology and how the brain works. For him, an organization behaves like a living organism. To avoid Darwinian extinction, it has to develop "techniques for survival in a changing environment" by adapting itself to "economic, commercial, social and political surroundings and learn from experience."[16]

Beer created a complex intellectual system based on assumptions about human and organizational behavior. Computer technology was at the heart of his philosophy of organizational communication, enabling the construction of systems to network information. Beer's sociotechnical system had the Orwellian name of the Liberty Machine. It allowed organizations to flexibly bundle information together and distribute the authority to make decisions to the workforce. Together with a Viable System Model, which connected autonomous parts of an organization, the Liberty Machine formed part of the Cybersyn project. Its objective was to marry together the need for centralized control with decentralized decision making.

Cybersyn, named after *cyber*netics and *syn*ergy, was a system to map and manage organizational and human behavior with the help of technology and access to data. The center of this cyber universe was the operations room, packed with screens monitoring production and with technology to automate production forces. Beer wanted to create organizations that were responsive to various economic signals affecting production. Although Cybersyn and its ops room have made people associate Beer with a military command-style organization, he defended it as a way to create decentralized organizations where labor, not management, controlled data flows and, consequently, managed their own work.

Today Beer's story is not unique; computer technology and software have reshaped production in many commercial areas. Networked information flows between autonomous parts of production are basic elements in standard, run-of-the-mill business information technology (IT) services. Most modern companies of size have automated information flows in their production and logistics, and these flows will prompt action even if there is no human being to command it.

But Beer's Cybersyn was not a product of Silicon Valley, the MIT Media Lab, or other places where big-data business models grow and artificial intelligence develops. He was not hired by Elon Musk, founder of SpaceX, nor in the employment of NASA or the University of Oxford's Future of Humanity Institute. He never had a Facebook account, and never tweeted his cybernetic vision. The long-bearded, Rolls-Royce driving Beer is fascinating because he is a product of history rather than the future. He died in 2002 and his grand cybernetic model was created over 40 years ago.

Cybersyn was not a project to improve corporates or capitalism. In fact, it was quite the opposite. Cybersyn carried a Chilean identity and was designed for President Salvador Allende's socialist government to monitor nationalized companies. It aimed to move ownership of production into the hands of workers. Launched in the early 1970s, Cybersyn attempted to marry cybernetics and socialism. It was a "planning machine"[17] – socialism with a digital face – a vision for creating a participatory socialism far distant from its authoritarian cousin in the Soviet Union. Its economic purpose was to repair one core defect of socialism, its "calculation problem": that bureaucrats cannot beat the market in channeling information from consumers to producers about what they actually want to buy. Cybersyn, therefore, was the socialist calculation to end all socialist calculations.

That is a Herculean task. Older economists of similar convictions had struggled to find ways for socialist economies to match supply with demand. Oscar Lange and Abba Lerner, famous economists around the time of World War II, had toyed with different systems of "market socialism" to substitute for bureaucrats in deciding what to produce. Several scions of socialism with an understanding of economics sometimes argued that socialism could only work if computers were strong enough to amass the information needed for producers to know what consumers wanted.

A member of the Fabian Society, the grande dame of British socialism, Beer thought he had the solution. From Beer's operations room, government managers could get real-time updates and respond directly to events disturbing production like a lack of resources due to coordination failures. Cybersyn was not a wholesale alternative to markets, but powerful computers with advanced software could network information better than the market and therefore become a superior coordinator of the economy. It was a utopian idea – and as with so much of technology futurism, the utopians behind Cybersyn were far more excited by the technology itself rather than trying to understand how technology interacts with individuals and societies. Capitalism, they thought, was not necessary to stimulate technological change or provoke innovation – pushing buttons was.

That character has not gone away. A good part of current technology futurism, especially from the prophets of the New Machine Age, charts a vision of technology and the economy that resemble the economic philosophy of the planning machine. While it seldom takes so extreme a form as Beer's fantasy, it builds on the same machine-like notions about how technology changes the economy and society. Contemporary scholars and thinkers about the future of technology often stumble into that line of thinking, assuming it is just a matter of time before idiosyncratic and erratic human behavior is replaced by smarter machines. Technological progress is considered inevitable. Quite often, innovation and technology are discussed as autonomous forces with not just a direction but also a clear idea of their destination.

Technology pessimists argue in a similar way. Physicist Jonathan Huebner, for instance, suggested in a much-debated paper that innovation peaked in 1873. According to Huebner, "we are at an estimated 85 percent of the economic limit of technology, and it is projected that we will reach 90 percent in 2018 and 95 percent in 2038."[18] Current and future innovation gains, he suggests, are limited by both economics and physics. And he is not alone. The low level of economic dynamism in the Western economy has prompted some observers to blame Western societies for lack of inventiveness or a falling appetite for new knowledge and innovation. In their view, it is technology, not the economy, that fails.

The idea, or zeitgeist, of the planning machine connects with old thinking rooted in Descartes and Francis Bacon's scientific civilization, with an open path from science to innovation, or from technology to the economy. Nassim Taleb, the New York University professor and author of *The Black Swan*, calls it the "Soviet-Harvard illusion" – the superiority, or primacy, of scientific knowledge and the religious belief in rationalism as a way to understand and change society.[19] Technological shifts are embraced for their revolutionary character, or unyielding ability to crush existing social and economic orders in their march through society. The relation between technological and economic change is like a beeline. In this view, it is technology that defines the shape and direction of the economy and society.

There are many ideological variants of this proposition. Several pundits have been quick to declare the death of capitalism with the arrival of the new digital age, assuming there will no longer be any need for an economic system that can bring profitable order out of spontaneous and unpredictable behavior. While this is an old fantasy of the utopian left – and a staple perception of the socialism that guided turn-of-the-century writers like H.G. Wells or the icon of America's socialists, Edward Bellamy – capitalism didn't perish, but rather anchored itself deeper in society as people and business prospered on new waves of technology.

However, this time it is different, or so we are told. Tech thinker Kevin Kelly has prophesied the rise of a new form of socialism as a consequence of open source technology and community-generated content.[20] Capitalism is a highly adaptive creature, argues the contrarian economic reporter Paul Mason, but it is not going to survive the current revolution in information technology.[21] Information, he argues, will destroy the price mechanism and new forms of collaborative production will do away with what is left of market capitalism.

On the other side of the ideological fence, the passion for technological determinism also thrives. "The Goliath of totalitarianism will be brought down by the David of the microchip," mused conservative icon Ronald Reagan,[22] who drew heavily from technology enthusiasts like George Gilder, an economist who later identified the billion-transistor chip as the cure to root out all economic evil.[23] A British libertarian politician has predicted that the new digital age will be the end of politics.[24] Neoconservatives similarly were quick to embrace the revolutionary promise of technology. In his thought-provoking but often misunderstood book *The End of History and the Last Man*, Francis Fukuyama charted the idea of a progressive relationship between technology in modern consumption culture and capitalism. It was the "ultimate victory of the VCR," he argued, to have homogenized the world upon liberal economic principles.[25] Twenty-five years later, after a crushing ideological defeat for the revolutionary view of new technology, Twitter was proposed as a contender for the Nobel Peace Prize. Microblogging, argued conservative cognoscente Michelle Malkin, would crumble Iran's theocracy "one Tweet at a time."[26]

While technological optimism is commendable, this is where it is time to part ways with modern tech determinists and their expectations about revolutionary change. They are portraying an idea of human beings and the economy as they hope them to be, but not as they are. They have a misguided view of technological change, neglecting its evolutionary character and rather slow progress through the economy. Importantly, technological change does not always lead to innovation because the two are not the same thing. Undoubtedly there are fascinating and sometimes breathtaking technological advances, and new technology will continue to surprise us in the future. Yet the expectation of revolutionary change is bound to disappoint, and the fear it often induces is misguided. Both the expectation and its opposition thrive on an illusion.

Being overly optimistic about the state of innovation today, or worrying about the prospect of innovation stealing our jobs, ignores discouraging realities in the modern economy. There is no shortage of new goods and services being put on the market, and in many ways innovation follows the Woody Allen principle of orgasms: the worst one is still great. Many innovations of the past decade have supported individual freedom and spurred choice, and we are much better off because of them. Yet the Western economies have slowed in their capacity to generate innovation that substantially restructures markets and improves productive behavior. The central worry should not be either no innovation or too much innovation, these are illusory projections: it is rather that the modern way of capitalism and regulation has reallocated money from big or radical innovation to incremental and economically uninspiring innovation.

In reality, innovation is defined by the economy and the capitalist system's ability to propel the diffusion of adaptation and economic renewal.

Innovation flourishes when it brings new opportunities for individual freedom, dignity, and welfare – when it connects with economic systems promoting such results. New technologies that cannot embed themselves in the structure of markets and industry, or in the way an economy works, hardly ever succeed.

This is why our concern about declining innovation is primarily about capitalism. Just as the West's economic takeoff in the late eighteenth century and early nineteenth century was a combination of technological progress and foundational economic and societal changes, the quest for innovation today is equally to do with the laws, practices, and market order that define economies. In other words, to comprehend the prospect for innovative change, it is first necessary to understand current capitalism and the way that Western economies evolve, and have evolved in the past decades. And, for us, that is not a happy story. The problem is not that capitalism is pushing societies to the cusp of fast and furious technological change, but that it is continuing its slowdown in the progress of innovative change. The chief reason behind the vapid performance of Western economies has less to do with what happens in tech labs than with the drama of capitalism as it has unfolded in the past decades. In our view, the existential challenge of today's capitalism is to break a habit of corporate and political reluctance to foster, transact and diffuse big innovation.

The problem is not about the limits of knowledge and human ingenuity – we are just as inventive as in the past, if not more so. The main story of the innovation illusion is the changing character of capitalism: the way the private corporate sector has evolved, often as a consequence of legislative and regulatory action, and how economies are changing because of factors like demography, globalization, and financialization. For the economy, innovation has always been more about what happens outside science labs than inside them. The economic power of innovation is not really about invention, but contestability and adaptation: how labor, investors, companies, and governments are pushed to improve their performance. And in the past three decades, the capitalist innovation engine has not been pushing much at all. To see why, let us turn to the health of Western capitalism.

Bound capitalism

Western capitalism is not in good health. For a simple diagnosis, just look at the West's saturated corporate sector: it is brimming with cash but glaringly short of ideas for how to use excess capital to grow companies and innovate markets. Or consider the pace of corporate renewal in Europe. In

Germany's DAX-30 index of leading companies, only two were founded after 1970. In France's CAC-40 index there is only one.[27] In Sweden, 30 of the 50 biggest companies were created before the start of World War I in 1914 and the remaining 20 were founded prior to 1970.[28] If you compile a list of Europe's hundred most valuable companies, none were actually created in the past 40 years.[29] America is different, but less different from Europe than it used to be. Indicators of capitalist renewal generally encapsulate a dreary trend in Western economies: they have lost much of their past savor for growth and dynamism. Their current passivity has nothing to do with the failure of governments and central banks to lift demand. That case could have been made a few years ago. Now, however, Western economies fail because the corporate and political sectors have dampened their aptitude for economic renewal. The chief economic problem of the West is its weak supply side, not its demand side.[30]

However much big companies on key stock indices are admired for their business acumen, Western capitalism has turned into a club with lifetime membership rights, where no one signs out. Like all other treasured and preserved societies, when no member makes an exit in corporate clubland, no one new gets in. Or alternatively, where nothing gets destroyed, hardly anything new is created. For new things to grow, "first, some things must wither," if you remember the economic gardening class by Mr. Chance, played by Peter Sellers, in the film *Being There*. Withering, as all of us middle-aged people unfortunately know, is never agreeable, but it is a central part of the capitalist ecology.

The history of economic progress is therefore one of many entrepreneurial failures. In a way, the unique character of modern capitalism is its ability to encourage economic experimentation despite poor odds of success. Take start-ups. Over 95 percent of all start-up investments fail to deliver projected returns, and as many as 30–40 percent burn all invested capital and completely fail, says Harvard Business School's Shikhar Ghosh.[31] What is even more striking is that many of them fail for the same reason, probably leading some to suspect that capitalism confirms the definition of insanity often attributed to Albert Einstein – doing the same thing over and over again, but expecting different results. Of all the internet start-ups, for example, three-quarters fail because of "premature scaling" alone, according to the Start-up Genome Report.[32] Yet here we are, with rising venture capital investment in internet start-ups – many of them rushing to scale up their businesses faster than the others.

Joseph Schumpeter, the Austria-born economist, argued along the same lines and, partly inspired by German scholar Werner Sombart, portrayed the capitalist innovation process as "a perennial gale of creative destruction." For Schumpeter, creation and destruction was part of the same process of economic renewal. In fact, in his "vision of capitalism" the entry of new technologies and entrepreneurs, and the exit of the old, was the central dynamo of progression.[33] Capitalism, in this school of thought, is not a reflection of the way Karl Marx had treated capital accumulation; a capitalist is not necessarily someone who is rich. Nor is it a synonym for a market society where competition is free and the market process determines prices. Capitalism is about the private ownership of firms. However, the actual attributes of the owner are equally important and, in capitalism, they are chiefly defined by vibrant entrepreneurship, rapid adaptation, and a culture of experimentation. In other words, what defines the capitalist is his or her disposition for economic dynamism and renewal – supporting both creation and destruction of technology, capital, and jobs.

For Schumpeter, innovation and capitalism are thus part of the same economic grammar; they are almost alternative expressions of the same phenomenon. Capitalism is a system for constant innovation, and for innovation to happen there has to be an economic system promoting entrepreneurial contestability and change. Modern definitions of innovation – and there are many – tend to look at it differently. Economists often think about innovation as invention or technology. In politics there is plenty of talk about establishing "tech incubators" or promoting "triple helix" models of collaboration between universities, businesses, and governments to drive innovation. Others are envious and want to copy the culture of Silicon Valley. While all these factors are important, the essence of Schumpeter's approach is that the concept of innovation is useless unless new technologies, combinations of products and technologies, production processes, or business models force markets to adapt through diffusion, adaptation, and imitation. A new invention is an input, but innovation is about output.

Capitalism and innovation are part of the same zeitgeist, and the perception of runaway innovation that guides today's debate about the Western economy is an illusion because far too many parts of our economies have become shielded from the real attributes of capitalism. Schumpeter's composite vision highlights capitalist dynamism. It is part of a market society, but it is not just any market economy. Capitalism is based on informal and formal institutions, and a culture of individualism, and it is thus embedded in a larger political and economic culture that promotes a spirit of constant renewal.

Schumpeter is the start, and not the end, of an inquiry into innovation and the economic institutions that feed or starve it. His views on innovation and capitalism have been criticized, and sometimes for good reasons. In the latter part of his academic career Schumpeter developed a rather dystopian vision of the future of capitalism. Like Karl Marx and Friedrich Engels in the *Communist Manifesto*, Schumpeter thought that societies could not stand the inequities and constant demand for change that followed on the heels of capitalism.[34] Capitalism, he argued, plants the seed of its own extinction and is "being killed by its achievements."[35] In the end, capitalism will innovate itself to death.

Schumpeter got the future of capitalism wrong, but the ethos that he, Marx, and other classical political economists described as the essence of capitalism and innovation is also our definition of capitalism. In fact, it is central to the entire book – it defines our narrative and the arguments we put forward. It also guides the way we select what is important and what is less important for a discussion about innovation in Western economies today. This book aims to step beyond individual examples or anecdotes about innovation and take account of the degree of innovation in the economy at large. Our quest is to understand to what extent modern innovation actually contests markets, or forces radical adaptation on businesses, labor, and governments.[36] Consequently, there are many aspects of innovation that are not covered for the simple reason that they are distant from what this book is all about: the intimate relation between capitalism and innovation.

Following Schumpeter's four-stage approach to innovation – invention, innovation, diffusion, and imitation – we are chiefly concerned with the latter three stages where capitalist adaptation happens, or not. Obviously, inventions such as new technologies are central for economies to improve their performance and to raise prosperity. However, it is not the technological attributes of new inventions that define their own economic impact or determine their own commercial success or failure. From an economic point of view, the really interesting part of new technologies is whether they prompt investors, companies, labor, and markets to change, or whether these factors and organizations of production resist the absorption of new inventions.

There is a historical point to be made, and one that can help in better understanding the concept of innovation that guides this book. What separates our time from eras in the past is not more or less creation of new technologies or our ability to imagine new inventions. The difference goes much deeper than that. Take technologies like tidal mills, the hourglass, blast furnaces, quarantine, eyeglasses, and the printing press. They are all examples of technologies used in Europe during the Middle Ages. And think about all the inventions that the same part of the world could import around the same time: paper, navigational instruments, the spinning wheel, wind power, and Arabic numerals.[37] What came out of all these new discoveries?

If the yardstick is per capita economic growth, the answer is "not much." England, for instance, had only 0.19 percent growth per annum between 1270 and 1700.[38] Gregory Clark disputes such optimistic figures and argues rather convincingly that real wages actually were *higher* in 1200 than in 1800, or later in that century, because societies were caught in a "Malthusian trap" with stagnant incomes and growing populations. "The average person in the world of 1800," says Clark, "was no better off than the average person of 100,000 BC."[39]

Malthusian trap or not, for hundreds if not thousands of years it was almost as if an invisible force was keeping humanity away from prosperity. Technologies were invented and imported, but they did not ripple through the economy and lift welfare. Nobel laureate Edmund Phelps captured the paradox in his recent book *Mass Flourishing*, and provided an illuminating example of the stagnant economies of the Middle Ages. In 1300, 58 bushels of grain were produced in a certain area in England, and a few hundred years later, in 1770, an equal amount of worker hours managed to produce 79 bushels. Productivity improved by only 21 bushels in 470 years, which amounts to *one* extra bushel every 22 years.[40]

If the difference between premodern and modern eras of growth can be reduced to one word, it is capitalism. Starting a quarter-millennium or so ago, it emerged during a period of profound change in the social fabric of the Western world. A product of the Enlightenment and that era's new ideas and institutions, capitalism was midwifed by economic and societal reforms that brought a greater degree of economic freedom to isolated territories of the economy. And that expansion of freedom gave people permission to challenge the established order, including markets and their incumbents. It allowed societies, and not just the privileged elite, to flourish. It gave birth to a grand modernization of entrepreneurship.[41]

The new form of entrepreneurship that grew from the late eighteenth century could experiment and contest in better ways than before. It was not unique because entrepreneurs now recognized opportunities to produce and sell what people demanded: that is an old economic habit. Nor was it different from past entrepreneurship because it could raise capital to fund new enterprises. Merchants, explorers, and voyagers had done that for centuries, but the fortunes of the trade they created never spread widely in the economy. The premodern economic system was full of speculative capital and asset bubbles, such as the Dutch tulip mania in the 1600s or the French Mississippi finance bubble in the 1700s. All past ages have had their own financial sharks and Bernie Madoff-type hustlers. A defining character of modern capitalist entrepreneurship, to follow economic historian Alexander Gerschenkron, was rather one of time: investments in big innovation needed far longer to generate expected economic gains. One of the factors separating past entrepreneurs from the new generation emerging after the modernization of entrepreneurship was the latter's understanding of uncertainty as a necessary ingredient to build private and societal profits.[42]

The twentieth century witnessed ideological experiments with other economic systems, but capitalism, for all its faults, has stood the test of time. It did so partly because it served as a better protector of individual freedom against coercion. Capitalism did not conquer just because it raised living standards and gave us products like automobiles, refrigerators, and color television. Its winning formula was that it made space for eccentric individuals with unconventional ideas. Other economic systems have failed because they were intolerant to dissent and treated nonconformity as a vice. The deserts of the Siberian tundra, for instance, never had a Burning Man festival like the annual gathering in Nevada's Black Rock desert that draws more than 60,000 techies, entrepreneurs and others for a celebration of creativity, ingenuity and self-expression. Without such freedom, investment, innovation and experimentation cannot thrive.

Capitalism, argues the erudite economist Deirdre McCloskey in a series of books on the bourgeois society, lived off individual dignity and virtuous behavior, but also helped their profusion.[43] Capitalism's political history certainly has dark moments of war and oppression. Nor is it the only form of economic organization that has encouraged new scientific discoveries. Various forms of command economies did as well – and they had people who understood the way of the world as well as Westerners. People in East Germany did not work shorter hours than those in Western Germany. Hard-working Chinese think about the same things as Westerners: their body aches, they long for a vacation, and they want to enjoy the fruits of the modern consumer civilization. Capitalism, however, engendered an appreciation of time, patience, and human behavior. As an economic organization, it is unrivalled in its proclivity for moving the innovation frontier, or impelling capital and labor to behave smarter.

Yet the Western form of capitalism is challenged from "state" and "authoritarian" versions of capitalism, or from "capitalism with Chinese characteristics" – or so it is said. Observers have been quick to release the obituaries of Western capitalism as growth rates in countries that are less open and democratic have outpaced the West. Jin Liqun, head of the Asia Infrastructure Investment Bank, has traced the illness of the West to its welfare state and "sloth-inducing, indolence-inducing labour laws."[44] Others, like Lee Kuan Yew School dean Kishore Mahbubani, have raised concerns about rekindled "competitive populism" burdening Westerners. Unlike Asians, he warns, "many Europeans have lost confidence in their ability to compete with the Asians. And many Americans have lost confidence in the virtues of competition."[45]

Much as some criticism of Western capitalism echoes actual realities, Schumpeter's "vision of capitalism" is hardly challenged by a better idea or better forms of economic organization. Nor are the variants of capitalism practiced in authoritarian regimes impressive. An economy like China's has improved its economic institutions, and the country's capacity for indigenous innovation to modernize the economy has been boosted by innovation inputs like research and development.[46] Furthermore, China, like other fast-growers, has over the past decades positioned its economy for faster adoption of new technologies, especially through enlarging the role of the market.

However, China is still far away from the spirit of capitalism and innovation. "Why can't China make a good ballpoint pen," Chinese Premier Li Keqiang recently complained, and the conventional wisdom held that it had not yet copied a Swiss machine for making good ballpoint pen tips.[47] The dominating view among China's minions is that innovation is an input in an economy rather than a consequence of institutions that support capitalism.[48] The country still suffers from an imperious state-directed economy whose five-year-plan mentality drains time, patience and energy from those indigenous long-term innovation processes.[49]

For a few years around the global financial crisis, China, Russia, and other emerging markets were claiming superiority over an economically dull and stagnant West. While their growth rates were far higher between 1995 and 2010, their triumphalism was hollow. Many emerging economies have still to prove their capacity for sustained long-term growth, especially "intensive growth" through better use of existing resources. Their growth rates have declined markedly in the past years – especially in Brazil, China and Russia. To a large extent their high growth rates in the past were the result of more labor and capital being added to production, or simply reflected extraordinarily high commodity prices. When these taps of growth have been turned off, growth no longer looks impressive. Emerging economies still need substantial reform to spur entrepreneurial competition and dynamism, but their political systems resist rather than encourage reform. They are still a good distance from the economic frontier of innovation and productivity.

Schadenfreude, however, is no comfort for the West. Capitalism may have a bright future, but not necessarily in the regions where it was born. The complacent, introvert, and incurious habits that rob economies of vitality are – yet again – unveiled, and more so in Europe than America. And in some respects, the similarities are greater than the differences between state-oriented emerging economies and the West. Politically and economically, Western economies have also moved in the direction of mercantilism and cronyism, and their economic policy is increasingly infected by short-termism and reluctance to address structural economic deficiencies.

Moreover, the past few decades of Western economic growth were, broadly, based on the same remarkably strong one-off factors that powered the emerging markets. In a way, Western economies could masquerade as high-growth societies because more labor and capital, at home and abroad, were connected to their economic arteries. In the last 40 years, net labor inputs grew as a result of an increasing working-age population and higher rates of female labor-market participation. The boost from labor was so strong that White House economists have called its initial phase "the age of expanded participation."[50] Net capital inputs also expanded remarkably fast, first through an emerging and, later, an accelerating debt supercycle, allowing firms and households to borrow and spend more money. The financial sector became the new master of the universe; there seemed no end to its ability to engineer new sources of capital. While savings increased in a few countries, such as Germany, they dropped in the majority of Western economies. In the United States, for instance, gross national savings fell from about 22 percent of GDP in 1970 to approximately 14 percent in 2010.[51] At the same time, US households expanded debt service payments as share of disposable income from less than 11 percent in 1980 to more than 13 percent at the peak of the credit boom in 2008.[52] Nonfinancial corporate debt-to-equity ratios jumped between 1970 and 1990, and yet again between 2000 and 2008.[53]

Economies at the frontier of innovation and productivity coupled with emerging markets as the opening up of the latter offered Western econo-mies exceptionally good opportunities to grow. Spurred by reforms at home that reduced restrictions on trade and product-market competition, globali-zation allowed them to source inputs and goods from more efficient producers. The entry of a billion people or more into global consumer and labor markets during the period of globalization was, to use economics jargon, a big "supply shock."[54] Western economies could import sources of growth – and for Europe, with falling indigenous economic dynamism, that succor from post-Soviet countries and Asia became more important than for other regions. It accelerated a positive transition in the economy from lower-productivity to higher-productivity sectors.[55]

But then the music stopped. It is a decade now since the West's financial sector began to crumble. Yet America and Europe still show a stubborn resistance to recovery to healthy levels of economic expansion. While some economies like Germany, the United Kingdom and the United States have returned to the levels of output they had before the crash, others have been unable to rise above those levels. None of the Western economies have returned to the precrisis trend of GDP growth. The West's stagnation, to paraphrase Hemingway's bankrupt in *The Sun Also Rises*, came in two ways: gradually and then suddenly. Its recovery, however, has been anything but quick.

Governments and central banks are often blamed for the weak recovery. However, they have also supported economies at unprecedented levels. Fiscal deficits and monetary supply operations have beaten most previous records. The real worry is that these economic drivers remain strong and, disturbingly, continue to be an important reason why Western economies grow at all. Moreover, most Western economies, with only a few exceptions, are still grinding the debt supercycle, gradually adding more debt to the economy.

We are close to a secular stagnation, argues Harvard's Larry Summers, and he suggests that growth cannot return to its historic trend without a faster rate of credit growth.[56] Secular stagnation or not, the thesis is based on some astute observations about Western economies today. Their natural interest rates, an indication of their underlying economic strength, have fallen continuously in the past decades. Even though that rate was not recorded or observed, investors got caught up in its decline. Short of opportunities to invest in safer types of assets, their capital was employed in extremely risky financial ventures, helping economies first to grow, then to crash.[57]

But to understand what went wrong, we have to look much deeper. Western stagnation has evolved over 40 years and is not the result of the crisis and its faulty policies for stabilization and recovery. The West's spirit level has fallen for several decades, despite globalization's supply-side shocks and incredibly cheap capital sloshing around the economy. The fault lines run deep and, in our view, are explained by a capitalism that has become increasingly bound. For those leaders in America and Europe who want to improve the West's economic expectation, it is time to address completely different problems than those associated with the crisis. What if Western economies are on a different trajectory because of a weak supply side, limited in its capacity to yield healthy levels of growth in the private sector? What if the modest growth in the past decades was just about high enough to mask our wretched capacity for innovation and economic dynamism? "Either he's dead or my watch has stopped," joked Groucho Marx, and you could say the same about today's economy. What if capitalism has lost its mojo?

Every now and then, history shows, economies evolve to a point where things just cannot continue as they were. That point has now been reached. The recent crisis was a breaking point, the end station on a multi-decade journey, when advanced and emerging economies alike could go for the easy pickings of extensive growth and global expansion. However, economies accumulated far too much debt because of a great illness in the capitalist system that started well before the Great Recession, even well before the end of the Cold War. Debt accumulation was just a symptom, not the cause, of a sluggish economic climate and a capitalist system that had become saturated.

Yet the combination of growing debt and falling consumer prices prevented people from understanding the direction of the economy. For a while global growth was better than good. Not only were consumers content; investors and executives were charmed by the period's offer of near effortless growth.

But effortless growth increasingly obscured the spirit of capitalist enterprise. Business owners and companies unlearned the lessons of uncertainty, experimentation and innovation as necessary conditions for sustained revenue and asset growth. Modern capitalism, perhaps like the rest of Western society, distanced itself from long-term thinking and instead came to inhabit that fast but impatient part of the brain that Nobel prizewinner Daniel Kahneman associates with short-termism.[58] Andrew Haldane, the Bank of England's witty Chief Economist, made his own summary: "Fast thought could make for slow growth."[59]

The thesis of a depressed capitalism is provocative – but it is what this book is all about. It challenges the conventional wisdom of today's capitalism and argues that capitalism no longer operates in the way we used to think of it, and the biggest change is that it no longer casts a role for its leading actor: the capitalist. Conservative financiers and money-holders are in abundant supply, perhaps more so than ever. They are around in all kinds of economic organization, probing every new opportunity for safe yield, but now they reign supreme. And when companies and their future strategies are funded from their hands, they incubate defensive habits rather than innovativeness, and that is when the capitalists' absence shows.

In a way, capitalism has lost its founding spirit of enterprise. While incumbents show little appetite for building future business through radical innovation, they compete by limiting the space for new entrepreneurs to oust the old. There are exceptions to every rule. Some sectors are experiencing a higher degree of contestability than before, and many who walk the streets of *corporateville* are eager to unleash radically new business ideas. Nonetheless, Western capitalism is cut off from the culture of experimentation and does not encourage much real Schumpeterian innovation. Western capitalism rather breeds bad habits and poor institutions, including a crop of corporate chieftains espousing a vision of capitalism as a safe, dull and predictable territory, free from taxing adventures and the stressful uncertainty that inevitably follows strategies to contest markets through innovation.

For 40 years, a virus of managerialism and excessive bureaucracy has infected Western corporate life. Ownership got separated from ownership – and capitalists from capitalism. The economy was living off the easy pickings of growth, and even if investors and executives knew that was not forever, the period changed their habits and transformed capitalism. The great paradox, at least for some, is that key factors behind the stagnation of capitalism were largely desirable. Few would wish them undone – or the last 40 years away. But to understand how Western capitalism stagnated it is first necessary to understand the big economic trends of the past 40 years and how they mobilized many companies to hide from rather than embrace innovation.

The four horsemen of capitalist decline

No one deliberately planted the virus in the capitalist world. But once there it replicated, just like any germ, and in this case with the assistance of four forces that from the early 1970s guided the economy. They are not the Four Horsemen of the Apocalypse, nor were they all undesirable, but they changed Western capitalism. And the more commanding they have grown, the more they have impelled the Western economy to resist change. Now they are pushing corporate defensiveness to an extreme, insulating companies from changes that naturally come as the world economy adjusts to the end of a four-decade long supply ride.

The four factors that have made Western capitalism dull and hidebound are gray capital, corporate managerialism, globalization, and complex regulation. These four themes are also at the center of this book. The past 40 years have witnessed a sharp increase in the capital and funding that is available to companies. No doubt the surge in capital chasing investments encouraged the financialization of the real economy, and a change in the structure of funding – from equity to debt. Highly leveraged finance is worrying, but the key point here is the influence of financialization on capitalism and corporate behavior. It changed stock markets from being a source of funding for corporations to a cash cow for savers and money managers. Companies had usually retained a high part of their earnings in order to reinvest, but starting in the 1960s, retained earnings have gradually dropped and investment decisions have largely moved from corporate leadership to financial markets. Western companies certainly have a lot of cash and other liquid assets, but a good part of them comes from debt and not from their own revenues, and if companies follow the trend, not much will be spent on new innovations.

In the early 1960s classic in corporate sociology, *The Conduct of the Corporation*, Wilbert Moore stressed the importance of retaining earnings in companies. When the control of capital in a company moves to financial markets, he argued, creditors will interfere in corporate strategy and management in a way they are not capable of doing. By contrast, companies retaining a high share of their earnings remain in power because capital is "entirely at management's disposal without any promises or guarantees."[60] Much can be said about economic evolution since then, but one thing is clear: corporate America did not take that advice. According to one estimate, retained earnings in the US moved from 50–60 percent of net income in the 1960s to single-digit levels in the 2000s.[61]

For a time, the financialization of firms was exclusively positive, leading to improved capital efficiency and new sources of financing, allowing firms to improve their access to funding. And while there are many critics of financial capitalism – lashing out against the "excessive financialization" of the real economy – most of them get it wrong. In reality, what cripples capitalist ownership is the incursion of what we call "gray capital," squeezing out core capitalist owners and promoting "gray ownership," or what can be described as capitalism without capitalists. Leading corporations in America and Europe now have anonymous core or controlling owners, such as financial institutions, which are simply not capable of taking ownership responsibilities. Remarkably, a big part of this gray ownership effectively invests on the premise that companies should go with the flow of the market rather than beating it. What these owners require is corporate managers steering a steady and predictable course, not entrepreneurs with a habit of economic renewal.

In that way, corporate managerialism rooted itself, and Western capitalism is now a habitat for *The Man in the Gray Flannel Suit*, if you remember Sloan Wilson's book about the boredom of organization.[62] While business leaders and gray owners talk about agile adaptation, disruption and revolutionary innovation when they describe their businesses, they stoop ever more as the Organization Man. Wilson's gray flannel suit was a phenomenon of the 1950s. Those who returned from World War II had a talent for organization, and that old perception of America, a place for rugged individualism, was about to be changed for a new vision of hierarchy and organization. The Organization Man was born – and William Whyte, in his classic tract on business sociology with that name, observed a new type of economic organization: more risk-averse but better at combining various talents in specialized organizations.[63]

Business got increasingly managerial. John Kenneth Galbraith, the icon of postwar American liberalism, argued in *The New Industrial State* that the real "enemy of the market is not ideology but the engineer."[64] And he was not alone. Business management "aims to minimize uncertainty, minimize the consequences of uncertainty, or both,"[65] concluded Robin Marris, the don of British managerialism, around the same time, in the mid-1960s. Like many others at the time, Galbraith and Marris, both men of the left, commended economic planning and trusted the corporate structure to manage uncertainty in a way that would allow investment and innovation. In fact, bureaucracy as a precondition for innovation formed a central part of their support for managerial capitalism. The more complex the technology, the more bureaucracy was needed to embrace it.

The managerial school of corporate governance lost many adherents in later decades. Yet in the corporate world, managerialism never faded away, but progressively anchored itself more firmly in companies. A custodian corporate culture has been proliferating in the corporate world and it has been bad news for the culture of capitalism and innovation. Corporate managers shy away from uncertainty but turn companies into bureaucratic entities free from entrepreneurial habits. They strive to make capitalism predictable.

Globalization exacerbated the culture of managerialism. Globalization came in two waves. The first pushed horizontal expansion and propped up business volumes based on already existing products sold on home and other markets. No doubt it ushered in contestable competition; when

foreign firms entered markets that previously had been home-firm dominated they often contested these markets. This wave of globalization
required some innovation ingenuity too, but it was primarily defined by the
organization and management of international expansion.

In the second wave, vertical globalization, companies redrew firm
boundaries and built global production networks based on a high degree of
supply and value-chain fragmentation. Global companies concentrated
their focus on market positions and the ability to influence, let alone
control, their end-customer market. They grew defensive about their
incumbency advantages and fearful of radical innovation that contested
their markets. Barriers to market entry went up as market concentration
increased and companies accelerated their specialization, making it more
difficult for incumbents to be ousted through innovation. The soul and
rhythm of competition changed.

The managerialist culture united corporate managers and regulators.
Like managers, regulators have responded to the increasingly complex
world by making regulations complex. As a result, regulations today cause
a good deal of uncertainty about what companies and innovators can or
cannot do. Two decades of economic liberalization did not change that
trend. While economic regulation became less restrictive as markets opened
up, other forms of regulation interfered with innovation. Stability and
predictability have shaped many of the new social regulations that have
spread since the 1970s. Together with all economic regulations that
have grown more restrictive again over the past 15 years, social regulations
have created a permission-based regulatory culture of innovation and
economic renewal.

The four factors reinforced the bureaucratic impulses of Western
societies. Instinctively defensive, operating under a compliance mentality
supported by their financiers and government regulations, companies lost
the entrepreneurial appetite for transforming markets with big innovation.
As the managerialist disposition for predictability and preservation seized
the corporate world, capitalism lost its orientation. It wrecked its compass
for economic dynamism and contestable competition. Now capitalism is
challenged; not from outside competition but the four horsemen of capitalist decline. The existential challenge of capitalism in the twenty-first
century is a growing inability to foster contestable innovation and entrepreneurial competition. Capitalism is no longer what most people think it is.

2

WHEN CAPITALISM BECAME MIDDLE-AGED

The long, dull, monotonous years of middle-aged prosperity ... are
excellent campaigning weather for the devil.

C.S. Lewis, *The Screwtape Letters*

In some quarters there is a remarkable degree of optimism about an
imminent turnaround in Western economies, led by a new wave of innovation and corporate investment. One can understand why. Respectable
futurists and leading journalists predict America and Europe will be
shocked by a superfast technological change, if they have not been already.
The corporate sector is brimming with surplus cash that could be used to
diffuse new innovation and power economic growth.

Unfortunately, pessimism rather than optimism seems like a better bet.
There is no compelling evidence to suggest companies invest just because
they have the means for it. Nor are cash-strong companies generally
investing more than companies under financing constraints.[1] Moreover,
big and global companies, those who keep most of this unutilized cash, do
not invest more than other companies.[2] The cost of capital may be close to
zero, and companies could take up almost free liquidity on markets, but
surplus liquidity is now used for other purposes than making it into working
capital. Today's Western economy is not just depressed by low economic
expectations about future demand. Western capitalism has become middle-
aged and shows every symptom of getting older. If there ever was a cathedral of capitalism, the painted ceiling would now rather picture someone
who is grey-haired, worldly and efficient, content and anxious at the same
time, especially about their own health. Divorced from past aspirations,

drifting from the pursuits of younger generations, this is a capitalism that is planning for those long, dull and monotonous years that C.S. Lewis associated with middle age.

In this chapter we will discuss Western economic developments from the early 1970s until today, and document the weakened capitalist ethos with some key headline figures on growth, productivity, investment – and defensive corporate strategies. While the period had its cycles of boom and bust, the general judgment has to be that the past four decades were not economically impressive.

In the 1970s a period began when countries at the economic and innovation frontier slowed down their creation of new gross domestic product (GDP). From 1950 to 1973, average growth of real GDP per capita in Western Europe and the United States stood at 4.8 and 3.9 percent respectively. Between 1973 and 2007, the combined economies of "the West" grew on average by 1.98 percent.[3] The growth in Western Europe in the 1950s and 1960s was part of the economic recovery after World War II, and once that cycle had ended, the rate of growth and increasing prosperity declined. What is remarkable, however, is that growth in GDP per capita continued to decline up to the precrisis boom in the 2000s (see Figure 2.1). While there were short growth spikes between 1970 and today, they were neither long nor capable of changing the trend.

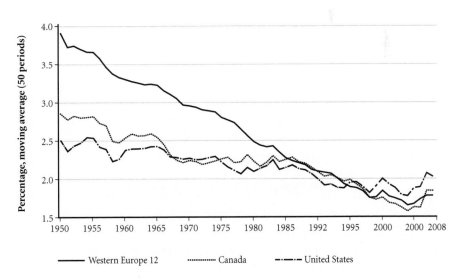

Western Europe 12 .... Canada —·—·— United States

* The years from 2008 on are not shown because the crisis and weak recovery make the decline much steeper.

Source: Angus Maddison, "Statistics on World Population, GDP and Per Capita GDP, 1-2008," updated to 2010, at http://www.ggdc.net/MADDISON/oriindex.htm.

Figure 2.1 Growth of real GDP per capita, 1950–2007

Nor are economic forecasters suggesting that the trend of stagnating growth is about to change. On the contrary, estimates of future growth suggest the trend will change only slightly. Between 2000 and 2020, suggests the Conference Board, growth in real GDP per capita will have fallen much further below its trend in the past decades.[4] While these forecasts are notoriously difficult, the Paris-based Organisation for Economic Co-operation and Development (OECD), for instance, estimates potential real GDP per capita between 2014 and 2060 to be a bit higher than in the past decade in the euro area and a bit lower in the United States.[5] Albert Einstein once said that compound interest, that is, savers getting interest on accumulated interest, was one of mankind's greatest innovations, and perhaps the same can be said of compound growth. In the long term, the average annual rate of growth makes a big difference. If the economy grows by 1 percent a year it will take 70 years to double GDP. If it grows by 3 percent a year, it will only take a bit more than 23 years – a generation – to double it.

The low long-term rate of growth presents the West with economic expectations that will disappoint hopes for better pay – or for more resources to be available for education, healthcare and other central parts of society. Equally important, if not more so, is that low growth expectations make people less excited about the future, and generally feed a psychology of anxiety. Aspirations in the West have clearly faded – and not just at the margin. It is acceptable now to assume that life and prosperity for future generations will be worse. Many students graduate from university only to find a labor market where the best offer is an unpaid internship. Parents are satisfied as long as their children get a job and manage to keep it. It is accepted that kids will live at home well past their twentieth birthday because they cannot afford a place of their own. Low-growth societies are low-expectation societies, and the raw economic numbers of a weak economy feed into imagination of an uninspiring future.

The bridges to Maddison counting

To better understand the West's declining economic esprit, we pay a visit to the Club des Chiffrephiles. It may sound like a club for people with odd interests, and in a way it is. But it is neither an aristocratic French club nor one of those modern elite private members' clubs for the well-to-do class. Its clubhouse is not located on the Champs-Élysées, alongside the landmark *grandes maisons*. In fact, it does not have a clubhouse. Nor does it keep a record of its members. Economist Angus Maddison founded the Club des Chiffrephiles, and its sole purpose has been to encourage people to dive deeper into the world's economic history with the help of numbers and quantified estimates of prosperity through two millennia.

For "economists and economic historians, who, like myself, have a strong predilection for quantification,"[6] Maddison became a source of inspiration and a central figure for all those who wanted to understand why some countries have grown while others have not. He helped to spark a far greater interest in the forces behind long-term rises in real prosperity, and what hides behind the numbers in historic league tables of economic growth. And for him, like every chiffrephile, the growth of an economy's productivity – a measure of how much output is created by the input to an economy – is the workhorse of prosperity.

"Productivity is not everything," Paul Krugman observed, "but in the long run it is almost everything."[7] It has been a staple perception among economists that variations in productivity growth explain why some countries are rich and others are poor.[8] And behind those variations is not just the economic organization of a country, but its ingenuity and the space given to experimentation and Schumpeterian innovation. That is not what you find in economic spreadsheets, but eventually these sources of prosperity translate into an economy's ability to innovate and adapt to new technologies.[9]

If there is one cause that explains the West's declining rate of growth in GDP per capita, it is the slowdown in productivity growth. It is the chief reason why Western economies are growing slower than before. America and Europe, it seems, have sapped their capacity for using and combining labor and capital in more productive ways. In particular, they have lost the ability to improve the performance of labor and capital through innovation.

Economists have a way of measuring the growth of productivity in an economy by looking at all factors of – or inputs to – production, called total factor productivity (TFP). It is the preferred indicator of productivity when the task is to measure how much innovation adds to the improvement of the economy. Yet economists are hedging their bets, and if you do not like this version of productivity, well, there are others. A second approach to grading an economy's productivity is labor productivity, for sure a better one if the task is to understand the relation between wages, employment and the health of the economy. In this case, however, there is really no need to spend much time on different approaches to productivity. Nor is there a need for caveats – or for us to hedge our bets. The trend is clear.

Productivity growth is going south – and has been doing so for several decades. Business productivity growth – taking account of productivity only in the business sector – had a longer upward trend in the 1980s and the 1990s, but has also fallen when viewed over several decades. The decline has been particularly strong since the early 2000s.[10]

Figure 2.2 shows this trend for TFP in a selection of Western economies, and it uses moving averages in order to delineate it. Over time the real observed rates of productivity growth have been above or below the trend shown, and the annual variations would have been larger if headline rates had been used.[11] But as far as the trend is concerned, it clearly shows that Western economies have gradually slowed down the rate of TFP growth. Their capacity to grow the economy by using smarter or more productive combinations of capital and labor inputs has declined. For every new input that is added to the Western economy, the output is smaller than before.

The trend is no more exciting if we look just at the productivity of labor. For advanced economies, labor productivity has been more volatile than TFP growth, surging in the US during the boom in information and communications technology (ICT) in the second half of the 1990s. But that spurt, which promised a lasting digital shock to the US economy, proved to be just that – a spurt.

Economist Robert Gordon has a sobering view for those who think past and future rates of US labor productivity growth are impressive. He has recently become known for swearing in the church of the New Machine

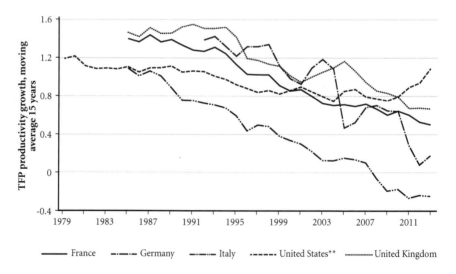

* Moving 60-year average calculated over the period of 1949 to 2014.
Source: OECD's database, authors' calculations.
Figure 2.2 Total factor productivity growth in selected EU countries and the US

Age by suggesting that the role of innovation for US growth is under-whelming and that it will not get much better. In a fascinating account of living standards in the United States, Gordon has computed labor produc-tivity for different periods and shown that while it soared in the US between 1996 and 2004, the periods between 1972 and 1996, and from 2004 until now, show a productivity trend significantly below the trends after World War II or after the industrial revolution.[12] After the post–World War II catch-up with the United States ended, Europe's productivity growth has been consistently below that of the US.

As Figure 2.3 shows, the direction of labor productivity growth in advanced economies has been firmly declining for several decades. The figure tracks the development of productivity in Group of Seven (G7) coun-tries – all economies at the technological frontier – and shows the average labor productivity growth between 1995 and 2012 to be 1.2 percentage points lower than that between 1970 and 1980. Between 1995 and 2009, Europe's labor productivity grew by just 1 percent annually.[13]

Like the United States, the other G7 countries seem to have exhausted the usual sources of productivity growth, especially the growth from the first (1760–1840) and second (1870–1970) industrial revolutions. That tallies with economist Tyler Cowen's catchy summary of declining strength in the American economy, that it has "eaten all the low-hanging fruits of modern history and got sick."[14] Translated into economic prose, this means that new technologies do not create much economic growth, or at least are

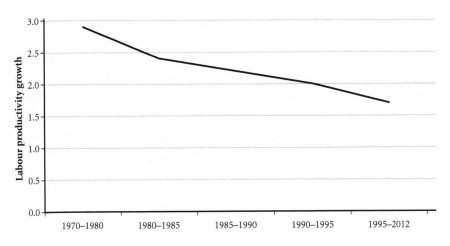

* G7 = Canada, France, Germany, Italy, Japan, United Kingdom, United States.
Source: OECD Stan database, at http://stats.oecd.org/Index.aspx?DatasetCode=LEVEL.
Figure 2.3 G7 labour productivity growth

not making as big a contribution as in the past. Many other studies confirm this view, and lead to the conclusion that the recent waves of innovation in sectors like software do not compare well with the economic effects of past achievements, like the combustion engine, electricity, and modern household technology.

However, explaining poor productivity growth is not just an issue about falling contributions from innovation and new technologies. For technology to create growth it has to be used and diffused, and there are many barriers to diffusion, let alone fast diffusion. In fact, the OECD suggests that the overriding task for advanced economies is to fix the broken "diffusion machine" so that new innovations are more easily shared between economies, sectors, investors, and labor.[15] Interestingly, while broader changes in "economic organization" in the past decades – such as urbanization and globalization – have accelerated the diffusion rate of innovations, they are still impeded from easy movement within the economy. Companies at the technological frontier, argues the OECD, grew their productivity at an average annual rate of 3.5 percent during the 2000s; by comparison, nonfrontier firms had negative rates of productivity growth.

The barriers to diffusion – including from frontier to nonfrontier firms – are multiple, have different origins, and vary between countries. While some barriers have been reduced (e.g. tariffs on trade in goods), others have been raised. A country like Italy, for instance, has problems in adapting to new innovations because of the high proportion of family-run small businesses in its economy. They are part of what two economists have called the "Italian disease"[16] – a defective institutional structure promoting cronyism and a culture of nepotism, preventing firms from igniting productivity and growth. As in other European countries, big companies in Italy are more productive than smaller ones.[17] If the size distribution of firms in Italy resembled Germany's, its exports would have been about 25 percent higher.[18] When they were surveyed about the most important factors behind financial success, Italian managers did not suggest hard work, education, or innovation as the top factors but ranked "knowledge of influential people" as the surest way to success.[19] Far too often small businesses stay small to avoid the crony culture and regulations that apply only to companies of a certain size (such as hiring and firing regulations), but that comes at a heavy cost for the economy. Small companies simply lack the resources to scale up production and turn innovations that can be imported from others into products and production processes. Italy does not have many firms competing to stretch the technological frontier, but a greater problem for its economy is its wrecked diffusion machine, which prevents

Italians from accepting and executing technological and organizational change.

Italy is Italy, you might say, but that is misleading, not to say wrong. Other Western economies, closer to the technological frontier, have problems too, and sometimes they are similar to Italy's. Canada, for instance, also has firm-size disadvantages, where the big population of small and medium-sized enterprises (SMEs) prevents the rapid absorption of new innovations.[20] Or take the United States. Its total factor productivity growth accelerated in the 1990s but then slowed down again. The slowdown is often associated with a weakened ICT sector, no longer pushing productivity growth to the same extent (we explore this further in Chapter 8, "Capitalism and Robots"). But an equally disturbing trend has been declining technological efficiency caused by a weakened capacity to diffuse new technologies across sectors and the economy. The likely villains are the falling adaptive capacity of human capital and the halted progression of investment in research and development (R&D).[21] Companies and sectors need substantial R&D resources in order to adapt to and imitate advances in other companies or sectors. When those resources are eroded, the speed of spillovers from one actor in the economy to another will also be drastically reduced.

By contrast, in Germany and France, falling levels of productivity growth are associated with stringent labor market rules. That is an old problem in Europe, but in past decades it has grown worse because stringent labor market regulations have prevented digital technologies from rippling through their economies. The combination of rigid labor markets and general regulatory heterogeneity in Europe's product markets is the key reason why digitalization did not greatly boost productivity growth.[22] For a country like Spain, to look at another set of barriers to diffusion, the surge in capital inflows in the 1990s and 2000s pushed the economy away from productivity growth in business sectors to sectors like real estate.[23]

The OECD also notes that a general barrier in the Western world is a shortage of R&D spending and skills, and mismatches of skills. There are constant reports about how companies cannot find the labor they need – and analyses suggest that many advanced economies suffer from skill deficiencies.[24] Pricewaterhouse Coopers (PwC) surveyed Western executives and found that 70 percent of them believed that there was a shortage of the "skills necessary to grow."[25] Others argue that a particular problem for the diffusion of innovation is the transfer of knowledge, know-how and labor from less dynamic to dynamic firms.[26] Forces resisting the reallocation of labor thus effectively clog the arteries of productivity.

How companies spend their money

The Western productivity slowdown did not happen by accident or default. There are multiple factors behind the decline, but businesses have not been innocent bystanders since the deceleration of productivity growth can be linked back to corporate decisions affecting growth. In other words, slowing productivity growth is a reflection of behavior in the real business sector, and especially decisions made by corporate executives and boards about their balance sheets. There are two areas of particular interest: business investment and R&D spending. Both are central for innovation, diffusion, and imitation.

The balance sheets of many large companies today don't look like products of capitalism. Companies have rarely, if ever, been so well capitalized. Estimates suggest that S&P 500 firms have approaching US$1.5 trillion of unutilized short-term cash balances.[27] Reportedly, in the first quarter of 2015, Apple had US$194 billion in cash and financial investments.[28] European firms, too, have what one study called "stashes of cash," prompting many to hope for a new period of accelerating capital expenditure to lift Europe's anemic growth.[29] Compustat, the S&P financial database, revealed *total* corporate cash holdings in the range of US$5 trillion in 2011 – with an annual growth rate of about 10 percent since 1995.[30]

The trend goes further back in time. Between 1979 and 2011, the ratio of cash to total assets for American firms increased from 9.4 percent to 21 percent.[31] While there are differences between individual companies (and not all companies are fortunate in having remarkably large liquid balances), the overall pattern clearly reveals that the expansion of liquid assets does not correspond with operational costs, or working capital. For a long time, the average levels of liquid assets in relation to short-term liabilities stayed stable at around 30 percent in nonfinancial US companies.[32] Now that figure has moved closer to 50 percent. In other words, companies have excess liquidity; they manage their balance sheet for a world that does not require companies to turn a higher share of liquid assets into fixed capital in order to be profitable.

Excess liquidity cannot therefore be explained, as some suggest, by the Great Recession and corporate reluctance to spend at a time when the future health of the economy is uncertain. No doubt the sluggish recovery has exacerbated corporate capital defensiveness, but liquidity has grown from levels that were already comparatively high and that is part of a longer trend. The OECD, for instance, observed several years before the crisis that excess corporate savings had been unusually large for many years.[33] While the corporate sector in the United States was borrowing around 15–20 percent of the value of its productive assets in the 1970s and 1980s, the same sector *lent* 5 percent of the value of its productive assets in the years before the crisis.[34] Remarkably, the typical multinational company today is a net contributor rather than a net user of savings, and that balance affects their ability to lift productivity. Moreover, it hurts jobs and salaries. As corporate savings have increased, labor's share of GDP has inevitably fallen. And that is the important relationship: when corporate capital is idle, labor usually takes a hit.

This alone should make alarm bells go off. There were good reasons, 30 years or so ago, to improve the net borrowing position of firms as inflation was brought down and changed the cost of capital. But for quite some time now, cash hoarding has been more of a defensive act, and it has served to protect the current stock of innovations, technology and companies against competition and destruction. Judging by current trends, this development is not about to stop or reverse direction. Companies look rather determined to keep strong liquidity balances and continue to mute their propensity to invest.

An accelerating pace of innovation and productivity in the economy requires growing business investment. For innovations to be diffused through the economy, the corporate sector has to invest. The same is true for governments and households. Their capital expenditure would need to go up for innovation really to be diffused at a much faster pace.

Take the example of telecommunications. The telecom sector has expanded fast in the past three decades. But for that expansion to happen, companies and governments needed to invest in network infrastructure and other fixed capital – and that is exactly what they did. In fact, business investment in the telecom sector has expanded by about one order of magnitude. Likewise, to use these networks, companies and households had to lay out capital expenditure in buying telecommunications equipment like mobile phones and broadband routers. And that is exactly what they did. This expenditure also went up by about an order of magnitude.

The telecom example, however, is not representative for entire Western economies. Business investment in Western economies is declining and does not show the pattern you would expect from an economy moving in the direction of rapid innovation and fast TFP growth. The long-term investment trend suggests that Western economies are more likely to stagnate than accelerate because of business investment behavior. Had there been an acceleration of innovation, companies would pour more capital into the economy. Business investment as a share of revenue or output or gross domestic product would be on the rise.[35] But as Figures 2.4, 2.5 and 2.6 show, business investment is anything but on the rise. Apart from a surge in the mid-1990s, the trend since the late 1970s has been going down. Business investment is generally following the same declining trend as total investment in Western economies.

Again, take the United States as an example. Compared to other Western economies, the US economy has followed a pattern of economic growth that is less reliant on a big trade sector but more dependent on Schumpeterian innovation and creative destruction. Figure 2.4 tells the story of business investment in the US economy between 1975 and 2014. The trend of US business investment has been declining since the late 1970s, when measured as a share of GDP.[36] Private investment as a share of business capital stock is on the same trend.[37] Just as for the West as a whole, there was a spurt in the 1990s, and during that period productivity growth in the US accelerated too as the business sector invested more money in absorbing new technology. The spurt was also more significant than in most other advanced economies. Another period of growing business investment happened just before the financial crisis. Yet neither of these have been able to return business investment in the US economy to levels last seen in the 1980s. Business investment during the spurts has taken it to the average ratio since the 1960s, but not to the peak rates during that long period.[38]

Nor is the trend of slowing business investment growth an exclusively US phenomenon. It has happened in other advanced economies too. In the

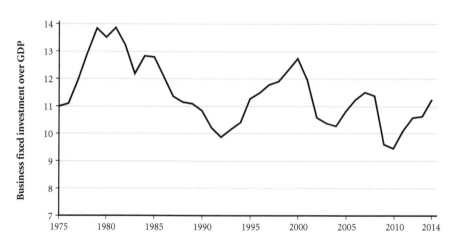

Source: Federal Reserve Statistical Release, Z.1, table F.103.

Figure 2.4 US business fixed investment/GDP

past 25 years, for instance, business investment in the UK has been compassed to go in mostly one direction – down (see Figure 2.5 and 2.6). Business investment as a percentage of GDP has fallen pretty dramatically also in Germany years, and even if other continental economies have not experienced a similar sharpness in the decline, their direction of travel has been similar.[39]

Traditional ways of measuring business investment in the economy have been incomplete for a long time, despite improvements by statistics authorities. Now they are frequently in the firing line and some critics contend that the entire approach is antiquated. In a knowledge-based economy, they argue, the important investments are in intangibles rather than tangibles. And the types of investments that determine success in modern economies – skills and competencies, R&D, intellectual property, brands, and so on – are only tangentially covered in national accounts of investment. Consequently, if data included all investments in intangibles, the trend of falling business investment ratios could be corrected. In reality, therefore, it may well be the case that business investment as a share of GDP or another relevant indicator has increased.

However, this approach to business investment data should be treated with caution. It is correct that human capital is critical for economic performance, but it is also predominantly financed by other sources than companies. They are rather the consequence of investments made by individuals and governments. Some forms of investment in brands, R&D and intellectual property are already accounted for in current national accounts,

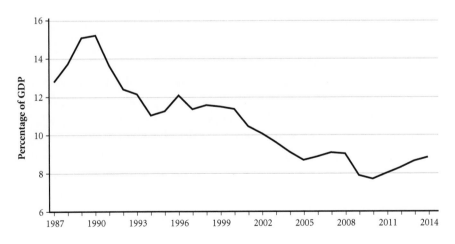

Source: Office for National Statistics.
Figure 2.5 UK business investment/GDP (at current price)

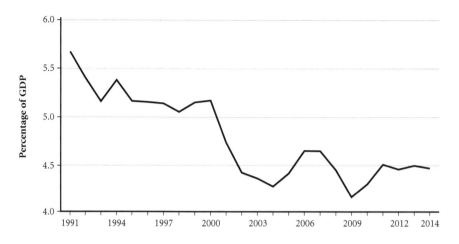

Source: Federal Statistical Office, Germany.
Figure 2.6 German business investment as a proportion of GDP

sometimes in indirect ways. Moreover, it is difficult to get a good numerical understanding of outlays on other forms of intangible investments, primarily because it is profoundly difficult to distinguish an investment in intangibles from an expenditure. Corporate accounts are far less reliable because firms making a distinction between investment and expenditure in relation to intangibles are more influenced by accounting and tax rules than in the case of tangibles. As the depreciation rates of many intangibles are generally unknown, it becomes a great challenge to separate net values from gross values in aggregated data. Importantly, some forms of outlay that are said to be increasing rapidly and need to be counted – such as investment expenditure on ICT software – have in reality not increased much at all.[40] More to the point (and as we will discuss in Chapter 4), significant parts of expenditure on intangibles are used to substitute for innovation.

There are several possible explanations for why the business sector's investment share in the Western economy is going down. Broad factors like demography certainly influence corporate investment and changing patterns of age might thus have pushed business investment down. Likewise, structural economic change, and a movement from manufacturing to services, could plausibly have influenced investment too, but there is no evidence suggesting that the economy has moved from more capital-intensive to less capital-intensive sectors.[41] Relative changes in the price of investment goods, making investment goods cheaper, could partially explain falling levels of investment. However, the increasing depreciation rate of investment goods would even out a good part of the decline in relative price. The explanations that we advance in this book are that broader changes in corporate capitalism have drained the Western economy of investment. Western companies have lowered their investment shares in Western economies because they were not expecting much growth there. A greater part of their new investments have been exploiting opportunities from globalization and these have been destined for emerging markets. Furthermore, changing ownership structures motivate companies to retain earnings and increase debt for other purposes than investment.

Neither are companies using a higher share of their expenditure for research and development any faster than the rate of economic growth. Many companies will disagree and contend that they are spending more than ever on innovation or in R&D. Headline figures will also give them support: R&D expenditure by many large firms has been steadily on the rise. That holds also for the entire corporate sector: it records a pretty steady increase in spending on R&D.

Total spending on research and development, including government spending, has gradually increased in the developed world in the past decades, but not by much. Total spending on R&D in OECD countries has on average been rather flat. Countries like Japan, South Korea and China have experienced a noticeable increase in business spending on R&D. Western economies, however, have not followed the same pattern of expenditure growth. While the ratio of R&D to GDP increased in the United States, countries like the United Kingdom and France have seen a rather flat development. From the early 1980s up to the crisis in 2008, they did not change their R&D spending habits much.

However, these figures are deceptive. They hide the fact that corporate expenditure generally has grown faster than GDP and that R&D expenditure has become increasingly concentrated in a few sectors across most of the mature economies. A parallel trend has been increasing gross revenue in the corporate sector. Hence, R&D expenditure has increased, but when viewed as a proportion of revenue it has largely been stagnant for many years in several Western countries.

Moreover, like the rest of society, the concept of "research" in the corporate sector has changed. While the image of corporate research still evokes places like AT&T's Bell Labs (whose scholars have received eight Nobel prizes) and Xerox's Palo Alto Research Center (PARC), the reality is that a declining share of R&D budgets is spent on research. Consequently, what many companies describe as research today is often less connected than in the past to big innovation – innovation aiming to introduce new products that reshape the market. R&D expenditure for many companies is spending on product adaptation, design and development – copying a feature or an add-on from another product, or adjusting the product stock to local demands. Corporate expenditures are hence mostly "D" and little "R."

Adaptation, imitation, and incremental change are good developments: a central theme of capitalism is that companies learn and copy from each other. Expenditure to that effect also powers the "diffusion machine," taking innovation from one sector into another. Perhaps companies also are using their R&D outlays in a better way than before, promoting an increase in their R&D efficiency. After all, innovation is a question of output, not input, and more money on R&D does not necessarily translate into more innovation. As economist Luigi Zingales recently joked: "If innovation was just throwing money at it, Greece would be the most innovative country in the world."[42]

However, the reallocation of resources from "R" to "D" does not sit comfortably with the hypothesis that modern and capital-deepening economies are increasingly reliant on innovation and that the business sector should be increasing its spending on big ideas and more radical forms of innovation. An economy growing on the back of innovation would surely see R&D spending growing *in real terms* and faster than *general expenditure*. If an economy is moving toward greater innovation intensity, this would show as a visible trend in the data. But the data do not generally support that view (see Figures 2.7 and 2.8).

What is missing in the general view is an understanding that data on ratios of R&D to GDP are based on different measurements. R&D expenditure is

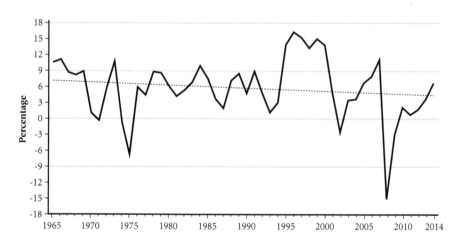

Source: US Bureau of Economic Analysis.
Figure 2.7 US real business R&D investment growth (change from previous year)

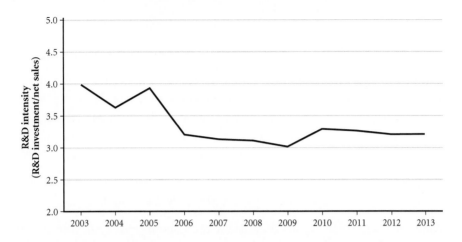

Source: European Commission, Directorate-General Enterprise and Industry, Innovation Union Scoreboard.
Figure 2.8 R&D intensity in the European Union (R&D expenditure as percentage of net sales)

based on the volume of expenditure while GDP is based on value-added. R&D expenditures should generally grow much faster than GDP. And when R&D is measured against another volume measure, the picture becomes materially different. The growth of real R&D spending in the US is on a declining trend. When measured against sales – as in the European Commission's R&D scoreboards – Europe's R&D intensity has been following the same direction. For the US, the National Science Foundation reports that its measure of R&D intensity has flatlined since 1995.

These data series cover a short period of time and far-reaching conclusions should not be drawn on the basis of only a decade. Yet many other observations point in the same direction and suggest that Western economies are not evolving in the way you would expect if there was a surge in innovation or if companies were preparing for it. Observations from companies suggest this is no coincidence. Big companies have for a long time reported difficulties in managing innovation or R&D, especially in aligning R&D with their business strategy.[43] In some sectors, R&D productivity has obviously fallen[44] – with less output for money spent on R&D – and many companies have reacted to problems with their R&D strategy (some of which relate to increasing regulatory costs) by "outsourcing" their R&D to smaller firms that can take bigger risks. Once the R&D investments have began to mature into innovative products, big companies have acquired them and integrated them into their sales and marketing infrastructure. Pharmaceuticals is one such sector. Time will tell if this strategy works or not. Perhaps it is efficient at the corporate level; perhaps it will destroy the innovation ethos.

Diminishing capacities for in-house invention *and* innovation have consequences for companies; they have far less control over their own long-term competitiveness. They have more exposure to market risks and need better capabilities to defend their market position against competitors and new entrants. This may exacerbate a strong existing trend in Western economies: companies are increasingly spending their money in defensive ways.

How companies play defense

Modern corporate life is less occupied with big innovation than with other concerns. The image of capitalism as a roaring lion, hungry for more investment and innovation, is a bit antiquated, a theme better suited to history books than contemporary accounts of economic development. The business sector in the West is now on a different trajectory. It is not sinking its rapidly growing share of capital into production and organization. Companies are generally not expanding their investment and R&D expenditures. But, you may ask, what are they doing with their money, if not investing for the future?

Large companies now seem to have a different idea about the future and what it will require from them in terms of investment exposure. It is difficult to escape the conclusion that a good proportion of leading Western companies no longer operate on the hypothesis that they raise capital to finance the investments needed to raise long-term revenues and profits. They are rather excess savers, and instead of growing the company through more investment and innovation, many of them use their excess capital for defensive purposes.

That is to say, the corporate sector has become conservative and complacent over the years. Generally, executives and investors appear to be planning for a future where liquidity will be needed to ensure that the effective return on equity is stable, partly through operations to hand back money to shareholders. No doubt they worry about their future competitiveness, partly because their asset base is aging. But they are not concerned to the degree that they activate a larger share of their cash balances for offensive and competitive purposes. In that way, capitalism today confirms its vices rather than its virtues. Short-term targets for investors often take primacy over long-term innovation and competition. Capitalism has become a platform for routine and almost risk-free savings rather than remaining a motor of economic and technological experimentation

Three categories of evidence point us in that direction. Our *first* point, and to reinforce the above: the corporate sector's status as a net lender of capital is neither new nor temporary. While there has been an acceleration in corporate net lending in recent times, data show that the development started before the crisis.[45] While the long-term trend has been a net borrowing rate in the range of about 0.8–1.2 percent of GDP, the corporate sector in the US has experienced surplus capital contributions to the rest of the economy by around 1 percent over the past decade (see Figure 2.9). There is a similar pattern for the United Kingdom, even if the data does not go as far back in time as for the US. While the business sector added capital to the UK economy in the late 1980s and early 1990s, there has been a consistent trend since the new millennium of net corporate lending (see Figure 2.10).

There are multiple reasons behind why the corporate sector has become a net lender rather than a net borrower. Generally, the past decades have been a good time for companies to reduce borrowing rates as inflation has come down. When the cost of capital is no longer an issue for companies they can allow themselves greater flexibility in their capital balances. However, a corporate sector that contributes capital to the rest of the economy is surely a corporate sector that on balance does not know how to spend its surplus capital to build long-term value. We now have a corporate sector where the management or the owners, or both, believe that the exceptionally low level of capital costs is not enough to raise investment.[46] Companies are preferring to slow investment, capital expenditure, and

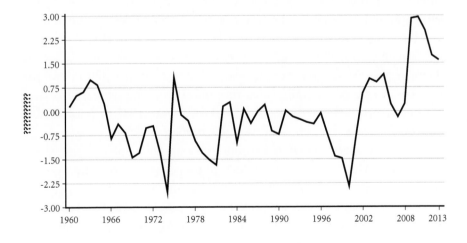

Source: Federal Reserve Statistical Release, Z.1, table F.103.

Figure 2.9 Business net lending and borrowing in the US (percentage of GDP)

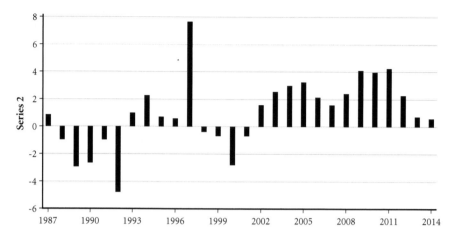

Source: Office for National Statistics.
Figure 2.10 Business net lending and borrowing in the UK (percentage of GDP)

R&D intensity because the captains of corporate America or corporate Europe believe the capital is better used for other purposes.

That takes us to the *second* point, that companies have used their earnings and balance sheet in the past decades to accelerate the number of mergers and acquisitions (M&A), which of course is an investment, too, but a very particular form of investment. The number and value of M&A transactions increased sharply from the mid-1980s up to the late 1990s, when it plateaued. In recent years there has been another spurt, and in 2015 a new global record was set for mergers and acquisitions as it passed US$5 trillion.[47] Given the general increase in corporate valuation, it is not surprising that the number and value of M&As also spiked.[48] The number of M&As has grown to such an extent that it has impacted the size of public markets and almost turned them into an advanced form of corporate dating service. M&As are the chief reason why the number of listed companies has decreased radically since the mid-1990s. Studying 15 years of delistings, a group of economists showed that "from 1997 to 2012, the US had 8327 delists, of which 4957 were due to mergers."[49]

There are several reasons behind the long-term increase in M&A activity, and M&As can generally help to propel an economy into greater efficiency, at least when they work in a textbook kind of way. When they do, M&As cut the costs of production. Globalization in the 1980s and 1990s, for instance, churned the acceleration of M&As because companies used acquisitions to hasten horizontal expansion and build scale. It was easier to buy a firm in another country and make it an affiliate than to try to set up a company from scratch. Importantly, it also cut the time of scaling up production.

Lately, however, M&A strategies have become associated with hide-bound business operations. They are intended to consolidate, rather than build competition. Hence they are sometimes, if not often, used in order to defend market positions – and, in that way, they form part of a different type of globalization that emerged in the 1990s and promoted horizontal expansion, vertical integration, and corporate attempts to create stronger network effects on the market.

More importantly, however, latter-year M&As are a sign of middle-aged corporates that have lost their ability to reproduce through innovation and have to get their vitality from other firms to stay on the market. Management and shareholders in middle-aged capitalism have made a choice between different alternative uses of their capital, favoring mergers with or acquisitions of other companies because they believe they can better control the returns of M&As compared to other alternatives on offer. Mergers and acquisitions are considered safer and more manageable strategies for future competitiveness. And that matters, says economist Robert Litan, "because when big companies swallow up others, it signals that acquiring companies have essentially outsourced their ideas rather than growing internally."[50]

Third, and last, the corporate sector has used the balance sheet to return capital to shareholders through dividend payments and share buybacks. This has been a topic of frequent discussion in corporate America in the past years, and exacerbated fears among observers that America Inc. is placing less faith in the US than in previous eras. There has been a remarkably strong trend in the past few years of giving capital to shareholders. Software giant IBM, for example, spent twice the amount of its R&D expenditure on share buybacks in 2014. And it is just not cash-strong firms that buy back shares. In 2013, calculates *The Economist*, "38% of firms paid more in buy-backs than their cashflows could support, an unsustainable position."[51]

However, this is not just a short-term phenomenon. Companies are not shrinking their equity base or paying high rates of dividends because demand is depressed. In fact, the US is well into a long-term trend of moving the ratio between spending on investment and spending on shareholders in favor of the latter. Ever since the early 1980s the trend in investment spending has been on the decline. Again, there was a short surge in the 1990s but it did not usher in a lasting shift to a growing use of capital for investment. A few years later, the US corporate sector had returned to a

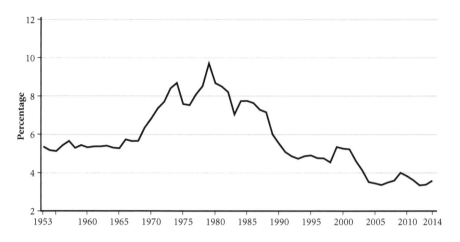

Source: Federal Reserve Statistical Release, Z.1, table F.103.
Figure 2.11 US ratio of investment/cash to shareholders

declining trend, and with a growing propensity to spend its profits on shareholders rather than investing them.

There is nothing wrong with returning money to the shareholders. After all, they own the company and have made investments on the presumption that they would get a good return. The key question is what the decline in business investment, and the growing propensity to spend money on shareholders, reveals about the capacity of corporateville to actually be or become the great champions of productivity growth or, if you like, to step into a new era of fast and furious innovation. The reality is that many companies feel high dividends and share buybacks are necessary to maintain or raise the companies' earnings per share. They are weighing down expectations of what levels of profit they can generate – and generally preparing for a future that is not very exciting. This does not sit easily with the projection of a pending, if not current, innovation revolution. The actual image of capitalism tells a different story, that companies are increasingly hesitant to invest and innovate, and that they are aging the asset base rather than modernizing it through new investment.

3

THE COLOR OF CAPITALISM IS GRAY

The colour grey is an unemotional colour, neutral, on the fence and neither here, nor there. Tis why old people's hair turns grey ... betwixt life and death.

Ursley Kempe, alias Grey (1525–82)

Hence the extraordinary growth of a class, or rather, of a stratum of rentiers, i.e., people who live by "clipping coupons" [in the sense of collecting interest payments on bonds], who take no part in any enterprise whatever, whose profession is idleness.

Vladimir Ilyich Lenin, *Imperialism, the Highest Stage of Capitalism*

"American by Birth, Rebel by Choice" was the infamous slogan of the Harley-Davidson Motor Company, or what is simply called HD. After 12 years, however, the American Machine & Foundry (AMF) wanted to be released from that rebel. After fighting a losing battle against foreign competition, and problems of poor quality in its main product, the AMF – a conglomerate in recreational equipment – decided to drop one of the most legendary brands of America Inc. The company was in a bad shape, and to many at the time it seemed there was no end to the perils it faced. It had been a long time coming from the early 1900s when William S. Harley had figured out how to fit an engine into a bicycle. By the time AMF got involved in 1969, HD had built a reputation for good quality, entrepreneurial pride, innovation ingenuity, and business drive. By the time it got out, that reputation was in jeopardy, if not already squandered.

Harley-Davidson is a story of capitalism – a story of the failures as well as the successes that capitalism breeds. Fortunately, HD did not go down. The "legend rolls on" – to recall its slogan – and today it controls more than half of the American heavyweight motorcycle market.[1] Its return to glory came after new owners arrived in the early 1980s and put the company back on track. Vaughn Beals and his coinvestors mounted a management buyout, borrowed $81.5 million on top of $1 million in equity, and bet everything they had on themselves and the hog.[2] It was quite a contrast with the previous owner.

AMF had not been a bad owner. In fact, it had invested quite a lot of money in HD and did what you would expect from a conglomerate proprietor, if not more, to raise profitability. But for AMF, HD was just one investment among many, allowing it to diversify its portfolio of companies and offerings. Yet for Harley-Davidson to share space with AMF's motley crew of automated bowling equipment, atomic research reactors, snowmobiles, golf clubs, and tennis racquets was like forcing Dennis Rodman out of the basketball court to play bridge with Warren Buffett. With the lack of fit of its identity and customers HD could not thrive, nor benefit from synergies with other parts of the conglomerate. It needed investors that let Dennis play basketball – and once such investors took control of HD, it became a successful example not just of capitalism but of the critical role that ownership and capitalists play.

That is the story of capitalism. Just like other failing or low-performing companies, HD needed a capitalist that made the company entrepreneurial, one that was not investing according to a finance theory formula. Capitalism and the market are not, of course, synonyms. While markets and competition have been unleashed, the conditions for capitalist ownership have deteriorated across the Western world. The ethos of the capitalist, if you like, is to get ahead of the market, even to monopolize it. The virtue of markets, however, is to make sure the capitalist fails on that mission. Capitalism is a system for the ownership of production and it simply cannot work without its main character, the capitalist. Think then where we are today – after 40 years of shrinking the role of capitalists in the ownership of public firms. This is the drama of the modern Western economy.

Capitalist owners today are a rare species. Apart from a dozen or so high-tech entrepreneurs who are household names, we no longer hear much about the big capitalists. True, they are not typical media material because they cannot be recognized by their extravagant living or conspicuous consumption. They are not jet-setting members of the Billionaire Club, trawling the world looking for happiness or escaping boredom. Nor are they the villains of Thomas Piketty's history of rentier capitalism and its return in modern times.[3] Big capitalists *do* belong to the "one percent." But they are neither cousins of the cold-hearted Ebenezer Scrooge nor come with the pedigree of greedy "big swinging dicks," the sharks of financial capitalism memorably portrayed by Michael Lewis in *Liar's Poker*. Capitalists should not be the targets of the angry left or right. Wall Street may have staged a quick recovery from the financial crisis and be richer than ever, but *people with money and capitalists are not the same thing*. Capitalists have money too, but they are different from other rich people floating around the corporate world in that they practice visible ownership, are entrepreneurial, and perform the critical role of controlling corporate development.

Unfortunately, we are gradually moving to the point when it is time to write the obituary of capitalist ownership. We are not there yet, but as we will show in this chapter, the tenor of ownership in the capitalist system has changed profoundly, and not for the better. Big capitalists still exist, and some new ones have been minted too, especially in the digital sector. Yet the color of capitalism has now turned gray. Just as in the epigraph from midwife-turned-witch Ursley Kempe, capitalism is betwixt – right in the middle of an unresolved development; neither one thing nor the other; not here and not there; between life and death.

And the paradox is that the *gray capitalism* that now governs the economy is a response to natural and partly desirable events. Yet the individual rationality does not hang together with the collective good. Gray capitalism has influenced business growth and ambition, and progressively made big companies embrace comforting bureaucracy and allowed them to defend themselves against uncertainty, innovation and contestable competition.

This chapter chronicles the rise of gray capitalism and introduces you to the stray ownership of corporateville. Gray capital, we argue, is defined by its absence of capitalist characters. Capital without capitalistic characters is often, but not always, related to the source of capital – where the capital comes from – and its intimacy with an aging and gray-haired population. Gray capital spawns a system of ownership that is *complex by design*, *allocates resources according to a rentier formula*, and *crowds out innovations*. If that was not enough, gray capital favors companies that espouse and guarantee predictability.

The color of capital is gray

Capitalism has turned into a riddle without an end. While it is a system for ownership, the distinguishing characteristic of gray capitalism is that no one knows who owns and controls a company, let alone who the diffused owners are. In a way, ownership has been separated from ownership, to use a phrase from corporate governance,[4] and as a consequence no one really knows what the owners want to do with a company. It is a faceless capitalism.

Big listed companies have multiple owners, and that has always been the case. But for most of the history of joint-stock capitalism, it has been possible to point to at least one big owner, or perhaps a smaller number of owners, and figure out the industrial or capitalist idea behind that ownership. They were not always good owners, perhaps not even capitalist owners. Big owners of the past sometimes also lacked ambition or business vision. However, it is different now. There is even less ownership competition, and capitalist owners control far fewer companies.

So let us start the riddle. Take General Electric (GE) as an example: a company that is quoted on the New York Stock Exchange with a free float close to 100 percent. Who owns it? The largest owner is the Vanguard Group, which – at the time of writing – held 5.6 percent of all GE's stock. That is not much and far from the levels of ownership necessary to have a controlling, let alone entrepreneurial function in the company. Yet it is far more than any other owner of GE. The biggest direct holder of floated stock in GE had collected merely 1.9 million shares, which can be compared to Vanguard Group's 566 million.

To know who owns General Electric it is necessary, as a first step, to ask: who owns the Vanguard Group? That turns out to be the wrong question, because the Vanguard Group is not investing its own money. It just represents Vanguard's different funds, and the company, which pioneered the market for mutual index funds, operates – like other funds – on a principle of diversified allocation of capital. Hence, Vanguard does not necessarily hold GE stocks because it has an idea for how to make a successful company even more successful, even if it is an asset manager that is a more active owner than many other asset managers. Vanguard manages assets of almost $3 trillion and invests in a great number of companies. Its principal interest is to manage other people's money – in fact, about 20 million savers have put money in its funds. Who are these 20 million savers that collectively are the biggest owner of GE? It is impossible to say, of course, but quite a number of them are not direct savers – they are beneficiaries of employers and others that have invested in pensions plans. Even if we worked the stairs down to the mezzanine or ground floor of savers, the group would be too large to ask what they want to do with their intermediated ownership of GE. It seems safe to say, however, that they are not putting their savings in Vanguard funds because they want an ownership role in GE.

If it is impossible to know the identity of the owners, it is equally impossible to know *what the owners want*. When companies are principally owned and controlled by owners whose agendas are, at best, arcane, capitalism turns gray. Most people do not acknowledge there is a problem in obscure and gray ownership. The basic rebuttal is that investors simply desire investment returns and if the company cannot generate it investors will leave. Yet while it is true, not to say evident, that everyone tends to be happy as long as companies make good money, it is equally true that the desire to make money is not what determines whether an owner is successful or not. Money can be made in many different ways. For the company to thrive, owners with highly dispersed ownership interests have to be aligned with the success of the the company. Sometimes they are clearly not. Many investment funds, for instance, have significant ownership in competing firms.

To complicate things further, owners differ in timing – stockholding periods – and risk levels, including their definitions of risks and uncertainty. They also perceive business development and ownership in varied ways, and that involves how boards should behave, act and be constituted, and the selection of manager types for certain markets and cycles of company development. If a manager plans to migrate the business into some other market discipline for good strategic reasons, he or she had better check with the owners first because they might have investment guidelines against it. Reporting and measurement of key financial ratios vary and change, and the control and influence over management follow from the selection process of board members – or lack thereof. All of these factors combined, ever subject to change, only begin to show the complexity of ownership and of knowing what the owner wants.

Take the case, admittedly stylized and simplified, of a fund or investor that owns two companies in two different markets that countercycle each other. If it has to draw down investment risks, it cannot just sell shares in one of the companies because that would upset the balance. The investor must either sell shares in the other company too, or find a replacement to recreate a balanced investment portfolio, even if it is satisfied with the investment. The decision will under any circumstance be influenced by portfolio investment concerns and not just the performance and future of the companies. Such investors buy shares in companies for a variety of reasons, with the performance and growth of a company being just one reason – and one that easily gets demoted as portfolio allocation risks take priority. In a world where a greater part of equity and debt holding follows such a formula, and where market and regulatory trends lead to far greater homogenization of investor behavior, the general profile of corporate ownership gradually comes to reflect broad macro trends and issues around systemic risks rather than the actual merits of a company and its future.[5]

So let us go back to the riddle: if no one knows who owns a company, no one knows what concerns the investors and why they have invested. It follows that no one will know if a company is following the wishes of the owners or not, or whether there is an alliance of interest between owners and companies. As a consequence, no one really knows whom the management serves. You see where this is going? It is an ownership structure based on *known unknowns*. That is what makes capitalism betwixt – and gray.

Add to that the global linkages of dispersed ownership. Global ownership of companies is connected together in a structure resembling a spider's web, where the ultimate ownership comes back to a small number of financial companies, or spiders. In a study of global concentration of ownership, penetrating into the ownership of as many as 37 million global companies, including financial companies and investors, it turned out that only 147 firms control about 40 percent of all corporate assets.[6] If this group of spiders is expanded to 737 companies, together they control 80 percent of assets. Notwithstanding some methodological problems, corporate interconnectedness adds a different complexion of gray to ownership. No one really knows the full scale of the connections or how companies relate to each other, and for that reason we cannot know the impact of companies owning each other.

We know, however, that savers largely define ownership and that the size and complexity of public markets force savers, institutions, and retail investors alike to rely on third parties for their investments. It is *this* development that has created the "financialization" of the economy in the past four decades, or the unparalleled growth of the financial economy in relation to the real economy. The late US economist Hyman Minsky called it "money manager capitalism."[7] It is not a new phenomenon. "I would rather see Finance less proud and Industry more content," argued Winston Churchill in 1925. But the economic gods did not listen to that wish, nor to repeated warnings about the instability of financial growth that is supported by state guarantees.

In Churchill's home country, the United Kingdom, the daily transactions of foreign exchange now exceed trade in goods and services by almost a hundred times. Yes, you read that right – a hundred times. The £7 trillion in liabilities managed by British banks is almost unrelated to production; only 3 percent of lending from banks goes to firms that produce goods and services. Payment proceeds in the UK exceed national income by 40 times.[8]

It is not much different on the other side of the pond, even if the American economy is much larger than the British. The financial economy's proportion of total US GDP, measured in value added, expanded from 4.9 percent in 1980 to 8.3 percent at its peak in 2006.[9] Total liabilities of commercial banks in the US are just below $15 trillion.[10] And for the entire world, the ratio between total global output of goods and services and financial assets was approximately 1 to 10 in 2012. So for every "real economy dollar" there are ten "financial dollars." If this relationship stays the same in the future, financial assets are expected to reach $900 trillion by 2020, compared to a GDP of $90 trillion.[11]

The size of the financial sector is daunting, but what are more worrying are the qualitative aspects of financialization, especially how it enabled gray capital to take over the core ownership role in capitalism. With little direct ownership but multiple intermediaries that are at best only occasionally aligned, there are bound to be consequences for companies, their long-term ambitions – and capitalism itself. Inevitably, gray ownership embeds itself into the structure, culture, and ambition of corporations – and, more operatively, how they allocate resources and investments. In most cases, gray capital does not invest in companies for the long term; nor is it common that the gray capital comes with a clearly defined business agenda for the investee. In fact, gray capital is more often than not invested on the premise that a company largely should follow the market trend. That is not a capitalist characteristic; it is rather a character of rentier capitalism.

Finally, capitalism has turned gray because a growing part of savings and shareholding is linked to the aging of Western societies and, as part of that, the growing role of retirement savings – in one form or another. "I say age ain't nothin' but a number," sings Saffire in "Middle Aged Blues Boogie." But as every asset manager can tell you, it is an important number. As people live longer, more money has to be saved to safeguard future pensions. With the growing instability of public pension systems, individuals today have a greater need than previous generations to save for their retirement. In that way, the role of savings that are invested in the economy gets changed. First, with the growing role of such savings, a greater amount of them and investment in corporations is channeled through intermediaries. In fact, the lion's share of the value-added created in the financial sector in the past 20 years has been made up from the fees paid to asset managers by savers.[12] Second, retirement savings have a preference for short-term over long-term payoffs. Consequently, a greater part of retirement savings avoids equity and rather funds companies through debt markets, additionally diluting the role of capitalist ownership and control.[13]

The irony is that gray capitalism is in many ways the effect of desirable and rational behavior by savers. For most of us, it is far better to save in funds and use the services of professional asset managers than to invest without any real knowledge of how savings are allocated, like betting all the money on one single stock. The paradox is that what is good for the individual saver is not good for economies, at least not in the long run as gray capital makes up an increasing part of the total financial economy. Gray capital, then, creates a capitalist economy where ownership is based predominantly on indirect ownership, or known unknowns. It promotes ownership without capitalist characters, and is increasingly dependent on gray-haired people, often investing their savings like a rentier.

Prospecting for capitalists: meet the owners

A few years ago one of the British tabloids ran a story about what is perhaps a usual sight on London's streets, but nevertheless drew people's attention. A $3 million Bugatti stood parked in Knightsbridge, outside the fashionable Bulgari Hotel. This was enough to collect admirers, yet next to it sat an equally expensive LaFerrari, a $1 million McLaren, and a Maybach – a budget trolley in comparison, but still worth almost half a million US dollars. Together, the story reported, the cars helped to build a crowd. This squad of horsepower and conspicuous luxury waiting on double yellow lines for its masters was not a sign of London bouncing back after the Great Recession. Nor was it the site of an annual meeting between Gordon Gekko, Sherman McCoy, Patrick Bateman and their modern, real-life incarnations in the asset management industry. The owners were "wealthy individuals from the Middle East" who had airlifted their four-wheeled toys to London for a short stopover. It costs roughly $30,000 for a car's return ticket with Qatar Airways, but considering that a customized paint job alone can exceed $40,000, probably no one complained.[14]

Stories like these get associated with capitalism. And, in a way, that is only fair. Even if rich people are oceans away from capitalist ownership, or the way companies work, there is no point denying that the way corporate and financial capitalism has evolved has spawned unearned riches – and reckless consumption. Capitalism needs capitalists that consciously and rationally seek to maximize profit in order to make the most out of whatever resources they have. To be a capitalist, or not, really has nothing to do with wealth. Likewise, to be rich does not make anyone a capitalist or reveal anything about whether someone has a capitalist character. In fact, someone with limited resources may be more inclined to make capitalistic investments than a rich owner, a rentier, or a superrich playboy flying insanely expensive cars between continents for their own shopping amusement.

This is an important distinction because it goes straight to the heart of current anxieties over tax, inequality, and whether capitalists should be squeezed harder. The latest financial crisis naturally ushered in that debate, not to mention the "Panama Papers" showing how investors have been hiding money in tax havens alongside thugs and kleptocrats. Unfortunately, however, the debate often stops where the interesting discussion should start, and never goes as far as addressing what type of ownership encourages bad versions of capitalism. There is a great deal of difference between various owners, and they tend to spawn different outcomes. While capitalists are rare creatures in today's economy there has been a very rapid growth of other forms of ownership. The problem is not that a lot of playboys around the world spend too much money, but that they have earned it through predominantly rentier forms of ownership. And many others have joined them in that version of capitalism. In fact, the separation of ownership from ownership has opened the way for increasingly rentier-like behavior by institutional owners like pension funds, insurance funds and others. It has made the financial economy and asset managers the masters rather than the servants of the real economy.

These trends are not separate events; and they did not happen suddenly. An institutional investor can be a principal owner and provide asset management at the same time. A bank is part of the financial economy yet it can own real assets, make direct investments, and contribute with active investment management. An asset manager might be legally detached from principal ownership, but the commitment letter can be so open that it almost resembles direct ownership. And all roles have gone through profound changes during the last decades. The financial sector has multiplied several times. Asset managers and professional investment institutions grew in importance as volumes of savings and investment jumped. Financial institutions expanded on the back of globalization and the need for professionalized investments, not least due to the rise in aggregate savings. They all underpinned the rise of gray capitalism and, in that way, are part of the big transformation of capitalism in the past 40 years.

That is not to say that every institutional owner and asset manager is a bad capitalist. Nor should the rise of the financial economy generally be blamed for causing the woes of current Western capitalism. Each and every actor in this development had rational motives. But they all conspired, unintentionally, to transform capitalism. Like a Greek tragedy in which every actor acts rationally, if not morally, yet still produces a bad outcome, the sources of gray capitalism have been taking Western economies for a ride toward a growth tragedy.

The financial sector in the Western world started to expand in earnest around 1980, and it was part of a larger trend of intermediaries investing, advising, managing and facilitating companies. Few characters have symbolized that early era of latter-day financial capitalism as much as Gordon Gekko, the villain of the 1987 movie *Wall Street*. Barring his criminal behavior, Gekko is in several ways a representative of the financial ecology that has grown in the past decades. The financial sector has expanded rapidly, and rewards its stars with exorbitant salaries. Total remuneration increased sharply and the sector's share of all American corporate profits went from well below 10 percent in 1980 to almost 30 percent in 2012. Gekko, like most other financiers, did not know how businesses are built, run and made productive. Presented with an opportunity to take over a failing airline, his best idea for how to turn the investment to profit was to plunder the company's pension fund. These masters of the universe are, for most of the time, managing other people's money, and they have only a limited and often short-term perspective on how value can be generated. They are asset managers and their distinguishing characteristic in gray capitalism is their role as intermediary.

The capital that asset managers administer often comes from other intermediaries such as insurance companies, investment funds, and pension funds. Together they held US$92.6 trillion of world assets in 2013, according to the OECD (see Figure 3.1). The largest parts come from investment funds, followed by insurance companies and pension funds. But the total sum of almost US$93 trillion equals the American GDP – five times over. Growth among all of them has been steady for years, naturally with a volatile development around the Great Recession. They recovered quickly, however, and between 2009 and 2013 investment funds increased by 6.7 percent annually, and pension funds by 8.2 percent.[15]

The rise of institutional holdings marks a shift from direct to professionalized ownership. Only a few decades ago, institutional investors were significantly smaller and, largely, just a background decor of capitalism. They were not nearly as numerous as they are today, and they were local rather than global. For instance, only 6.1 percent of total outstanding equity was institutionalized in 1950 compared to 50.6 percent in 2009. Natural persons owned approximately 40 percent of all outstanding public stocks in the US in 2013, down from around 84 percent in the 1960s. In the UK, natural persons owned 11 percent of outstanding public stocks in 2013, down from 54 percent 50 years earlier.[16]

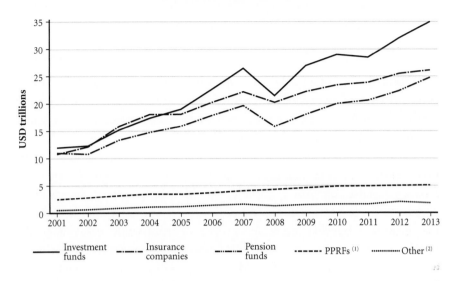

Source: OECD, "Pension Markets in Focus, 2014," 9, fig. 1.
Figure 3.1 Total assets by types of institutional investors in the OECD, 2001–2013

The proportion of invested capital coming from direct ownership no longer plays an important role. People saving for retirement prefer to use funds to manage what they invest for them. Companies allocating resources for their employees use professional intermediaries, and governments saving for their citizens use professional investors for all types of investments, ranging from private equity to real estate investments. These professionals, the asset managers, follow very patterned behavior, almost as if they were drones managed by someone at a remote location. They have a portfolio guide that defines that allocation of their investments. The higher up in the food chain people get, the more time they will have to spend on making sure they stay on a highly mapped territory. The benchmark is not how fast they move from point A to point B in that territory, but how they perform compared to others moving in the same terrain.

In addition to detailed internal instructions, there are fiduciary duties and laws defining how to perform their responsibilities, and with the passage of new financial regulations in the West, these duties and laws now add up to such an amount that if they were put in a normal book, it would likely deter any young aspirant from taking a job. As in previous rounds of regulations, asset managers now also get credit ratings agencies poking their noses into what they do, and the standard formula for any manager who wants to get a share of the gray capital is to avoid doing anything that would make rating agencies take a deeper interest.

You probably see where this is going. The point we are making is not to pass judgment on the performance of individual asset managers. It is rather that these money managers are completely different creatures than the capitalists that most people associate with corporate ownership. While capitalist ownership is about responsibility and control, asset managers are ultimately actors who cannot practice ownership control and responsibility. He or she simply cannot be a capitalist.

In 2012, after the recovery from the Great Recession, the global asset management industry managed 36.5 percent of assets held by pension funds, insurance companies, sovereign wealth funds, high-net-worth individuals, and the mass affluent. Asset managers are not the only form of intermediaries, but they represent a great proportion of the gray ownership in Western economies. And as GDP has expanded in the West, the asset management industry has followed – and, going forward, is likely to grow faster than the rest of the economy, according to PwC. In 2020, the industry is estimated to have expanded to manage more than 45 percent of total holdings. If the forecast is correct, the industry will then have US$130 trillion under its administration.[17] And looking at recent growth, it is not difficult to see why the expansion could continue. EFAMA, an industry body, claims that the European assets managed by the industry increased by 11 percent in 2012 and 9 percent in 2013.[18]

Intermediaries have seized capitalism and their expansion has continuously led investors and governments to demand greater control of the system. While understandable – and, indeed, needed if you consider all the bad apples in the business – these control systems have broadly exacerbated the anticapitalist nature of the asset management industry. Many of these controls have in effect enabled asset managers to contract away the responsibilities that come with owning significant stakes in any company. But it is unclear to whom they have been contracted. Regulators are part of that unknown gray quantity, for sure. And so are rating agencies, industry bodies for self-regulation, and – of course – the savers that are presented with page after page of legal-financial lingo when they begin to save in a fund. In that way, the controlling and entrepreneurial role of the capitalist owner is passed around among many different individuals and institutions. And when things go wrong, the buck does not stop anywhere, it just continues to move.

Empowering intermediated and external capital market funding of companies has consequences for how companies manage their capital and other assets, and encourages corporate cash hoarding or strategies to keep capital liquid. Companies that age their asset base often do it because they need to improve their cash liquidities in order to ensure predictable returns for their gray owners. Just as cash hoarding in Japan has partly been determined by its ownership[19] and corporate governance structure,[20] Western corporates are pressured by the short-term earning demands of their intermediary owners. Firms with a big and controlling owner are always at risk of rent extraction, or that the owner transfers capital out of the company. A similar logic seems to operate in firms with no sizable but many intermediary owners: they seek to extract rents from the current asset base – and take capital out of the companies. Firms cannot retain a large part of their earnings and use them for long-term investment but are pushed out to an external capital market for funding that has shrunk its interest in long-term value generation but stays eager to make sure that the company plays the numbers game.

Sovereign wealth funds and the socialization of private companies

A new kid on the corporate block is the sovereign wealth fund (SWF). Clearly, such funds are the first choice for some governments when allocating excess earnings, like revenues from oil and other natural resources, and they have grown to be influential actors in the modern corporate world. Their influence is actually now so large that the SWFs constitute the greatest socialization of corporate assets in the West since the socialization of Central and Eastern European economies after World War II. Their role in the ownership of firms is already felt in corporateville and, while there are differences between them, they have the effect of making companies even less capitalist and more political.

SWFs are run for the benefit of government owners that sometimes are democratic but more often do not exactly come with stellar records of democracy, civil liberties, and economic freedom. Like a pension fund, SWFs are based on savings put away for a rainy day when current income streams do not flow anymore. They also sterilize the economy from inflation and the so-called Dutch disease that spreads in the economy when one sector generates disproportionate foreign earnings and lowers the competitiveness of other sectors. They are "golden pension schemes," as someone once put it, and deeply embedded in the political governance of a country. Therefore, they usually share all the bad characteristics that come with authoritarian regimes, like cronyism and lack of transparency.

While the beginning of SWFs can be traced back to 1854, when the Texas legislature appropriated $2 million "for the benefit of the public schools of Texas" and created the Special School Fund, it was a rarity until recent decades. In 2014, the Texas fund, now called the Permanent School Fund, sported $36.3 billion in total assets.[21] Long before then, however, it had been distanced by younger SWFs, like the Kuwait Investment Authority (KIA), which had grown to take a top seat in the SWF asset race. In 2015, KIA held US$548 billion in assets.[22]

However, it was not until the turn of the millennium that SWFs became high-street fashion for governments swimming in money from the sale of commodities. Thirteen of the 20 largest SWFs in the world were actually founded in the first decade of the twenty-first century. The name "sovereign wealth fund" itself was coined as late as 2005, and between 2008 and 2015, SWFs more than doubled their total size from US$3.05 trillion to US$6.31 trillion, although some argue that to be too low an estimate.[23] At any rate, at that size, SWFs now carry a lot of influence and ownership power. To take just one example: Norway's SWF alone manages about US$860 billion and owns 1.3 percent of all corporate equity in the world.[24]

Most likely, SWFs will expand over the foreseeable future and continue to mitigate economic booms and busts for their government masters. Their growth is expected to continue, with 7 percent compound annual growth rate until 2020, according to PwC. By the same token, the total SWF volume is expected to reach US$9 trillion by the same year.[25] Their strategies for asset allocation will likely continue along trend as well. They will go on investing in foreign currencies like the greenback, the euro and the Swiss franc. Wall Street, Nasdaq, the London Stock Exchange and other key stock markets will get a good portion of their capital as well. Investment in private companies and infrastructure are also favored investment targets – and more so recently as their traditional assets have become more volatile.

If SWFs were a country, they would probably rank lower than Zimbabwe on Transparency International's ranking. The Linaburg Maduell Transparency Index (LMTI) measures their transparency and, to cut a long story short, if there are problems understanding the ownership motives of investment funds, these are light years ahead of the SWFs. SWFs are more like dark matter – known but not observable. Differences exist, of course, but SWFs are generally secretive and only one of the ten largest SWFs in the world – hey presto, Norway! – gets the highest transparency grade. Seven of them rate so poorly that it is impossible to know what they really own. In 2015, these "secret seven" together managed over US$3.46 trillion in assets.[26]

One can understand why many SWFs are shy about the outside world. SWFs are pretty much about politics, and to be frank about it, it makes little difference if the fund sits in Oslo, Riyadh or Beijing – it is still politics that dominates the governance of the funds. Cash-rich entities connected to governments will always attract political attention. Just like placing a sugar cube on an anthill in springtime, the SWFs attract admirers, beggars and cronies.

Norway is no exception, even if it is an open and transparent country. With a size that is almost twice as big as Norway's GDP, the country's SWF has become the subject of heavy politicization. When its Chief Executive Officer, Yngve Slyngstad, was ranked number four in the top 100 "most significant and impactful public investor executives of 2014" by the Sovereign Wealth Fund Institute, the reason given was that "faced with pressure from NGOs, politicians and think thanks, the sovereign wealth fund has *tried its best* to take a logical approach to investing" (emphasis added).[27] The domestic connection between politics and SWFs is strong through the symbiotic relation between them in the ownership and management of hydrocarbon reserves. Take Norway again. Its SWF is but one player in the system, and the Norwegian government exercises control over the exploitation of energy reserves through Statoil, co-ownership of energy transport infrastructure, and through its role as regulator of transport prices, licenses, resource exhaustion, and more. And then it taxes energy production, and quite heavily too. Hence, the conduct of the fund is an integral part of a system of political management. If that is the political anchor of Norway's SWF, imagine then how the SWFs in less open and transparent countries are run.

Politics likely motivates the asset allocation of SWFs too. Simply put, they do not have a capitalist agenda, and given how much revenues for SWFs fluctuate with the course of commodity prices, they can also be unreliable owners as they may suddenly have to change track. And it is not only the revenue side that diverts attention from a capitalist agenda. In an attempt to appease the public during the Arab Spring of 2011, to take one example, Gulf States suddenly and radically cut allocations to foreign investments. The calls to "balance fluctuations" went out of the window virtually overnight. Despite increased revenues, up 6 percent from 2011 to 2012, Gulf States cut transfers to SWFs by almost 40 percent. At the same time, SWF investments in the Gulf rose to 54 percent, up from 33 percent the previous year.[28] It is possible, at least theoretically, that this change was for strict investment reasons, but in reality the sudden change of asset allocation was politically motivated. The SWFs had to return capital back home in order to help governments to stem opposition.

The sovereign wealth funds have done much to burnish their political credentials. In the aftermath of the financial crisis, their critics were quickly silenced when Western corporates pleaded with SWFs to invest and to save credit-dry Western companies from bankruptcy. Companies desperate for funding, neglected by strained banks, did what they could to survive, and perhaps that is why so many were kowtowing to SWFs, even calling them "white knights."[29] Like every actor with liquidity, big money can be created in crises and downturns, but their role in Western corporate ownership is turning into a problem as the model presupposes that capitalism can work even if the financial impulses come from government offices. The OECD has rightly voiced concerns about SWFs' "financial stability, corporate governance and political interference and protectionism."[30] Yet there is an entire gray dimension to SWF ownership that is deplorable too.

The funds stretch themselves over continents, just like other institutional investors, and they use intermediaries. When they are not making political investments, they tend to follow standard diversification formulas and hence behave just like the herd. They are riddled with agency problems and if you take a country like China, it is the Central Committee of the Communist Party of China, that puzzling institution, which owns ultimate decision-making power for the country's SWF. The Norwegian SWF is different, yet it owns shares in 9,000 companies, dispersed over 75 countries, and no matter how it organizes itself, it is impossible for it to use its ownership for capitalist purposes.[31] Nor does it want to. But given the diffuse ownership of many big firms, an institution like this can get significant power in a company since it belongs among the larger shareholders and has such a diffuse ownership role which is combined with political demands about the risks it can take and the returns it should seek. The AMF fumbled when it came to its ownership of Harley-Davidson – yet it only managed a handful of interests at a time and never came close to the diffused interests of the Norwegian SWF and its colleagues.

Pensions and retirement savings

Pensions were a small financial matter when Otto von Bismarck radically broke with tradition and introduced the modern pensions system. Today, pension systems are chronic headaches for Western economies. When Bismarck introduced state pensions it was hardly a financial gamble to offer retirement from the age of 70 when life expectancy at birth was roughly 40 years in Germany. Still, the Iron Chancellor was labeled a socialist – someone who put Teutonic fiscal cameralism in jeopardy. Today is different – and radically so. Life expectancy in Germany is 81 years – and climbing. With an effective retirement age of 61–2, and large cohorts of people who are getting close to retirement, Germany like other countries is facing a raid on the public purse. While the country is strong at least fiscally, Germany still has no developed idea for how to protect fiscal policy from getting plundered by the costs of pensions, healthcare and elderly care.[32]

Still, Germany is in a good position compared to some other countries. Its additional costs for pensions, healthcare and long-term care up to 2050 have been estimated at 7 percent of GDP. In other words, assuming that the tax burden is not going to increase, Germany needs to find a way to free up close to one-sixth of its current government expenditure. For the euro area as a whole, the additional public spending necessary is close to 9 percent of GDP. By comparison, Spain needs an additional 13.5 percent of GDP, which is about one-third of government expenditure.[33] Under the scenario of high economic growth, it could possibly be manageable for some countries. Yet as Western economies see falls in their economic growth rates, it looks increasingly impossible for aging to pass unnoticed in fiscal budgets.

Yet the fiscal effect of aging is just one side of the coin. On the other side is, perhaps paradoxically, a warning sign that savings related to aging are occupying too much space in corporate ownership and funding. And the role of aging for the volume of gray capital is only going to increase. In 2013, says the OECD, pension funds and so-called public pension return funds (PPRF) in the OECD summed up to a total of nearly US$30 trillion. A fraction of future pension liabilities, but nevertheless a substantial sum when transformed into corporate holdings. Add to that all *private* pension assets together – including those sitting in insurance companies, banks and more (excluding PPRFs) – and we get to US$36 trillion.[34] Yet not even that tells the whole story as people save for retirement indirectly as well, buying property or stocks, for instance, or investing in collectable items.[35]

While there have always been savings for the silver days in the modern economy, the growth of retirement savings has been fast, and will be even faster in the future. Retirement is no longer the end of life. People today are planning, indeed yearning, for a period of active aging, and modern healthcare allows people to have full and healthy lives decades after retirement. They know, however, that future taxpayers will not foot the entire bill for their lifestyles, so they have to save even more. While perfectly understandable, the incentives for the individual do not hang together with the interests of capitalism when savings are intermediated by institutions. More money in retirement savings then means an expansion of gray capitalism. The institutions get bigger – and as people close to retirement prefer to invest in debt instruments rather than equity, the savings pattern can lead to both a diminishing role of equity and depleted capitalist ownership.

The life cycle thesis of savings holds that people save for retirement when they work, but when they reach retirement age they start spending money instead. Not all countries look the same, however. Saving rates are higher in Japan and Italy, for instance, compared to the UK and the US, even if the trend is similar. In most countries, turning 30 apparently awakens the will to save and, nearing the retirement age, that urge gets cooler, unless you are an Italian. Like so much in life, aging brings a different perspective, including on savings, and at the age of 65, people find it less compelling to store money. After all, why continue to save when life is moving closer to its end?

But not only do older people save less; young and old also save differently because of their age. It makes no sense for old people to embrace high investment risks because that requires the luxury of having a relatively longer investment perspective. It is easier for a young person to afford higher risks, as they are likely to yield better returns in the long run even if the journey there is shaky. Old investors prefer safer investments, like real estate – at least they did before the crisis. They favor mutual funds and cash equivalents to bonds and stocks. Diversification, not a single stock strategy, is the preferred allocation. Moreover, stocks with less volatility are considered better than stocks with higher volatility.

The average pension-saver may not make these preferences clear when setting aside money on a monthly basis, or having their employer do it for them, but money managers do. Anyone who has ever met a pension investment fund manager knows the importance of age. The level of professionalism in risk management has greatly increased over time, and actuarial conditions now dominate professional pension saving. Naturally, this is good for the investor, but the actuarial investment code makes capitalism grayer.

And the future will hold more of the same. Aging of populations happens fast in high-income OECD countries. Only 9 percent of the population in high-income nations were 65 years or older in 1970, but in 2013 over 23 percent belonged to that age group.[36] Unless immigration shakes those numbers up, Western economies will become ever more like a retirement home.[37] Less than 22 percent of the total population will be 19 or younger in 2030. Some countries will change more than others. Germany, for instance, is expected to have only 18 percent of its population between 0 and 19 years in 2030, compared to a 65-plus generation that will make up 28 percent of the country.

But economies are not only getting older; the population in many countries will even decline, and anyone daring to peek into the future to see what that implies should travel to Japan and walk around in the suburbs of the major cities to see what happens to a society when populations go down. Today, 8 million homes have been abandoned in Japan due to population decline, and by 2033 almost 22 million homes will be empty.[38] Shifting demography affects the economy as well as capital allocation in a society. While economies are not preprogrammed in how they respond to aging, there will be an acceleration in gray capital in the forthcoming decades, and the relative relationship between long-term and short-term investments in various assets will most likely reduce the West's propensity for capitalist ownership even further.

Gray capital makes capitalism gray

Gray capital has been transforming capitalism – and will do so even more in the future. Capitalism has changed in several ways, but, as noted, three aspects are central for this analysis. Capitalism has become *complex by design*; it now favors the *allocation of resources according to a rentier formula*; and it *crowds out innovations*.

At a distance, company ownership in the Western world seems progressive enough for capitalism to work well. For some, capitalism may not appear complex at all. Rules guide the separation of roles and responsibilities in what appears to be appropriate, if not ideal, governance, with a chain of interest – from principal owners, via investment representatives, to companies – that is distinct and unbroken. But the closer you get, the more the chain looks like a complex patchwork of conflicting interests and complicated regulations. Gray capital spawns a gray capitalism that is *complex by design*.

The patchwork is not harmonious, to say the least. In fact, it separates owners from companies. The use of asset managers and trustees, sometimes through layers on layers of intermediaries, has become the norm for most investments, and they stand between the ultimate money source and the subject of an investment. Legal and practical reasons motivate each independent layer. However, the complexity of the system generally undermines capitalism. It was never the intention to blur ownership, but it is nevertheless what happens when the multiple layers between money and investee create an agency problem. Capitalism has got trapped in a principal–agent foxhole.

The agency dilemma is as old as capitalism and essentially concerns nothing less than human nature. The question asks who companies and management really work for – the shareholders or themselves? John Kenneth Galbraith used more colorful prose to explain the essence of capitalist agency. To think that companies should work for shareholders, he argued, "one must imagine that a man of vigorous, lusty and reassuringly heterosexual inclination eschews the lovely and available women by whom he is intimately surrounded in order to maximize the opportunities of other men whose existence he knows of only by hearsay."[39]

Galbraith broadly got it right – even if he was ahead of his time, writing before others had coined the principal–agent theory. His flair for language caught the imagination of people, but there were others before him who had touched upon the same type of conflict inside joint-stock companies. Adam Smith, for instance, tendered the same view in his classic tome, *The Wealth of Nations*, where he made the point that "being the managers rather of other people's money than of their own, it cannot well be expected that they should watch over it with the same anxious vigilance with which the partners in a private copartnery frequently watch over their own."[40]

The OECD has also offered pointed skepticism about what happens in firms with highly diffused and intermediated ownership. The link between corporate performance and shareholders' income, argues a study from the Paris-based economic organization, "is broken by an increasingly complex universe of intermediaries whose business is to manage other people's money."[41] Companies with highly diffused ownership tend to have less engaged owners. Asset managers in the United States, for instance, complain that they have too little time, and too few staff, to engage with companies that they are investing in.[42] In Europe, studies have shown, companies with a more concentrated form of ownership have a higher turnout at annual general meetings and also more dissent from owners.[43] In other words, those managing other people's money have little time to be a responsible owner.

And it is all perfectly understandable. The agency problem with intermediaries that own small shares of the total stock is that the gain for them from investing time and knowledge into a company is too small. If a fund owns, say, 1 percent of the total stock value of $100 million and makes a serious effort to raise the stock value by 5 percent, that gain will be distributed among all the owners, and only 1 percent – $50,000 – of the increase will go to the owner that made the effort. Raising the share price by 5 percent is no small feat, and would require costs that may outweigh the gains that a small owner can take home as a consequence of the effort. This simplistic example shows one thing: the connection between performance and shareholders, and between owners and companies, is compromised in today's capitalism. That connection makes up the control room of capitalism. Destroy that connection and a key feature of capitalism is lost.

Adolf Berle and Gardiner Means, running with Smith's old insight, raised this concern in a classic study first published in 1932. What happens, they asked, to companies that have diffused ownership fraught with agency problems? The separation of ownership and control, they argued, will eventually lead to companies that get led solely by management and executives because owners have far too little supervisory control.[44]

Management legend Peter Drucker answered the Berle and Means question when they predicted a power change in the control room of capitalism because of the institutionalization of ownership and increased pension savings. In the mid-1970s Drucker stirred up feelings in corporate America by pointing out the obvious, albeit provocatively. If socialism, he said, is defined as "ownership of the means of production by workers," then "the United States is the first truly 'socialist' country."[45] The accusation of socialism did not go down well in all quarters of corporateville. But his observation is correct. Pension savers, then as now, have limited supervisory control. However, like any other form of socialism, ownership would end up in bureaucratic rule. Whatever pension savers do to express their views on the companies they have invested in, it would be neglected by all those bureaucrats who stand between owners and the company.

Just because the phenomenon is old, and known to investors today, it does not mean they have addressed the problem. In a way, investors have contained it, but they have done it in ways that have turned many large companies into bureaucratic labyrinths. Ownership tools to mend agency problems have been developed and practiced for decades. In their clearest form, they involve shareholder and ownership agreements, mirroring business and strategic plans, which are carefully penciled to avoid misunderstandings and suboptimal behavior. In large or small companies, stocks and vested stock option schemes are given to key employees because owners want managers to behave like owners, and make sure they make the most out of every decision from the owners' perspective. Investors sometimes bring sticks as well, insisting that key individuals in the companies they are investing in should have "skin in the game." In younger firms, that usually means that entrepreneurs are required to coinvest alongside an outside investor; this sometimes even goes as far as demanding that entrepreneurs mortgage family homes for the purpose of locking owners and management together – the capitalist version of a Mexican standoff.

Much as tools for ownership control have improved, they have not solved the principal–agent problems. In fact, the grayer that capitalism has become, the more acute it has become for owners to make sure that their capital is not going to get squandered. Shareholder and ownership agreements have tied management to a bureaucratic notion about the company. Moreover, owners have increasingly been incentivized to change the allocation of corporate funding – from equity to debt – and to cut the agency problem restricting management access to the cash flow. Companies have therefore seen a smaller share of their earnings being retained in the company – and a bigger share of it distributed to shareholders. Both trends have reinforced the complex and ambiguous character of capitalism by diffusing the structure of decision-making about how firms should get funded. Today it is neither owners nor executives who sit with that power, but external capital markets.

That brings us to the second reason why gray capital turns capitalism gray. It *allocates resources according to a rentier formula.* Any eight-year-old would tell you that the sum of six plus three is more than the sum of four plus four. Still, any professional investor would prefer the latter if the numbers reflect stable and yearly returns from an investment. Professional investors have a hard time managing volatility and try to avoid it in a number of ways.

Part of that harks back to 1952 when Harry Markowitz introduced what today is called modern portfolio theory, explaining how investors should allocate capital for maximum expected returns for a given risk level.[46] This theory is all about diversification and it quickly became the weapon of choice for professional investors, almost regardless of what type of investment they were picking. It is easy to understand why. Diversification is an excellent idea as it decreases volatility and, armed with the theory, investors can allocate resources in far safer ways. However, a side effect is that it turns high volatility in the portfolio into a sign of poor investment management, and that it renews the attention to volatility the more frequent it becomes. Markowitz received the Nobel Prize in 1990 for his contribution to portfolio theory, and that served as a perfect symbol of capital markets and the way they had expanded in the 1980s.

By then financialization had rooted itself in the economy. Only a few years earlier, the chairman of the Securities and Exchange Commission in the United States observed that the country's capital markets "are by far the best capital markets the world has ever known."[47] A stock market crash hit the United States only a few years later, and it showed how ownership and corporates had disentangled. Modern portfolio theory was by then software code for ownership capitalism. And that is just how it should be. Stanford professor Paul Pfleiderer has observed dryly that statistics "show diversification reduces risk, and that you are better of diversifying than not." It is that simple and, he asked pointedly, "what is the alternative?"[48] And that is the point: there are no real alternatives for professional investors and asset managers. They all end up using the same code – or chasing the same type of investments. They all tend to prefer aggregated risk balances that in their totality prefer predictability before anything else, sometimes including higher returns.

Undoubtedly diversification makes sense when you are a professional investor. Likewise, if you manage your savings on your own, it is better and safer to stick with investment allocations along the lines of modern portfolio theory. But it also has side effects – or unintended consequences. First of all, it dilutes ownership and weakens the investors' voice in each company invested in. And, second, professional investors that use variations of modern portfolio theory give too much weight to assumptions that are not correct. They tend to base their decisions on the assumption of perfectly functional markets, but all actors in a market do not always behave rationally, and they do not all have access to the same information. Above all, historic company performance is not always a good guide for future innovations.

Markets are never perfect. Markets help to organize partial and incomplete information and knowledge. Investors using opposing assumptions tend to let the historic performance of a company or a market motivate expectations about future performance. More often than not they end up extrapolating. Again, that is not a bad assumption – for most of the people and most of the time, today is pretty much like yesterday. Capitalism, however, was not supposed to be a system based on such an epistemology. Capitalism was supposed to be a system for motivating and managing change, innovation and contestable competition – and for ensuring that those companies that were not performing well yesterday, or did not exist then, should perform better tomorrow. But if the funding of corporate capitalism increasingly follows the playbook of modern portfolio theory, it basically means that funding for the unknown is drained.

Gray investors increasingly have come to prefer shorter stockholding periods. One US study shows that investors' stockholding periods, measured as a mean (or average) duration, went from seven years in 1940 to seven months in 2007, and that the same trend can be spotted on major stock markets all over the world.[49] In 2015, average holding periods of American stocks traded on all marketplaces was 17 weeks, according to Credit Suisse.[50] Data from the New York Stock Exchange show that turnover rates have increased since the beginning of the 1980s, but also that turnover rates were significantly lower after the onset of the Great Recession.[51] For sure, measuring holding periods is trickier than it sounds. There are big differences between various types of investors. Stocks are traded on more markets today compared to before, complicating historical comparisons. However, the trend is real and it tells a tale of short-term targets stealing attention from what builds value in stocks over time.[52]

Legal guidelines and tools for the alignment of interests preoccupy gray ownership. They emerge from the best of intentions, but nevertheless tend to have negative effects. Companies become conservative and stay away from important components of business building, like innovation. They shy away from market opportunities that are uncertain because tools and guidelines order management to behave in a certain way. They favor corporate managers that can organize rather than build businesses – bureaucrats instead of entrepreneurs. Foremost they encourage companies to command full control of the map and the reality, in the name of predictability.

Predictability is not an asset of capitalism, but gray capital does not want much of a gap between ownership expectations and business planning, on the one hand, and revenues or dividends, on the other. The quest to eliminate such gaps fixes the attention on financial performance at the same time as it conceals business performance, or the business itself. Financial results become more important than building a business. Long-term value is all too often sacrificed at the altar of short-term results.

Demands for predictability ripple through ownership plans and shape investment agendas, leaning on boards and managers to allocate their attention in that direction. Good management for gray capital owners becomes equal to planning; leadership delivering predictable returns year after year gradually becomes the arch idea of good leadership. For decades, careers have been built upon delivering according to schedule; a remarkable proportion of the West's corporate captains were rewarded by owners for that quality alone. Managers with a penchant for business building, however, have gradually found their masters unhappy, especially if they did not have a disposition for predictability. For several decades, gray capital's pursuit of predictability permeated the psychology of companies and forced everyone to follow that formula. It rewarded companies increasingly hostile to the unknown, and defensive about business plans that strayed from the rather monotone machination of delivering according to expectations.

And as aging and saving for the silver years increasingly dominate corporate funding, owners force companies toward greater predictability. It is almost as if gray capital owners no longer want companies to be companies, but rather saving platforms. It may sound like nitpicking, but it is not. Many gray investors no longer invest money in companies, they save money in companies as if they were banks. While saving money is commendable, and highly desirable for the economy too, done in this way it takes the edge off capitalism. When companies try to capture the interest of gray investors they have to show their credentials as safe savings accounts where money can be stored and ideally grown. Saving platforms have to be conservative, like banks used to be. But one of the great changes in capitalism in the past 50 years is that banks have become more prone to risk while nonfinancial companies have become more conservative. They are no longer supposed to go for big changes in the market; they are supposed to keep things stable.

By stealing talents, and focusing too much on financial needs and political stewardship, gray capital *crowds out innovations*, and that is the third reason gray capital is turning capitalism gray. Since the 1980s, talent has been excessively attracted to finance and, sure enough, it is easy to understand why when wages are compared. Between 1980 and 2006, wages increased on average by 70 percent more in the financial sector than comparable work in other industries.[53] MBA graduates from Stanford choosing careers within financial services in the 1990s became reunion party poopers as, on average, they earned three times the salaries of previous classmates who started careers in other industries.[54]

Yet it was not only talent that got lost when financial services mushroomed. It is highly likely that growth in the real economy was damaged too, even if it is a difficult proposition to prove. "There is a clear negative relationship between financial sector growth and real growth," argued two economists at the Bank for International Settlements (BIS) after having studied finance and growth in 20 countries over 30 years.[55] The causalities are a bit ambiguous, but they suggest financial sector growth leads to lower productivity. Perhaps the effects are real; or perhaps financial sector growth is not causing productivity declines, but the two phenomena have just happened to occur simultaneously in mature economies. The same economists, however, have been able to demonstrate beyond doubt that there is a tipping point for financial sector growth – when it no longer supports GDP. That tipping point seems to come when credit to the private sector exceeds 80–100 percent of GDP.[56] With the put option to the financial sector – the implicit or explicit government guarantee of financial sector survival – the price of insurance of risk in the financial sector has been artificially low, leading to a general growth of financial sector assets.[57] Consequently, money has flowed toward the financial sector rather than the real economy.

Western financial markets are highly developed and financiers are generally very skilled in finance; otherwise they would not survive in the market. But no one would put forward the view that these skills in finance make financiers good carpenters, automobile engineers, or long-distance runners. So why is there an implicit assumption that financier owners are good at building businesses and long-term corporate value? The difference between financial and business-building skills is quite significant, and this is why most companies separate out corporate finance from business development. Management consultancies, for instance, usually make a separation between strategy development and financial services, because if they mix the two up they will get a financial solution to the problem they have been tasked to address. If you have a hammer, the whole world looks like a nail.

Hence, when financial services expand, business development tends to be pushed out. The BIS economists discovered that in one of their studies, and argued that "productivity tends to grow disproportionally slower in industries with lower asset tangibility."[58] Many others have suggested a similar type of problem. "The emphasis on earnings per share," argue Harvard's Clayton Christensen and colleagues, "diverts resources away from investments whose payoff lies beyond the immediate horizon."[59] Another way to put it, and to simplify to an extreme, is that an investor owning a stock for only a few months has little interest in supporting costly investments today that might pay off years in the future. Undoubtedly the capital deepening of a company builds stock value, but not necessarily in the short term – and it is actively deterred when it erodes the short-term earning capacity of firms.

Business creation as it was intended has almost become an associate ambition for owners and investors, not what makes them tick. Gray capital instead favors firms with a political character. Internal politics permeates most big firms today, and crowds out business creation and new innovations. If you have experienced a big company from the inside you will know that internal politics now plays a leading role in how time is allocated at many levels of management; success at work has become as much a contest of political wit as business acumen.

Politics extends beyond the immediate boundaries of the company too. Companies need leaders with political skills to sell an image. The successful boss needs to be particularly skilled at managing stock markets – the political playground for investors. Investors shift allegiances, buying and selling equity in seconds, and if confidence in a company or a leader dries up, they vote with their feet. Stock markets challenge companies in numerous ways, but one sin is greater than all others: never surprise the stock market. Every corporate director knows that mantra by heart. Oddly, whether the surprise is positive or negative makes a smaller difference than you might think; overperforming is almost as bad as underperforming, a sign of loss of control. While better-than-expected performance surely is good news, and drives stock prices up, in the long run it undermines capital market trust in the company, especially for that part of the capital market that demands predictability. Hence, listed companies with gray ownership follow targets of predictability – they maximize stability, not necessarily maximizing performance, and have innovations play second fiddle.

Through the growth of gray capital, modern capitalism is about to become a rentier capitalism, if it has not already. For the rentier, capitalism works like a bank, or a savings account – a safe place to store and grow value. The modern rentier is, to quote Lenin, "clipping coupons." It is not the classic Marxian rentier capitalism, defined by usury, which is emerging. Nor does today's capitalism resemble the rentier society in Piketty's chronicle, which concerns the widening gap between the returns on capital and labor.[60] The modern version of the rentier society is defined by new forms of owners that place little significance on capitalist ownership, market renewal and innovation. Rentiers make the economy hidebound.

4

THE RISE AND RISE AGAIN OF CORPORATE MANAGERIALISM

The modern large Western corporation and the modern apparatus of socialist planning are variant accommodations to the same need.

John Kenneth Galbraith, *The New Industrial State*

Modern corporate behavior increasingly conforms to the spirit of managerialism. Gray capital helped to shape such corporations, but firm managers equally assisted in the gradual corrosion of capitalism. Today, the appetite for creative destruction, the zeitgeist of capitalism, is all too often displaced by a custodian corporate culture that is defensive about the future and protective of its privileges. It is a culture that incubates habits, strategies and models that cannot be married with uncertainty or a disposition for radical innovation and contestable competition. Managerialism has become an undisputed meta-ideology of the business world. Companies plan more than ever. The more complex the world gets, the more they search for certainty and control.

Take the case of Nokia. In 1865, Fredrik Idestam, a Finnish engineer educated in Germany, opened his first wood pulp mill in Tammerkoski Rapids, Finland, and what eventually would become a world-renowned cell-phone company was born. The story of Nokia tells us all we need to know about how innovation and corporate behavior have changed over the past decades – and, with Finland's post-Nokia depression, it is also a good example of how mismanagement of innovation can have disastrous consequences for the economy. The company was – and still is – a pioneer of technology. Its first innovation was built on using wood rather than rags to produce pulp for paper. With increasing demand for pulp and limited supply of rags, Idestam created a technology to turn Finland's forests into a success story of pulp production. As the business grew, it expanded into many other sectors and eventually presided over an industrial conglomerate producing everything from electricity and telephones to toilet paper, car tires and rubber boots.[1]

Like many other big conglomerates in the West, the 1970s and 1980s were not kind to Nokia. During a short period in the late 1980s and early 1990s the company, under new management, boldly stopped developing, producing and marketing virtually everything that had thus far made it profitable. This included Finnish Cable Works, manufacturers of telephone and power cables, and the production of TV sets, a market where it was once Europe's third largest producer. It was an audacious strategy, to say the least. Many Nokia pundits at the time thought it was idiotic, creating turmoil not just in a flagship company but also in Finland – a small economy whose fortunes had been so closely tied to Nokia. Nokia's standing in Finland is special and the company has been compared to the strange and invisible creature Sampo in the Finnish national epic *Kalevala*, a magical engine of eternal wealth.[2] Nokia had such a dominant role in Finnish business that when a former Prime Minister of Finland moved from politics to the post of Senior Vice President of Nokia, locals quipped that he was getting a promotion.

Nokia divested itself from a range of businesses in order to focus all its attention on the nascent GSM technology by developing mobile phones and related products. In hindsight, the decision was astonishing. Many industrial conglomerates have divested but few have divested to move capital into what could only be described as a very uncertain sector. Nokia's new strategy was decided long before the cell-phone market revolution had gathered speed and one can only admire Nokia's decision to abandon what was familiar for something uncertain.

The strategy paid off – handsomely. Thirteen years later Nokia had sold over 1 billion phones. It mastered, even spearheaded, the practice of new market sales and lean operations through globalized supply chains. In 2007 the Nokia brand was the fifth most valued in the world. At its peak, the company's stock market value was in excess of US$350 billion.

Nokia is an example of a company that did not just develop a technology but brought it successfully to market through a good deal of creative destruction. It was not afraid, at least not at that point in time, to practice the logic of destruction: hiving off products to make space for something else that could generate greater profits. Moreover, it banked on the expectation that the mobile market was going to change and that Nokia could contest that market. It tirelessly worked to move its capital, skills and business to assets that could yield most value. In that way, Nokia did what many other big and global companies would do later, or wish they had done.

The bold spirit that guided Nokia in the late 1980s gradually diminished and the company became, like so many other big and dominating firms, fearful of markets changing too fast because of innovation.[3] Nokia became an example of a company getting trapped in defensive corporate managerialism, and of downgrading the spirit to contest markets. Managerialists squeezed out entrepreneurs. For a while, Nokia was exactly the type of company that made capitalism lose its mojo.

Nokia is a good example of the theme running through this chapter, the growing dominance of managerialist thinking in big and global companies, and how the tools of corporate management have gradually become devoid of entrepreneurship and the spirit of contestable innovation. There are many successful companies that compete, contest and innovate in a way that forces everyone to behave better and smarter, and this chapter covers some of them. However, a growing number in the world of big companies have been trying to shield themselves from such habits. Companies like Nokia go through life cycles, sometimes independently from how markets develop. Periods of more technology creation are followed by periods of less. However, innovation, in its essence, is not just about creation; it is, importantly, about the adaptation and renewal of markets. While many companies can rightly boast of their talents for creation, an increasing number of them have worked themselves up to market positions where they are afraid of the consequences of their own inventions and the changes they can bring. They prefer a slowdown in the pace of market change.

Innovation and corporate destruction

How the mighty fall! Nokia's history of producing mobile handsets is now, well, history. It sold its mobile unit to Microsoft for a little more than US$7.2 billion a few years ago – much less than what Microsoft paid for Skype, and many times below Nokia's peak value just a few years earlier.[4] Nokia stumbled – and squandered shareholders' money. It failed to do what the company prided itself on – "changing with the times, disrupting the status quo," as the company's own hagiography put it.[5] Companies with new business models and technological applications relevant to the mobile sector outcompeted Nokia on the handset consumer market. Similarly, one of Nokia's main competitors during its golden days, Motorola, was snapped up by Google – a company few had heard of around the time of the millennium (a stripped-down version of Motorola was then sold to Lenovo).[6]

Did the smartphone revolution catch Nokia by surprise? Not really. Aside from its boldness in the late 1980s, Nokia had hidden most of its advanced software innovations for smartphone-type products in its product portfolio. It knew it was sitting on a proprietary business model and a product stock that by and large would lose traction among customers. But in the short term, a strategic move away from its own portfolio of hardware-based intellectual capital and its product stock of low-margin mobile phones would risk eroding the value of the company, perhaps radically so. Its technological developers understood the emerging software revolution in mobile phones; it was ahead of Apple both with apps and maps. The business side of the company, however, was afraid a software shift would cannibalize its hardware profile, which dominated at the time. Steve Jobs once said that "if you don't cannibalize yourself, someone else will." Nokia did not take the advice. Rather than swiftly destroying that hardware value and making room for something new, it went for a strategy of killing it softly.

Nokia's problem was not that it lost its ethos of inventing new technologies and products. Its decline was related to how it managed its business and to expectations of diminishing returns on its current stock of products if it introduced new technology too quickly. This was the same technology that the company needed to upgrade its product stock. It did not expect Apple or any other company to disrupt the mobile phone market; Nokia thought it could wait a bit longer to shift technology. But that made Nokia a laggard. Eventually it had to rethink its business model and move into mobile software through a partnership with Microsoft – a company with similar problems of finding a viable business model in the fast-changing world of mobile software.

Nokia is not alone. Many companies find it difficult to abandon products, markets, processes and methods, or perhaps even business models. The new parent of Nokia handsets, Microsoft, has struggled with transforming its business for quite some time. Once the unrivaled leader in the world of technology, it has been competing a good distance from the technological frontier – at least in the consumer market. Its Windows-led strategy has gradually become less profitable, perhaps even a burden for the company. Many in the tech analyst community would say it prevented Microsoft from quickly seizing most of the defining trends in the past decade of ICT growth.

Like many other firms, Microsoft had a clear – and, as it turned out, prescient – idea of how markets and products would evolve. In 2000, at the height of its antitrust problems in the United States, Microsoft explained what the future of computer software and hardware would look like. Steve

Ballmer, the then newly minted heir to Bill Gates, described how Microsoft would create a "unified platform through which devices and services cooperate with each other."[7] Microsoft predicted the need for interconnected web services that could be used across platforms and shared between colleagues or family members. It understood what would come in location-aware devices, voice-control services, and photo sharing. Microsoft even predicted the services, or variants thereof, that later became known as Facebook and Skype.

However, Microsoft did not reshape the consumer market with these products. Since the millennium it has been trying to catch up with the kinds of new devices and services that have made the shareholders of other companies rich. While it is only natural that fast-growing and technology-intensive markets have many successful companies, it is remarkable that Microsoft – given its dominant market position for operating systems – could not lead the consumer market with new products and technologies it knew was coming.

As past innovations represent sunk costs for firms, market progression should happen by a constant succession of innovations on the winner's stand. But that is not the logic companies always follow. Nokia and Microsoft share with other companies that have had similar experiences a structural reluctance to innovate markets that challenge its current product stock. Microsoft was too tied to its "defend and extend" strategy, which is code for an imperial ambition for Windows. While other innovators deserted Windows, Microsoft was too afraid of destroying the value of Windows by launching stand-alone products that worked in other ecosystems. It believed in a future based on a Windows-controlled ecosystem for all devices and services – *one ring to rule them all*.[8]

This philosophy helped shape a corporate culture that grew arrogant and missed many of the developments in the market. Steve Ballmer's colorful speech just after the launch of the iPhone in 2007 is indicative of the culture that permeated Microsoft;

> There's no chance that the iPhone is going to get any significant market share. No chance. It's a $500 subsidized item. They may make a lot of money. But if you actually take a look at the 1.3 billion phones that get sold, I'd prefer to have our software in 60% or 70% or 80% of them, than I would to have 2% or 3%, which is what Apple might get.[9]

Six years after Ballmer's prediction, only 3 percent of new mobile phones used Microsoft's operating system while Apple's iOS had close to 50 percent of the market. And he is not the only executive to have made spurious claims about their products. Around the same time as Ballmer's brash dismissal of Apple, Research in Motion (RiM) ridiculed the iPhone as a marginal event in the market for cellular phones. But that arrogance seemed daring, even at that time. The parent company of BlackBerry had grown from a small Canadian pager company to a major, multibillion dollar mobile company in just a few years. It had made its fortune by mobilizing computer services, enabling people to read and write emails from anywhere in the world using a QWERTY keyboard. It could not have been a distant thought that there would be demand for a new mobile device that allowed people to surf the web everywhere too.

And it wasn't a distant thought. RiM understood that change was coming. But the profits it made from its blockbuster email device were still too substantial and tempted them to stick just a little bit longer with the old, instead of moving to a new product that had a different keyboard and a screen suitable for web services. Moving into web services was seen as a risky move at the time. In the end, the company had to apply the logic of destruction – literally – as unsold BlackBerries were sent to the Tech Street shredder.

Kodak, Sony, the New York Stock Exchange, and many other firms can also testify to the dangers of maintaining products that are still profitable but increasingly vulnerable to new technology and business models.[10] Not only is it difficult to build a viable innovation model, but avoiding innovation makes them protective and defensive, a posture that, once adopted, tends to stick with companies. IBM is an example of a company that managed to rebuild its success by doing just that. Recalling Nokia's fearless move away from nonmobile businesses under Jorma Ollila, Louis Gerstner joined IBM when it was running out of money and turned the company upside down. In the early 1990s, the tech giant experienced three consecutive years of financial losses. It had failed to adapt to agile competitors like Microsoft and Intel which had trespassed on its market territory over the previous few years and now they were starting to poach its customers. IBM barely managed to survive.

Why all this drama? After all, IBM had the best people available to understand and interpret the big changes occurring in the market and in technology. Yet despite the awareness inside IBM about the need for a radical change, it failed to adapt because the company had grown so complex. IBM reached 300,000 employees at around the same time as its competitors started to aggressively challenge it with new innovations.[11] Large corporations tend to build complex and bureaucratic organizations – and IBM was no exception. Its decline into corporate bureaucracy appeared related to its excessive managerialism, not to say corporate socialism – a suspicion fanned by IBM's philosophy of offering lifetime employment. The company's turnaround, into one of the most innovative businesses in its field, was the result of a ruthless destruction of the company's culture, organization and product portfolio. The key decision for IBM was not what it was going to continue doing and producing, but *what it should stop doing or producing*. What had deprived the company of success was not an absence of ideas or inventions, but an organization so complex that it increasingly became dependent on defending its market position.[12]

Withering, if you remember Mr. Chance's rule for cultivating the economic garden, is a central part of innovative and contestable capitalism. However, it is difficult to practice at the corporate level. Withering is ruthless, to begin with, and opposition to it extends far beyond products and services. It requires constant changes in the organizational habitat. People, rules, procedures, processes and structures have to change as well. Companies may have to dismiss their "intangibles" – their corporate culture, values, legacies, and myths. Abandoning the old, however, is only easy if you do not think too highly of the past.

Complexity tends to breed bureaucracy that reduces the ability of companies both to wither and contest markets with innovation. And the standard strategy of managerialists is to face the increasing complexity of the world with ever more complex organizations. As globalization required companies to become big, expensive and complex, bureaucracy naturally increased, making creative destruction even harder. Every organization needs internal bureaucracy – and bureaucracy is not the same thing as managerialism – but the combination of bureaucracy and a far higher degree of production specialization made it difficult to wither something old to make space for the new. The better you get at doing something, the more it costs to stop doing it and start with something else. While the principle of specialization is about honing the absolute or comparative advantages of an individual, company or economy, the world of innovation is based on the destruction of something you are currently doing. Nokia, for instance, did not fail because it was bad at producing mobile handsets. Nokia failed because it competed in a market that others were contesting. In a way, Nokia's fortunes were squandered because it was remarkably good at what it was doing: it ran one of the most efficient production networks in the telecom sector. It was too profitable to abandon.

There are companies that manage to combine global scale and specialization with the ethos of creative destruction, but most firms do not. For those that have successfully reached global scale there is usually a far bigger preoccupation – ensuring that the barriers to entry are so high and thorny that new rivals will not bother to cross into their territory. Protecting markets can be difficult, and big companies can fail to do it even in markets where competition is concentrated among a few big players. Over the last decades, however, firms have become more skilled at market and incumbency protection (see Chapter 5) and they invariably use the same formula as Nokia: increasing production specialization and optimization.

Nokia got a second chance. It lived to fight another day, or as a Finnish politician memorably put it: "I guess one could say that the iPhone killed Nokia and the iPad killed the Finnish paper industry, but we'll make a comeback."[13] Everyone is not as lucky, though. Some die fast, some bow out slowly. Most, however, continue to stick around even when they are no longer successful. Capitalism is in many ways a history of failures, and to understand the current version of capitalism it is necessary to understand why so few actually do fail.

The formula of failure

Success, it is said, has many fathers, while failure is an orphan. That is not a soothing message for entrepreneurs who have crashed, or for companies that are still around but whose light went out a long time ago. Markets usually get the blame, but corporate failure occurs from the inside-out and is connected with the firms' structure and how they try to play the market. The larger companies that fail surprisingly often have one thing in common: they have become excessively managerialist.

Failing or low-performing companies mostly understood the technology frontier of their sector and were not surprised by a new technology they had never considered themselves. Nokia, for instance, was the first company to bundle internet services in what we today call an app store. Apple, among others, did not outperform Sony because the Japanese electronics powerhouse did not understand the future of mobile devices and their connection to classic electronics. Microsoft, as previously noted, knew exactly what technological change was emerging. The New York Stock Exchange, to take another example, was familiar with the trend of falling margins in stock exchange trading and knew that profits were increasingly made on other parts of the market (e.g. derivatives and clearing) that worked in different ways.

In other words, failing companies had the expertise, perhaps even among owners and managers, that recognized what was coming. They were aware that rival companies could wreck their market positions through innovations and that they had become too attached to their own product stock, services or revenue model. As in most other companies operating in markets where there are quick product and technology turnover rates, the managements of failing firms also know that over time there is only one question that should keep them awake at night: should we destroy our own offering, or should we let another company do it for us?

Still they failed. And to understand the mechanics of failure we need first to understand the firm and why it exists. There is no better starting point for that quest than Ronald Coase, the Nobel laureate in economics who rebelled against "blackboard economics" and made the firm the center of economic inquiry. Coase started from a simple, almost banal, observation – surprisingly controversial at the time. Companies, he argued, are not black boxes that cannot be understood by economists. Nor are the successes and failures of firms mysteriously shielded from generalized observations about how economies work. Coase, who came from an institutionalist school of thought, was not all that impressed by Joseph Schumpeter's almost Nietzsche-like admiration of the strong and individualistic entrepreneur. Entrepreneurs, Schumpeter later wrote, act "with confidence beyond the range of familiar beacons," a trait "present in only a small fraction of the population."[14] Nor was Coase satisfied with the residual treatment of firms in much of the economic thinking at the time; a perception of firms memorably described by Cambridge economist Dennis Robertson as "lumps of butter coagulating in a pail of buttermilk."[15] Schumpeter, like other economists with similar interests, could not give a reasonable explanation for why companies exist, and failure to understand such a basic component of economics clouded their views about the role of firms in the economy.

Coase challenged the prevailing ignorance with an idea of the firm and its boundaries.[16] He argued that firms and their boundaries (their size, functions and, to use a modern definition, "demarcation between the organization and its environment"[17]) are defined by transaction costs. Or to put it further into the language of economics: the marginal costs and benefits of contracting out production through the market's price mechanism versus combining necessary parts of the production "in-house" through the firm. You can also call it the make-or-buy question: should companies produce themselves or buy from others? It is a basic question, yet it is one that many economists and business observers ignore.

Companies have different origins and thrive for a variety of reasons, but they all have one thing in common, Coase argued, that if capital and labor miraculously found each other spontaneously – firms would become pointless. The market would coordinate all that was needed to produce something. Firms, after all, are complex social constructs, permeated with operational slack and inefficiencies that a perfectly functioning market could root out. Companies are hardly seamlessly connected and easily managed entities as described in glossy corporate presentations. Companies that fail often do so because internal transaction costs are too high.

Yet firms also exist because of high market transaction costs. And, in a way, the higher they are, the better it is to have companies, because the transaction costs partly set the value of a firm. Firms, if you want to be provocative, exist because markets fail, at least in a theoretical way. And the greater the failure, the more space there is for an upward valuation of companies. Coase put it a bit more dryly: "The main reason why it is profitable to establish a firm would seem to be that there is a cost of using the price mechanism."[18] A successful firm can bank on the value of its unique combination of ideas, management, capital, and labor – or of what it has that cannot easily be reproduced by the market, or copied by another firm.

Companies exist because they reduce market transaction costs. Yet if this is the case, then why has the process of capitalist competition not coalesced all firms into just one gigantic unit? Why is there not just one single company in a country, let alone the world, that rules the market?

It is not just markets that have transaction costs; companies have them too. Companies can grow but there is a limit to the scale benefits received. Big companies that invest in expansion will sooner or later reach a point where it no longer saves costs and makes them more competitive. And if we run along with Coase, the limit of the firm is intimately linked to the weakened capabilities of the entrepreneur to manage a company that has grown too big. When the entrepreneur can no longer manage the firm efficiently by relying only on entrepreneurial spirit, complexity typically overwhelms the company. Internal transaction costs suck the energy out of business development and value creation. Matters of less importance, and not what makes or breaks firms, begin to occupy them instead. When firms grow big, internal rent-seekers are empowered. So the good news is that the size of the firm is not predetermined, but it depends on how managers balance internal and external transaction costs. That balance does not just change because "business men will be constantly experimenting, controlling more or less."[19] It also determines whether companies can thrive, let alone survive. Companies go out of business when internal transaction costs get too high. Companies with internal transaction costs that are too high are companies that have lost their entrepreneurial spirit and allowed excessive managerialism.

Corporate managerialism – ideology on the rise

Coase's philosophy is the start, not the end, of an inquiry into the rise of corporate managerialism and the economics of organizations and how companies set the boundaries of the firm. And those that are academically minded will know that there is a heated debate about the nature of the firm, with different schools of thoughts.[20] Yet his basic concept is irrefutably simple and it is easy to see how it immediately manifests in companies through organization, coordination and agency costs.

To manage increasing complexity, a big company needs to organize itself into divisions and subgroups, but those often turn into silos that sometimes get so entrenched that the left hand does not know what the right hand is doing. Divisions and subgroups create hierarchies among each other. Human virtues and vices get in the way, like pride, vanity, jealousy, and – on the brighter side of human nature – the spirit of winning. Microsoft, Sony, and IBM, before its turnaround, are examples of companies that became trapped in what *Financial Times* journalist Gillian Tett calls the "silo curse."[21]

Corporate executives are no strangers to organizational complexity, but they struggle to fend off its downsides. They try to avoid them by appointing more managers and writing new internal rules in order to get divisions and subdivision to coordinate with less friction and at lower cost. They design performance indicators to create transparency and enable control, and new groups of managers are appointed to measure performance and report failure. The typical complex company has built layer after layer of management, coordination and monitoring. And if that is not enough, new managers are added to control and distribute responsibility. Sometimes it benefits business development and value creation; most of the time it does not. People spend hour after hour in meetings that add little but take time away from value generation and lead to frustration for any with a touch of entrepreneurial blood running through their veins. In a typical company, argues Boston Consulting Group thinker Yves Morieux, between 40 and 80 percent of the working time of managing teams is waste.[22]

For companies that are truly big and global there is an extra markup in internal transaction costs, because they have to manage, coordinate and control operations across markets and cultures. Though such costs often increase the productivity of the firm, when good practices are taken to divisions and countries where the organization works less efficiently, the simple point is that these companies often need more layers of management in order to benefit from trade opportunities – and transfer those opportunities to the market.[23] This is true also after the introduction of new communication technologies in the last decade. Perhaps somewhat paradoxically, to benefit from size and international reach, companies needed to build complex organizations and that complexity is one of the factors helping companies to fan greater productivity into the rest of the economy. Yet such complexity is not cost-free. There is a limit to diversification and to the degree of organizational complexity a company can muster, and the closer companies get to that limit, the more costly it is for companies to coordinate internally.[24]

If a truly big and global company joins the bandwagon of vertical globalization, by fragmenting production and outsourcing the supply chain, it has even stronger reasons to add layers of management and control. The more a company outsources various inputs, the more resources need to be spent on ensuring a clear division between the core assets of a firm and its linkages to the sourced inputs and the companies that produce them.[25] Contracting out inputs to the market has benefits, but it does not reduce the need for managers to control contracts, execution and coordination.

The market mediation that occurs when a company gets into sourcing structures with outside firms drives scale and specialization. It provides input for innovations, better quality, faster "time to market" – and in most cases improves efficiency. There are also other gains: companies that operate in a market characterized by change and uncertainty about the future can diffuse the cost of uncertainty throughout value chains, across a larger number of companies, and the firm will be able to switch more easily between input technology and sourcing firms. Mitigating uncertainties by outsourcing is similar to how the insurance industry spreads risk between firms, absorbing shocking events, like earthquakes and forest fires. Markets are generally much more flexible than the hierarchy inside a firm.

While a branch of business economics has preferred to view vertical partnering and contracting as cost free, or free from transaction costs, the reality is that there are substantial costs associated with it. When a firm chooses between "make or buy" it has to weigh the transaction costs of both alternatives. While it saves money in the short to medium term, it moves companies into operational realities that are not just complex but reduces their appetite for contestable competition. Moreover, any relation that a firm creates with an outside supplier also requires continuous investment, and the bilateral relation that is created quite often becomes inflexible, and make companies biased, although that was never the intention. Sometimes bilateral relations behave as monopolies, locking contractors into a relationship that is costly to switch from because of sunk costs. So while the flexibility gains are real, they are balanced by organizational necessities and habits that follow on the heels of complexity.

This explain why big firms – although only a fraction of companies – have such a profound impact on markets. Small companies follow big firms like planets orbiting around the sun. Anyone who has worked for a small supplier knows that implementation of new technologies, legal procedures, rules, time plans, and other issues of a similar nature are decided by big firms, with limited influence for others. Only consider payment cycles. Mars, Kellogg's and Anheuser-Busch require 120 days payment time from their suppliers, and they are no outliers.[26] Big firms use their strong position to delay acknowledging work completion and payments. Suppliers become part of the external capital market funding the big company.

One way to get on top of complexity and big firm market dominance is to view it through the lens of contracts. The greater the role of external supply – for whatever reason – the greater the need to contractually specify the relationship between supplier and buyer. Yet contracts create their own transaction costs and the closer parties intend to interact – to jointly develop products, for instance – the greater the complexity of the contractual relationship. In advanced production systems, even small disruptions can be very costly; just think of a car-plant assembly line forced to stop production due to failure on the part of a supplier. The liability aspect of any contractual arrangements increases complexity to such a degree that it often serves as an obstacle to cost-sharing development projects. The cost of downstream innovation then goes up. While companies usually retain full control over specific parts of the value chain – the parts related to its core assets – the more investments in human and R&D capital that are made outside the firm, the higher the costs for accessing that capital and its results. The paradox is that, for the company as well as the larger economy, vertical development of industries, especially globally, tends to raise both efficiency gains and the cost of innovation.

Responding to a complex world with a complex organization might be inevitable, but it has negative side effects. Corporate culture, for one, gets changed – and not in a good way. The complexity of a big and diversified organization tends to promote bureaucratic managerialism and hierarchies that stifle natural coordination, productive human interaction and entrepreneurialism. The greater the degree of diversification or verticalization, the more the success of firms relies on ensuring and improving internal coordination and organizational optimization. The attention of companies naturally shifts to internal models of control and coordination. And the direct administrative or management costs that arise when a firm needs more control and monitoring is just one part of the negative side effects. More importantly, internal transaction costs also trickle up – defining business ambitions and in particular what firms need to do with their boundaries. Companies excessively occupied with internal transaction costs have to put greater emphasis on protecting their boundary and market position. They need to organize in a way that allows management to keep better control of the firm's core assets. In particular, they have stronger incentives to specialize and protect sunk costs associated with specialization.

This can be thought of as the nexus of corporate control and specialization. Although defined differently, all firms need to control their core assets, or what really drives value. And that control is not just about targeting competitors, but perhaps more importantly, people inside the firm. This may sound like paranoia but, as the former owners of Fairchild Semiconductor discovered, it can have huge repercussions, including unwanted notoriety. One day two of its leading managers walked out of the company to start their own firm – and the technology that allowed the new company to succeed was something that had been developed inside Fairchild. This may not seem like a big deal, as it happens every day. But that new company was not just any company. It was NM Electronics, better known by a shorthand for "integrated electronics": Intel.[27] Fletcher School's Amar Bhide observed some years ago that of all the firms on Inc 500, a ranking of the fastest growing firms in the United States, people who replicated or modified an idea they had picked up in their previous position as employee with another firm had started 71 percent of them.[28]

Control is not just an issue of managers, contracts, and systems of internal oversight; it has to permeate the organization to actually work. One way for companies to build control is to push through as much specialization as possible. Specialization, apart from everything else, breaks up the value chains and production processes – and also makes it more difficult for staff to access the core assets of a firm. Firms can then appropriate or defend their assets with greater ease. Raghuram Rajan and Luigi Zingales pointedly observe: "In the vertical hierarchy, the entrepreneur controls access to the critical resource so as to draw forth specialization, and then uses specialized employees strategically to control the actions of new employees."[29]

In other words, specialization through verticalization creates both efficiency and control gains, provided the firm and its owners appropriate the value it generates by adding complementary assets to the inputs the company has sourced.[30] Therefore, specialization through verticalization is a corporate instinct that guides executives and investors. It affects how companies draw their boundaries – but it comes at a cost, sometimes a very heavy cost of complex structures, higher sunk costs, and a shifting of focus away from innovation and radical change in corporate strategy.

Most big corporations, or profitable companies, can offset such costs through one of their core advantages: they have an internal capital market – defined by revenues, debt, and equity – that should be better than external capital markets for funding innovation investments and allocating investments to the right targets. However, the big disadvantage of gray capitalism, as we noted in Chapter 3, is that decisions regarding innovation have all too often been outsourced to external capital markets – the banks, funds, and other institutions that control money. So the advantage that was real and applied a few decades ago does not seem to hold sway anymore. At the least there is much greater variety between firms. The reality now is rather that big companies fail at promoting a better allocation of investment resources. Why?

Owners, to start with the obvious, have preferred to take capital out of the firms – effectively draining big firms of their core capital allocation advantage. But they have done it for understandable reasons. Clearly, investors want to avoid big agency problems from giving executives too much freedom to use the cash flow.[31] Furthermore, executives of big firms do not have a compelling record in general. In fact, there is not much evidence in favor of big firms being better at investment allocation, other than during times of distressed, dislocated or underdeveloped capital markets.[32]

Stock markets understood that some time ago as conglomerates have been trading at a discount compared to other firms.[33] Investors do not seem to appreciate the argument that big firms are better at raising and allocating capital. In fact, they rather seem to go with the idea that big companies suffer from a disease that has been called "corporate socialism." Internal capital markets in big firms all too often promote an inefficient use of investments because productive investments finance less productive investments, or strong divisions finance weak divisions. While such an investment profile can occasionally be explained by firms making long-term bets on future value – many investments perform weakly before they start to pay off – the general view is rather that agency problems inside a firm spawn inefficient use of capital and investment spending.[34]

The exact nature of these agency problems varies, but the usual suspect is a misalignment of interests between owners, board executives, and management. Misalignment permeates most large organizations and helps to explain many of the unproductive habits of a firm. Rent-seeking behavior, such as the desire to maximize the budget for a division even if it would be better to allocate resources to other parts of the firm to create value, preoccupies management. Sometimes executives can correct misallocation. However, quite often they, and perhaps even the owners, conform to rent-seeking bids and behavior because – to continue with the example – they need to "bribe" division heads or other key managers in the firm. In this way, misalignment of interests makes organizations succumb to the process of internal politics.

Those of you who have worked in a big company probably recognize the habit. If you have not, there is plenty of research pointing in this direction.[35] If a company has a badly performing unit the last thing it should do is try to turn that unit around by reducing its budget. Cutting back will not attract the type of management that a badly performing unit needs. So management acquiesces to budget demands, allocates investment resources there, but adds new layers of control to avoid multiplying agency problems. In short, the firm spends time playing politics instead of developing its business.

Lately, the role played for big companies by external capital markets has exacerbated corporate managerialism and affected the way companies plan for their earnings. The postcrisis era has offered extraordinarily good conditions for corporate funding, predominantly because central banks have boosted money supply and cut interest rates. And that has been good for companies and their investors. Yet while stock markets have grown fast, business investment has been muted. Companies have taken up a lot of new debt, but they certainly have not been using their borrowing to invest for the future or spend on capital. They have rather returned a significant share of their capital to shareholders through high dividends and growing numbers of share buybacks.

Something is not quite right when fast growth in corporate borrowing is combined with low investment growth and high ratios of dividends and share buybacks. It also proves – yet again – that business investment rates are not helped by extraordinarily cheap capital. Take nonfinancial US corporations. Their operating cash flow has been growing at a declining rate since 2010 at the same time as their net debt has reached the peak levels of a year before the crisis started. But this new debt has been used not to raise the capital stock – to invest in future earnings – but to drive up stock values and give investors predictable returns. In other words, the debt-fueled feedback loop has allowed companies, and especially managers, to mitigate the fact that, in reality, their earnings have not been all that good.

It is a combination that reveals what occupies minds in corporateville, and what sort of future they are planning for. The companies that have been exploiting the opportunities from monetary easing have greatly increased the role of external capital markets and financial planning for the firm. With leverage ratios of the kind seen in the past years, corporations have turned their attention away from investments, innovation, and the future. Managers and organizations have focused on external capital markets instead of cultivating innovation plans and development of core businesses.

The role of external capital markets has led corporate politics – internal and external – to define more of the day-to-day management and ambitions of firms. Companies exposed to competition are always vulnerable to change, and when they become focused on finance rather than market contestability, they need to find other ways of protecting the boundaries of the firm and their market positions. That protection is increasingly about playing zone or company-to-company defense of markets. Those that have been around in corporate life know that, aside from specialization, there are several ways to do that. They include lobbying, branding, marketing, design, and incremental changes in products that give the pretense of development. Corporate social responsibility (CSR) and general public relations campaigns emerged later but are today part of the same toolbox. Together they all help to create customer loyalty and political protection. What used to be the icing on the cake – activities to support innovations and real business competition – have become more important than innovation itself to combat competitors.

The use of private standards has gained prominence, too. Large and global companies are increasingly behaving as regulators as they set standards for companies in their supply chain and for entire sectors – standards that are usually above those determined by governments. While this is partly related to reputation management, many dominating companies have also found that these private standards raise the entry barriers to markets and make it easier for them to capture the advantage of having drawn a firm boundary that can operate as a market boundary.[36]

All of these activities are perfectly legitimate – and they can be used as part of a strategy for market contestability. However, they are increasingly used for protective or defensive purposes, and they all too often substitute for real innovation in companies or strategies to contest markets. Lobbying often pushes legislators to protect old innovations – and targets new entrants that either want to step into the market or gain a stronger foothold there. Branding is for positioning and building loyalty, but changes little in product configuration. Marketing is for price and features, but when promoting old products and technology it becomes more like dressing the bride. Cosmetic aspects of design are for appearance and feeling but should not be confused with product innovation – although some would argue that they are closely linked.

Defensive actions usually have a good payoff, especially in consumer markets where the customer "experience" or "identity" of a product is central. Apple's iPhone and its strong market position is a good example. While the first iPhone was truly innovative, later versions have failed to give customers much more value than previous models. However, that has not restrained customers from embracing the iPhone. A study shows that almost 60 percent of iPhone owners admit to "blind loyalty" to the product.[37] That sort of loyalty is worth tons of gold because Apple's customers do not switch when they purchase a new phone, even when they think that the iPhone is not a particularly good phone. Only 28 percent of Apple's *loyal* customers think of it as the best phone on the market. In other words, Apple does not have to bend over backwards to come up with a new innovative phone, at least not for a period of time. It can release new models with limited improvements. A model that has a slightly changed design, a bit more storage capacity, a somewhat different screen size or perhaps slow-motion video-recording technology, is enough to get customers to pay good money for a new phone.[38]

However, such improvements, valuable as they can be for some, are not innovation. That is all "D" but not "R," to put it generously. It is natural that companies spend resources on lobbying or other ways of informing and influencing regulators and politicians. Just as economist Gordon Tullock once argued, given the sizable and growing role of the government in the economy, it is surprising that companies do not spend more on lobbying. But lobbying, like branding and public relations campaigns and the rest in that category, is often connected to a business strategy aimed at taking the pressure off firms and markets to innovate and give customers better value for money. For managerialist companies, such strategies are often better than putting resources into research and innovation because they conform to the general belief that it is better to control markets than advance real and contestable competition.

Corporate managerialism is thus a confluence of actions and events pushing the company and its leadership, including its financiers, to operate on the zealous extreme of what, with a reference to Coase, can be described as "non-entrepreneurial planning." Complexity and size are then no longer in balance with transaction costs. While Coase's ideal firm thrives on the entrepreneurial spirit, companies that have succumbed to managerialist versions of capitalism have corroded that spirit to such a degree that, often, only planning remains.

The logic of planning

The corporate planning machines are not new, but they have grown in size and importance over the past decades. They typically defend a product stock rather than competing with new innovations. Big, complex and slow-moving entities, the planning machines are fearful of contestable competition and convinced that they deserve market (and political) privileges because of their past successes, but most of all because of their size. They tend to think of themselves as simply too big to fail. However, the typical planning machine generates productivity and growth for economies, and is therefore seen somewhat paradoxically as an engine of capitalism, competition and innovation. Corporate titan Pehr G. Gyllenhammar revealingly expressed this ideology and drew attention to the paradox of planning when he noted in the late 1980s:

> today we talk about entrepreneurship versus bureaucracy. "The entrepreneur" represents all beauty in life. It represents progress, optimism and eternal success. The entrepreneur does not need to care about the rest of society. This constant talk about entrepreneurs is dangerous. We can't afford many of them. . . . The main part of industrial activity and societal maintenance is not built on so-called entrepreneurship.

This comes from a representative of a typical corporate habitat, an industrial conglomerate that initially reaped the benefits of what several entrepreneurs had done in the past, but later turned it into something else. Business management is all about planning, not creation, Gyllenhammar continued in his eulogy of corporate managerialism:

> It is a stable and routinized activity with limited space for imagination but vast space for competence. We are going to produce tomorrow what we produced yesterday, hopefully with somewhat higher quality and at somewhat lower cost. We cannot afford rapid shifts in production. We can't change it just because someone gets an idea. . . . We need little creativity, not much.[39]

Gyllenhammar's view has not exactly aged well – and he is perhaps not keynoting conferences on technological entrepreneurship and disruption. Yet he is far from alone in holding the managerialist view and it corresponds with the dominant strand in corporate governance and business development from the 1960s onward, when ideological stalwarts like John

Kenneth Galbraith measured up the corporate world. "The inevitable counterpart of specialization is organization," wrote Galbraith, and this is "what brings the work of specialists to a coherent result." He went on to argue, presciently at the time, that "so complex, indeed, will the job of organizing specialists become that there will be specialists on organization and organizations of specialists on organization."[40]

Gyllenhammar and Galbraith broadly got it right; they knew what was required to run large and growing corporations. The latter's worldview fell from grace when America's big corporate giants began to crumble in the 1980s. Gyllenhammar's Volvo conglomerate – a growing empire of trucks and cars, pharmaceuticals, beverages, and more – bumped into similar problems and was forced by markets to dismantle. But their corporate managerialism never went away.

The desire for predictability and the aversion to uncertainty buttressed corporate managerialism. Pledges made to money managers, investors and other stakeholders asking for predictable returns bolstered demand for greater corporate control. As corporate returns do not evolve randomly, a planning system to facilitate stable returns had to be developed – and that system espoused a general thinking about corporate development that favored slow and incremental change. Once the economy began to transform itself through computerization and globalization, big corporates had to put even greater emphasis on developing corporate managerialism and exercise greater market control.

In a way, these transformers "democratized" the economy, at least initially. Costs of starting businesses decreased, or at least it seemed that way. Tools to manage companies were spread widely and technologies that could destroy slow-moving companies became available to many. Suddenly, it seemed, a handful of ambitious tech geeks gathered around a couple of Atari computers in a dark basement could challenge the establishment. For a while, competition became much more unpredictable, firewalls between markets less impenetrable, and, above all, lack of business experience could be compensated for by computer knowledge.

Undoubtedly these changes challenged corporate philosophies. One can even argue that they freaked out titans in the old corporate establishment, who wished for a predictable world without radical innovations and disruptive technological leaps. They were suddenly pressured to change their business models to compete with this new crop of tech entrepreneurs who brought promises of sudden and galloping innovations. This was generally bad news for those who had something to protect; many did not even know where to start. Measures had to be taken to contain the risks of larger societal changes bringing corporate structures to an end. But those measures only half-heartedly involved an embrace of new technology and market opportunities. Some companies initially joined the bandwagon, but for most of the big corporates it took time.

The initial reaction of the corporate establishment was much like the Krikkiters, in Douglas Adams's blockbuster *The Hitchhiker's Guide to the Galaxy*, when they discovered they were living in a universe with stars and planets and, in fear of what that would do to their society, concluded: "It'll have to go." Once they turned to digitalization and globalization, however, they did it in their own way, and without importing the entrepreneurial spirit of the new companies that had emerged in digital hardware and software. Instead they emphasized preservation of the firm's boundaries, market control, and managerialism. In that way, computerization, digitalization, and globalization first promised the arrival of a new era of capitalism but later came to fuel planning and bureaucratization throughout the corporate sector.

The impact has been astounding. Boston Consulting Group's "index of complicatedness," for instance, shows that in five decades, bureaucracy in companies increased by almost 7 percent *annually*. This exercise measures how companies respond to an increasingly complex world. Companies spend more time managing, controlling and organizing than ever before. Forty percent of a manager's time is spent on writing reports and up to 60 percent in coordination meetings, the same consulting group claims.[41] It is not difficult to imagine the impact on companies and their staff. It is not just that time is wasted; bureaucracy and planning also change the composition of people working for large firms. Not many entrepreneurs, for example, would endure a working day writing, rewriting and filing reports and coordinating meetings.

Another way to measure bureaucratization is to count interactions. And as you would suspect, companies are overwhelmed with them. Management is now forced to handle collaboration "noise" on a level never seen before. Thirty thousand "external communications," for instance, is what the average executive receives annually, and that is a 3,000 percent increase from 1970 when a manager received approximately a thousand external communications annually.[42] And that is not because management in 1970 was made up of slackers. Nor is it a consequence of companies investing more in R&D, innovation and other more complicated areas. It is rather a direct reflection of complex and bureaucratic companies – and, indeed, an increasingly complex world – where more time is spent on the control and monitoring of divisions, firm boundaries, and market positions.

The quest for predictability is natural. Just ask yourself, hand on heart, how often you prefer uncertainty to predictability? Most of us prefer predictability to uncertainty. Similarly, the dominant thinking in big companies is not just that they can but that they *should* plan and operationalize in a completely predictable way. Planning, however, does not guarantee predictability – but it turns uncertainty into risks.

Converting uncertainty into risk is essential for modern companies and a central part of growing corporate managerialism. The Chicago School theorist Frank Knight made the distinction between risk and uncertainty in his classic tract *Risk, Uncertainty, and Profit*, which is often profoundly misinterpreted.[43] Knight differentiated between two worldviews, mechanical and organic cognition, and defined the first as a machine-like idea of predictable human behavior, whereas the latter was subject to change and new iterations for development. The mechanistic approach to the economy – much in the mold of the same cognitive philosophy as Robert Rubin's probabilistic approach to uncertainty (discussed in Chapter 5) – is important for the company because it can work with normal functions of the market. Risks can be priced, for instance, just as is done in an insurance contract.

Take card games as an example of mechanistic cognition: if a card is randomly picked from a deck of playing cards, it is impossible to know which card will be picked, but you know it will be one of 52 cards. Now, based on this information, everyone with basic knowledge in algebra can compute the likelihood of a certain outcome, such as the probability of picking the queen of hearts or a combination of cards that add up to 21. In a similar way, mechanistic cognition helps to turn complex issues into standard risk formulas that mathematically guide corporate behavior.

Uncertainty, however, is different in the sense that it cannot be contracted out: neither internally within a firm nor to the market. It is inherently linked to partial and incomplete knowledge of an individual and an organization, making it impossible to reduce it to probabilities that can provide guidance. Importantly, potential outcomes cannot be modeled or foreseen under Knightian uncertainty – such enterprises become, at best, "an estimate of an estimate." In the end, the only way to deal with uncertainty is through individual judgment and, in a firm, that judgment cannot be diffused between different functions or management roles; it can only rest with the owner (in this case the entrepreneur). Responsibility for and control of firms are inseparable, and the greater the distance between a firm and its owners, the more it shrinks the capacity to deal with uncertainty.

These observations were made in a different world. Knight's book was published in 1921, and it was an attempt to write "pure theory," a bullet of abstract economics taking aim at other economic thinkers in his age. However, as psychologist Kurt Lewin argued, there is "nothing so practical as a good theory," and Knight's insights – like Friedrich Hayek's views about human behavior under incomplete knowledge – are applicable to modern firms. Knight's theory was bad news for big corporations and, in particular, decisions relating to the individual judgment. In short, companies get it wrong.

Knight's idea of the role of ownership in managing uncertainty explains the West's modern capitalism. Uncertainty requires an institutional form or presence and capacities distant from the corporate bureaucracies, gray ownership, and agency conflicts that define much of today's corporate world. Corporate managerialists are not equipped to handle uncertainty and quite rightly choose not to do so. Together with the different breed of owners that have emerged, planners have squeezed out entrepreneurs, and while companies have grown skilled at measuring and handling risks, they have crippled their ability to deal with uncertainty. Corporate management has become mechanistic, like a software program operating in confined environments with modeled outcomes of possible risks.

The first casualty of managerialism is the corporate ability to work with uncertainty. Uncertainty is essentially absent in today's corporate playbook because ownership and control have been separated – and because there are not many real capitalist owners left who can exercise that judgment and have that capacity Knight suggested was essential. When deciding about the future, boards and managers often ignore alternatives that are fraught with uncertainty because they do not fit the corporate software code, and because they represent a different breed of ownership.

By ignoring uncertainties, however, boards and mangers also sign away their capacity to influence their own future. The future is inherently uncertain and those actions that can truly empower future business are surrounded by oodles of known and unknown unknowns. This is especially true of radical innovation. Without innovation a company becomes trapped in its own current market – and, for the larger economy, the technological frontier does not move much. In such a situation, the company has to spend far more resources to defend its market position – and such business planning reinforces the vicious cycle of bureaucracy because it requires more monitoring and control at the expense of entrepreneurship.

Plan, plan, and plan

There is one particular actor who knows how to embrace uncertainty: the successful entrepreneur. They do not just possess a unique ability to handle uncertainty. Uncertainty is in fact much of their *raison d'être*. Therefore, when corporate managerialism contracts out uncertainty, and when investment evaluations have largely become number-crunching exercises, it does not just disrupt the innovation ethos but disunites entrepreneurs from the company as well.

In the big companies that make up much of corporate America and Europe, the space for entrepreneurs has shrunk at the same pace as corporate managerialism and bureaucracy have increased. And these companies are important. While only 1 percent of US firms employ 500 people or more, this adds up to 50 percent of private sector employment.[44] It is true that big firms still employ people with entrepreneurial orientations – and some of them are still led by the founding entrepreneurs – but their bureaucratization in the past decades has taken on a life of its own. Perhaps this is what should be expected. Max Weber, both defender and critic of bureaucracy, prophesied that the bureaucratic system would embed itself in an organization.

Competition still compels companies to regularly change techniques and operations, and corporate leadership reinforces that trend with routine changes of corporate metrics and diagnostics. Bureaucracy and managerialism, therefore, are not synonymous with laziness and sloth. On the contrary, staff in bureaucratic organizations usually work longer and longer – but not smarter and smarter. They become trapped in a perpetual process of creating more bureaucracy for every new work process, business intent, and operational activity.

Bureaucracy, then, becomes the epicenter of organizations, influencing the way companies define themselves. Everything that can be planned is planned, and everything that it is not possible to plan, like uncertainties, is planned away. Corporate *strategy* development, if defined as creating something new, has lost its influence and has been replaced by corporate governance entrenched in the managerialist culture. Companies that are addicted to predictability, and shun uncertainty, are not strategizing for something new. That does not prevent them from paying lip service to strategizing. But most of the time their managerialist disposition will lead them to do just what they did before – plan for predictability.

Failing companies are different in that they have taken managerialism to the extreme, given too much power to gatekeepers, or been complacent in thinking that protecting their firm's boundaries will protect them against change. They almost uniformly fall into the category of companies that excel at planning. It is easy to blame fallen corporate titans – like executives Jorma Ollila of Nokia, Steve Ballmer of Microsoft, Jim Balsillie of Research in Motion, or Richard Grasso of the New York Stock Exchange – for the way their companies evolved. However, failure is hardly ever the result of one individual but the result of an evolutionary process that has changed the corporate identity and the way the company thinks about business development in general, and strategizing for something new in particular. W. Chan Kim and Renée Mauborgne, professors at the INSEAD business school, concluded after years of case studies that the difference between high- and low-growth performers is strategy – and more to the point, conventional thinking versus "value innovation." Value innovators are less concerned about benchmarking against rivals, and rather than limiting opportunities to market specifics and existing capacities they start by asking "what if we start anew?"[45] It is a basic question, but one that few companies ask themselves.

Given the time and money that corporate leaders spend on talking about strategy it is surprising how little attention is given to entrepreneurial quality and the capacity to manage uncertainty. Originally a military concept, "strategy" has been reinvented and renewed, and over time has slowly changed. From the beginning the changes followed management fashion and were almost a contest between the long term and the short term, between planning and execution, between top-down and bottom-up, and between levels of complexity. Peter Drucker, once called by *Business Week* "the man who invented management,"[46] had a crucial impact on defining strategy. Most notably, he spearheaded what in the postwar era were novel assumptions about how companies operate: from being seen as army-style top-down command-and-control units to complex organisms of interdependent parts, much as we think of companies today.

In the 1980s, Japanese car manufacturers introduced a structured and lean process of company management by combining high quality with low production costs. The American car industry quickly signed up to it and lean production soon became the ruling doctrine in corporateville. But the methodology of lean had its limits, and it was but one example of how business migrated from a recipe of contesting markets to more rigidity – still it was strategy many companies adopted. The famous strategist Michael Porter, however, dismissed anything that underestimated the complexity of business development. In 1979, he revolutionized business development by introducing into strategy the concept of competitive forces. Juggling the combined impact and bargaining power of suppliers and customers, and the threat from new entrants and substitutions – within any industry – was the essence of competition and that in turn was the essence of strategy.[47] Competition, markets and companies were a more complex habitat, and strategy the means to guide companies.

Business development and Porter's strategy quickly became the undisputed canon. Yet even if his perspective has been the intellectual decor for many executives, its most striking fate is that few of his ardent followers managed their companies on the basis of strategizing to contest markets. While companies, almost by default, ended up searching for Porter's competitive advantages in the era of corporate globalism, operational day-to-day concerns and other short-term targets became substitutes for bolder development steps. Strategy generally became defensive and confined, and not a real search for the corporate soul and entrepreneurial edge – or a tool to manage uncertainty.

While strategizing to create something new became scarce, improving operational performance moved straight into boardrooms. It is easy to understand why: operational excellence was handmaiden to the mindset of planners and managerialists. Responding to the growing demand for quick answers to complex business questions, the business community became awash with easy-to-use and one-size-fits-all performance tools and methods. Most of them had nothing to do with contesting markets, although many gave that impression. And it changed the perception of strategy.

Only think of "strategic planning," a strand of strategizing that became popular decades ago and still guides many managers today. It was partly a response to demand for bridging strategic goal setting and operational implementation. Companies often struggled to complete the chain from beginning to end, and failed to operationalize efficiently after having done all the strategic thinking. However, as strategic planning evolved it was, over time, almost cut by half. When companies today refer to strategic planning, it is not really about strategizing for something new. For the most part it is all about planning within a confined business space. Goal setting is reduced to what the company already knows about and currently operates in. Benchmarking, metrics, SWOT analyses (of strengths, weaknesses, opportunities, threats) based on the firm's boundaries are inputs, while other evidence and knowledge do not get much of a hearing.

Performance tools are great for augmenting operational performance. There is nothing wrong with that aspiration or the tools themselves; all companies perpetually need to improve, and using best practice is indisputably efficient. But apart from connecting measurements with actual improvements, the platoon of executives graduating from business schools came to believe that the tools were the answer to everything, including how a company should strategize for something new to make money in the future. While the recipe for corporate success cannot be found in a textbook, and everyone is not an entrepreneur just because they have read a book on entrepreneurship, the dominating notion was that strategizing for something new was almost equal to finessing costs by a few percent every year, gradually improving sales tactics, analyzing a key performance ratio here and adding another staffer there, and generally being opportunistic.

In that way, business development has gravitated toward more of the same and toward copying from others rather than shaping an identity and positioning for the future. Copying can be very successful. However, it is a shortcut that makes companies vulnerable to changing circumstances as it gives a false impression of strategic control, and it seldom plays out well in the long run. Copying is almost like learning a song lyric in a foreign language by heart. Anyone might be able to sing "Ne me quitte pas" in French like Nina Simone, but it does not turn them into a native French speaker. And when change in the strategic model is required, companies do not know what to do, or how to change. It is quite telling that 95 percent of a company's staff, according to a study, "does not understand its organization's strategy." The same study concluded that strategy was discussed less than one hour per month in 86 percent of the executive teams surveyed.[48] A manager who never discusses strategy becomes unintentionally ignorant, if not blind, to both strategic opportunities and threats – and certainly is not equipped to contest markets.

Moreover, it makes prioritizing difficult. What separates a truly strategic manager from the rest of the herd is an ability to grasp what should come first, and to identify which is the most important among many important tasks, and to make decisions accordingly. The quality of decision-making, together with implementation, separates high performing companies from the others, and one study found that only 15 per cent of companies were configured to excel in this area.[49] But as strategizing for something new and managing uncertainty is out and planning is in, prioritization of firm decisions is increasingly ignored because a planner does not have the disposition for it.

In 1955, for example, between four and seven "performance imperatives" were standard for the average CEO compared to between 25 and 40 today, according to a company study from the Boston Consulting Group.[50] This implies that CEOs today are less focused; they are split between many equally essential executive tasks. Or to put it bluntly: a company with so many performance imperatives is trying to move in different directions at the same time and cannot really know what it is doing, or perhaps even where it is going. The imperatives are increasingly in conflict as well. "Companies want to satisfy their customers, who demand low prices *and* high quality. They seek to customize . . . *and* standardize . . . They want to innovate *and* be efficient," the study summarizes.[51]

The goals are desirable but they cannot be implemented without causing an advanced form of corporate schizophrenia. Low price and high quality seldom go hand in hand. A company cannot customize and standardize at the same time. Likewise, a company cannot promote innovation without demoting efficiency. Conflicting goals are tripwires for managers and the source of confusion in organizations. It is certainly not a formula for those planning to contest markets, because it opens the floodgates to uncontrolled internal planning politics. Numerous studies describe how politics has permeated companies. A study of British managers, for example, found that 93 percent agreed that "most managers, if they want to succeed, have to play politics at least part of the time," and 83 percent concurred that "politics is played at all organizational levels."[52]

Strategizing to contest markets was over time traded for internal politics, performance enhancing tools, and business imitation. Strategy became a tool to defend and work within firm and market boundaries. But that is not the end of it. When corporate strategy emerged, and especially when it was more frequently used, sights were set on exploring opportunities by taking companies to unique market positions. The essence of positioning is to have a case-by-case approach to creating something new. And creating something new means finding a place in the market that no one inhabits, and that is financially attractive. Positioning of companies was especially popular for its connection to Porter, but also Russian-born Igor Ansoff, the so-called "father of strategic management."[53]

Positioning was in the vicinity of the "mechanical world" of Frank Knight and emphasizes the importance of calculations and numerical facts. If taken too far, corporate positioning falls into the managerial trap of trying to turn the world into a comprehensible and controllable place.[54] Getting numerical facts about business positions (and strategies) right is important, but taken too far, it makes the real world rigid, it collapses strategy development like an overcooked soufflé. Contesting markets implies going beyond what is quantifiable. In a rigid environment, a position that cannot be quantified often fails to qualify as a strategic alternative. And if the bar is set too high, business strategy turns into operational planning because that can be quantified. This is what happens in many companies today: with the best of intentions, and because strategizing for something new became too mechanical, unquantifiable realities are demoted, and with them, ideas, visions, methods, systems, services, and products that could have challenged markets.

To look beyond what is quantifiable from current markets and aim for something new is pretty much the whole idea behind innovation, too. Before penicillin was invented, the market for it did not exist. Before the internet, the market for domain names or web designers was unknown. Before the automobile, who could calculate the return on investment in the car market? Henry Ford is famously quoted: "if I had asked people what they wanted, they would have said faster horses."[55] If rigid planners had been in charge then, Ford might have bred a faster horse rather than built a car. All these inventions and many more would have been halted by gatekeepers had there not been entrepreneurs strategizing for something new, looking beyond the numerical probabilities of today, and willing to work on investments that had uncertain outcomes.

Managerialist planning has simply gone too far. Strategy is not used for something new, nor is it a tool to manage the unforeseen and the unknown. What overwhelms managerialists and makes them disinclined to strategize for something new is that the concept travels beyond the confined and controllable habitat of risks and operational improvement. Kim and Mauborgne touched upon this issue in their celebrated book *Blue Ocean Strategy*.[56] Strategy, they argue, cannot be about pushing for gains in a confined market space with inherent and fixed competition (red ocean), but is about creating a new space in the market grid that does not exist today and thus harbors no competitors (blue ocean). This is a philosophy for contesting markets, not competing within them.

Another way of putting it is that competition is for losers.[57] Successful business development must aim at building future monopolies in a new market space that will not only last but also provide the company with the opportunity to avoid descending into markets with tougher competition and falling margins. It demands entrepreneurial qualities throughout the organization, and real strategizing aimed at contesting markets – not a corporate managerialist agenda of performance tools, rigid positioning, internal politics, and copying.

Meet the sheriffs – gatekeepers against change

Corporate scandals and financial crises spawn not just new but tougher regulations, invariably based on the misguided assumption that there has been too little regulation, too few regulations. Yet regulations have not really improved; they have, more than anything else, just become more complex (see Chapters 6 and 7). To rectify the complexity of regulation, a favored approach in recent years has been to expand the role of compliance officers and empower legalistic thinking inside firms. And that approach is not limited to finance. Compliance officer roles are on the rise in most types of companies, especially big firms. It is probably the corporate profession that has seen the fastest growth in the recent decade. The *Wall Street Journal* has called it the "hottest job" in America. Looking at the growth in jobs and salaries of compliance officers, you can see why. About 75,000 new compliance officers have been added in the past ten years and the average salary has jumped by almost 20 percent in less than five years.[58]

There is a logic to it. "Why isn't Wall Street in jail?" journalist Matt Taibbi asked in a famous *Rolling Stone* article about the recent crisis.[59] The frustration is understandable. When the crisis erupted and the financial swamp was drained, everyone could see what stumps and junk had been hidden under the water. Even if most of it was legal, or at least not illegal, a lot of it was proof enough that many financial firms had products so complex that no one really understood how they worked or what their consequences were for the stability of a firm, let alone the entire market.

Everyone began to hunt for someone to blame. Just as in previous crises and scandals such as the fall of Enron and WorldCom, legislators responded by changing laws and rules. The Dodd-Frank Wall Street Reform and Consumer Protection Act followed just a few years after the subprime mortgage crisis. In Europe a few years after the crisis, European Union institutions prided themselves on having proposed more than "40 legislative and non-legislative measures to build new rules for the global financial system," including prudential and consumer protection regulation.[60]

For sure, every organization needs enforcement agents or compliance officers to defend rules and order. Compliance is a central function, and a company that grows bigger and more complex need disproportionally more of it. These agents – lawyers, auditors, but often also people with other backgrounds – ensure that companies comply with legal requirements, that they obey the law and act diligently also when laws and regulations are ambiguous, and follow internal rules. They play an important role, especially in light of fraudulent behavior, a phenomenon that occurs with some degree of regularity in every form of economic organization. Even to follow up on business ambitions and market performance, compliance perception is sometimes handy.

Yet the tail is now wagging the dog. Compliance agents in organizations that have no entrepreneurial direction exacerbate bureaucracy and managerialism with their desire to monitor and control, and above all else quantitatively analyze, all aspects of the company. Organizations are ever more dominated by managerialists with Excel sheets containing hundreds of cells of data that need regular monitoring. They operate on the assumption, to use a phrase by Hayek but contrary to his view, that "the pretence of exact knowledge" is better than "true but imperfect knowledge."[61]

Compliance agents naturally follow this philosophy because they need to protect themselves. They have little choice because their role is to be the fall guy. When a problem or scandal occurs, not just the company but regulators will "round up the usual suspects" – and those "usual suspects" are now the officers and teams tasked to guard companies against misjudgments, errors, and scandals. Consequently, with increasing jurisdiction, practicing what one compliance officer calls "preventive law,"[62] the compliance agents who used to monitor legal affairs have now turned on pretty much anything in search of behavior that does not conform to their defensive standard. Their brief is much larger and the new role is to police companies in accordance with written and unwritten rules and regulations.

But that mentality erodes the business culture of a company. Management and staff are fearful of uncertainty. They hedge themselves. Overly complex internal rules are invented and they often just help to pass around responsibility because no one really knows what the rules mean in complex environments. Accountability thus becomes an illusion. The rulebooks have contingencies for every occurrence but they do not allow for change and human ignorance. They rather take away the Knightian disposition for uncertainty. Managers prefer to seek the advice of compliance agents for all sorts of behavior, and if that officer is prudent and aware of who is going to be blamed in the event of problems, he or she knows that the safest answer to every question is no.

Even the budget process increasingly resembles a political battle between forces pushing expectations in different directions, often in the name of avoiding future blame or coming under the scrutiny of the compliance officer. For anyone to emerge on the losing end of a budget process, or to fall short of budgetary expectations, is a sure career stopper. And the way to avoid it is not necessarily to excel in business, but to manage budgetary expectations long before any business is ever done. Therefore, instead of focusing on business success, managers spend far too much time managing expectations and their future legacy of delivering planned and compliant results. Time is spent on structures defending against potential deviations, let alone criticism, and not on building operations to beat expectations. And when most managers think and act in the same way, the whole organization loses its competitive vitality.

The role of compliance officers has expanded heavily in recent years. Tougher legislation and growing market and regulatory complexity have fueled the rise of the trade.[63] "The age of the compliance officer arrives," the *Financial Times* recently concluded.[64] In Europe alone, suggests McKinsey, the Basel III rules will require banks to hire up to 70,000 new compliance officers.[65] A survey of the US Federal Register estimated that the 30 "Dodd-Frank rules" that had been introduced a year after the full Act came into force (representing no more than 10 percent of all "Dodd-Frank rules") would require banks in the US to put in an extra 2,260,631 labor hours every year.[66] In 2014, a study by PwC shows, almost 50 percent of companies across US industries increased the number of compliance officers, while only 5 percent of companies reduced them.[67]

This is disturbing news for anyone who does not view corporate guardians as having a positive impact on a corporation's dynamism, experimentation and innovation. Armed with the right to monitor all corners of the company, compliance officers reinforce corporate managerialism and make companies even more allergic to uncertainty. Like any substance consumed in inordinate dosage, excessive consumption of compliance can turn good things bad and poison the bloodstream of a firm. A CEO who ignores or objects to a recommendation by a compliance officer risks attracting criticism, and a CEO reluctant to change always finds an ally in compliance. The incentive structure of a compliance officer is not aligned with the goals of a company that needs to experiment and innovate. On many occasions, a compliance officer has nothing to lose from stopping innovations and nothing to gain from approving any. Much as overly complex regulation may lead doctors to oversubscribe medicines, the obscure role of compliance officers results in companies being excessively treated in a regulative compliance mode.

This mentality has incited a greater role for the mechanistic culture of companies and intensified the habit of making calculable risks out of uncertainties. Companies routinely translate what they do into numbers, and without them, companies could not operate or even exist. What is measured gets done, especially in firms that care only for numbers. Numbers indicate performance and get managers and workers to focus. Yet there are limits to what can be described numerically – and if there is one thing that cannot be turned into a mathematical function, it is the future. "It is difficult to make predictions," it is said, "especially about the future." While the future can be guessed at or estimated in better or worse ways, the point about guesses and estimates is that they are nothing more than that.

The numerical instinct has many other sources. For many companies, however, the compliance mentality has ignited greater urgency in turning the future into plannable and numerical scenarios. But there are increasingly signs that numerical planning has gotten out of hand. Take measurements of performance within hospitals, which have skyrocketed over the past few decades. Professionals get overburdened by performance measurements, and when a study showed that doctors in emergency rooms clicked the computer mouse up to 4,000 times in total during a busy ten-hour shift, spending 44 percent of their time entering data and only 28 percent with patients, it is hard to disagree.[68]

Consider how many companies, when investing, rely on quantitative valuation tools such as the net present value of an investment, calculated for instance by using discounted cash flow models. Qualitative approaches carry little weight, even if it is known that the qualitative aspects of an investment are at least equally important as the quantitative ones. This is perhaps to be expected; at the least, it makes investment decisions easier, or rather less open to criticism. However, the risk is that ignoring nonquantifiable objectives pushes companies to make the wrong investment choices: it becomes too mechanical, and that is a particularly acute problem when dealing with investments in innovation.

The use of standard quantitative valuation methods, argue Harvard's "innovation guru" Clayton Christensen and colleagues, "causes managers to underestimate the real returns and benefits of proceeding with investments in innovation."[69] In other words, companies risk failing to accurately predict future cash flows by making incorrect assumptions about the future. But to make it even more intriguing, myopic companies also become overoptimistic about the not-to-invest scenario when modeling current investments quantitatively. Companies simply fail to appreciate that declining performance of investment and products is not linear, that the decline often picks up speed, that it is exacerbated by sticking with old technology or old business models. An inflated belief in the status quo is a human proclivity – and for companies, too, if the old technology or business model is viewed as sunk costs. An added benefit is that maintenance of the old rather than investment in the new saves leaders from having to explain to capital markets why new capital is needed.

Instead of doing what is right in the long term, management focuses on the short term. Christensen et al. hinted at this motive when they wrote that when the usable lifetime of an asset is "longer than its *competitive* lifetime," managers "may stall in adopting new technology" because they fear the reaction of capital markets.[70] In that way, numbers have become more important in many companies than the business itself. They have become the masters rather than the servants of business. This may seem like bizarre behavior to those who haven't experienced the corporate numbers game and the associated demands from the market, but those who have will know that the average manager would prefer to *destroy* economic value for the sake of keeping numbers predictably up.

According to a 2005 survey among US chief financial officers, 75 percent of managers would "sacrifice some economic value to achieve smooth earnings paths." Furthermore, approximately 80 per cent of the 401 executives in the study would "decrease discretionary spending," including R&D, to avoid coming in short on a quarterly earnings target. Half of them would prefer value-destroying delays of projects to mitigate the same problem.[71] Numbers have evidently become, at least for some, more important than real economic value. In an odd sort of way, numbers have become gatekeepers against change.

5

THE TWO FACES (AND PHASES) OF GLOBALIZATION

– What does (Art Vandelay) do?
– He's an importer.
– Just imports? No exports?
– He's an importer-exporter. Okay!?

Conversation between Jerry Seinfeld and George Costanza in *Seinfeld*

The best of all monopoly profits is a quiet life.

John Hicks, "The Theory of Monopoly"[1]

There does not seem to be a wrong way to hate a big and global corporation. Western public opinion appears convinced that they dodge taxes, pollute the environment, and have crony relationships with politicians.[2] London's *Economist* magazine once called them "everybody's favourite monsters,"[3] and if you follow the debate about globalization you will know that this monster unites leftists and conservatives. Where the left finds conspiracies against democracy, the right sees corporate elites wrecking traditional social orders.[4] In the West's climate of rising economic populism, it is a minority view that big business, or business without any adjective, is good for society.

It is easy to see how critical views of big companies have proliferated in the recent years of economic crisis. Yet what is more revealing about multinational firms is that they hardly conform to the political myth of footloose and faceless machines, crushing everything standing in their way. Lately, it is rather that these behemoths – with notable exceptions – have numbed competition, grown obese and complex with all their bureaucracy, and do not seem to think the future is all that exciting. At least, they seem to think that life is a bit too good to motivate game-changing innovation or other efforts to contest their own or other markets. In several sectors, the growing influence of large and global firms has increasingly had the effect of slowing down market dynamism and reducing the spirit of corporate experimentation. Barriers against innovation competition have gone up, not down. Many multinationals have instead absorbed the mentality of the planning machine, and paradoxically, globalization helped them to reinforce innate habits of managerialism.

It is true that multinationals are different from each other. They come from different parts of the world, have different identities, and reward shareholders in different ways. Some are old; others are not so old – just as some are successful, while others are not. But the things that unite them, apart from the cold rejection of many ideologues, are intimately linked to globalization and the way it evolved over the past decades.

First, multinationals have played a supreme role in global trade and foreign direct investment (FDI), and their skills in exploiting the global market have defined the scale and scope of globalization. In a way, multinationals are almost synonymous with globalization.

Second, multinationals have reshaped large parts of production and organization, and there are not many places left in Western economies where companies can hide from them. Global companies have made economies more efficient; they have especially played a critical role in converging lagging countries closer to the technological frontier. Their growing role during the age of globalization influenced the entire hierarchy of firms, down to the smallest mom-and-pop store. The way they work is a testimony to human ingenuity and the private sector's talent for organization. Setting foot in a global company for the first time is a humbling experience. Today's global company is a far more sophisticated entity than the international company of 20 years ago.

Third, the big firms have partly changed their own character as a consequence of globalization and progressively grown far more defensive about contestable competition, including innovation. As a group of economists quipped in a study, global firms have a good deal in common with Art Vandelay, the alter ego and imaginary friend of George Costanza in the TV comedy *Seinfeld*.[5] Like Mr. Vandelay, the global company is now functionally an "importer-exporter." In a way, it can be described as a giant logistics hub – but one with a brand, technology, R&D operation, and internal financial market. That change also forced companies to reevaluate how they compete – and protect themselves against competition.

There is a larger story about capitalism in this transformation of companies, and this chapter will argue that the acceleration of globalization in the past decades has made companies allocate their resources and competitive drive into building organizations and business models that place little importance on innovation. Globalization has two different personalities, or faces, and the second one has changed capitalism. The first face is about adaptation and market renewal. Starting from the end of World War II, globalization had the effect of exposing local or national incumbents to contestable competition, predominantly from multinational firms. Competition accelerated the process of innovation – both the diffusion of new technology and the disruption of markets.

The second face, by comparison, is about saturated markets dominated by stale and bureaucratic companies. This effect of globalization is more recent. It has cohabited in the world economy with globalization's first face in the past 25 years, but gradually weakened contestable competition, adaptation and experimentation. Multinationals shifted strategy from contesting markets to defending their positions, partly because the fragmentation of value chains pushed companies to draw their firm boundaries closer to their ownership advantages. The benefits were obvious, especially as it allowed a greater degree of specialization in the economy. Companies could contract away the less important part of their value creation to other companies, and reallocate resources to assets generating their core value.

However, that process also prompted many of them to aim for stronger market control over their end customers. In that way, the second face of globalization reinforced the role of corporate bureaucracy and its defensive attitudes toward experimentation. Many big companies got bigger and gradually absorbed the mentality of the planning machine in their thinking about innovation and contestable competition. Those who got infected by that zeitgeist gradually came to think of innovation as technology input, not as market adaptation and experimentation. Big companies had bureaucratic personalities long before the emergence of globalization's second face, but now it became dominant. Those who initially had embraced big innovation gradually came to fear it. The paradox of this form of globalization is that it ushered in more competition, but less space for contesting markets.

The two different effects of globalization also reflect two phases of globalization. The first phase was defined by the horizontal expansion of big firms – firms stepping into new geographic markets with largely the same products. From the 1960s onward, billions of people were stepping into the world economy, and they did not desire different products from those that existed in the developed world. Rather they wanted to close the gap with the frontier economies and become destinations for the corporate "diffusion machine." Multinationals quickly responded.

During its second phase, from the 1980s onward, globalization pushed companies in a vertical direction and to restructure a greater part of their value chains. Globalization also became more varied, with a greater role for services and new markets from which to source inputs. It was then that companies accelerated the move toward their ownership advantages and made their entire production structure respond to the globalization of supply and value chains. During the peak of globalization's second phase, the big task facing any leader of a sizable firm was the quest to absorb and make use of the comparative advantages of different geographic locations.

Both faces and phases of globalization were dominated by multinationals and reinforced their managerialist ethos. Obviously, globalization did not give birth to that bureaucratic culture, but the mentality of managerialism grew stronger during globalization, especially in its second phase. Globalization moved from markets into firms, and the world stepped into a period of corporate globalism. That phase required, more than anything else, skills to understand economic specialization. It also boosted the number of mergers and acquisitions, because companies needed to become bigger than before to capture the specialization gains from a growing world economy. There was little demand for innovators and entrepreneurs fanning that "perennial gale of creative destruction," and that demand naturally declined as companies turned into logistics hubs. Executive recruiters were not scouting for entrepreneurial people like Elon Musk or Mark Zuckerberg to take up key positions in multinationals. They wanted executives with specialisms in optimization, management, logistics, capital markets, and other key operative functions of a firm. They wanted trusted partners from the "technostructure" of managerial capitalism, to quote John Kenneth Galbraith.[6] And these partners were planners, not entrepreneurs.

In this way, globalization helped to move Western economies away from Schumpeter's vision of capitalism. It is true that the vision of globalization generally embodies an idea about greater economic freedom and connectedness – a worldview that planted, accompanied, and also spread from actual globalization. Corporate globalism, or the second face of globalization, is a habit. It is a corporate practice, a system for optimizing an organization to profit on the back of falling transmission costs and the market entry of millions, if not billions, of new consumers and workers in the past three decades. Yet it is a habit connected to its own ideas about the global society and the principles that should power it.

That is where this chapter starts: an inquiry into the globalist worldview and its growing affinity for predictability – for risk rather than uncertainty, for market stability rather than market contestability. We then step into the economic world of globalization, partly to show how globalization changed face – from the first to the second unbundling of globalization – and partly to couple globalization with a particular form of corporate behavior that is more focused on defending market positions than winning new market territory with the help of contestable innovation. Globalization, we conclude, was a windfall for the economy, but it changed Western capitalism.

The globalist worldview

Beginning in the 1980s, the globalist worldview was essentially characterized by how a lot of smart people made economic life simpler. The economic world could be powered by modern algebra, executed by corporate executives, financial engineers, McKinsey wizards, central bankers, Treasuries, and folks with advanced degrees from the Faculty of Spreadsheets. With the help of globalization, they had cracked the code of modern economic growth, free from the persistent macroeconomic irritations of the past, let alone systemic crises. The future had only one direction: undisrupted ascension. It was a predictable future; it was – to quote from a book title released at the height of triumphalist globalization – *A Future Perfect*.[7]

For a long period, the master of the globalist worldview was Alan Greenspan, the prescient chairman of the US Federal Reserve, who ruled the republic of central banks for almost two decades. Portrayed as the "maestro" by Bob Woodward,[8] Greenspan became famous for digesting vast quantities of economic statistics, data employed to regulate the temperature of the US economy and manage imbalances, bubbles, crises, and other threats to the economy. Contrary to his libertarian ideology – and his public persona, often espousing humble doubt – he revered the central bank as the economy's *pater familias*, an authority that could protect and guide the economy, if not control its fate.

In Bill Clinton's economics team Greenspan had an intellectual companion. Robert Rubin, who managed the White House's economic policy portfolio before becoming Secretary to the Treasury, was an American liberal but shared Greenspan's idea of knowledge. Together with Greenspan, he was one of three wise men in *Time Magazine*'s "Committee to Save the World,"[9] a group occupying central posts in US financial governance during a number of crises in the 1990s that threatened to rip the world economy apart. Both men had a philosophical view of the world and one that acknowledged uncertainty. Yet Rubin was not burdened by unpredictability because clever people had an excellent cognitive tool to conquer it: "probabilistic decision making." Crafting it at Harvard University and his Goldman Sachs trading desk in the 1960s, Rubin looked at economic policy through the prism of probability and turned uncertainties into calculable risks and alternative scenarios through self-defeat tests.[10] The complex economy could be made less complex – and a rationalist approach, with government intervention, could protect it from shocks and crises.

Greenspan and Rubin, with their roots in two very different branches of American ideology, became symbols of an era. Powered by a renewed belief in market forces, infinite growth in the financial sector, and globalization, the era represented an aspiration to build a stable system for international peace, freedom and prosperity on the back of cross-border trade, investment and capital flows. Never mind capitalism turning gray, the inflow of capital to the corporate sector was going to diversify risk. The world would be made safer from greedy financiers speculating against currencies and countries. In a way, multinationals became merchants of peace and freedom. Tying economies closely together, and embracing countries that previously had sealed themselves off from the world, global companies were no longer villains exploiting natural or human resources in faraway countries. They were part of a larger mission.

Globalization is an enticing idea. Clearly, the era of globalization deserves a central place in future history textbooks. Markets were liberalized. Inflation was brought under control. New forces of productivity were unleashed, lowering the price of goods and raising real income. Newly opened markets first offered good opportunities to source inputs and production in a way that forcefully drove down costs. That is the way China and other Asian countries stepped into international markets. In the second place, they became important markets in their own right. And these markets were not small, peripheral economies. They were large and populous. Billions of people have released themselves from the prison of poverty in the past 40 years, especially in the second half of that period. It is a great example of how changes to economic organization can unleash human talent and release prosperity. For many countries, the start of this era was equivalent to the industrial revolution in the West. For their economies, it was their point zero, or as Germans might say, their *nullpunkt*.

Yet it is a fantasy that this era was the construct of Friedrich Hayek, Milton Friedman, or other ideologues of free market capitalism. Clearly it was not. While globalization accelerated, governments in mature societies taxed and spent a higher share of GDP. Globalization did not shrink governments. Nor was the emerging system of global governance a synonym for neoliberalism. It was rather "embedded liberalism" – a Keynesian and social democratic vision of the management rather than the liberalization of global affairs – that guided politics.[11] Economic freedom in the world expanded and regulations were changed. Yet regulations were not abolished; nor were reforms of regulations embraced by the Mont Pelerin Society, the group faithful to classical market liberalism.

During the second phase of globalization, the parallel trend to market liberalization was a reconstructed belief in the capacity of smart people to control complex economic aggregates. Together with other believers in a mathematical approach to economic life, the likes of Greenspan and Rubin propelled an economic cosmos that was made and managed by political fiat. They laid the tracks for the global economy – or so they claimed. Not only could they determine its direction, they could almost control the timetable of the world economy with the same precision as a Swiss train conductor makes the trains run on time.

But this idea of the "man of system," to quote Adam Smith, grew hubristic and failed to understand the intellectual arrogance in the globalist worldview. Financial crises, they thought, could be addressed by omnipresent geniuses in central banks, ready to flood markets with liquidity if a crisis occurred or a bubble was popped. Confident Treasury ministers like Gordon Brown, Britain's Chancellor of the Exchequer from 1997 to 2007 and later its Prime Minister, declared that the brutal forces of boom and bust had been paralyzed. Wall Street alchemists and hustlers thought they had figured out the formula for selling junk in a safe and foolproof way, even if a growing amount of money was chasing safe assets. Their collective historic achievement was to have made the world economy predictable.

That view, and the spirit of economic policy and behavior it heralded, collapsed in a spectacular way with the financial crisis. The world that these "men of system" modeled was too dependent on recent history and did not factor in the probability of a giant and systemic financial crisis, or other big events changing the direction of the economy. Such crises had not happened for a long time – and taking exactly that long view, most Western periods of low growth in the past decades had been manageable hiccups. Nor, they thought, could crises be a consequence of their own actions – like ultrarapid money growth, "Greenspan Puts" (propping the securities market with liquidity in the event of crisis), and misconceived bank regulations – let alone the basic principle of their economic worldview: the almost unconditional trust in rationalism. They were "apt to be very wise in his own conceit," as Adam Smith described the flaw in the man of system.[12]

The globalist worldview, despite differences among believers, became defined by a machine-like expectation of economic behavior. Its adherents were seduced by the simplicity of extrapolation. The worldview became a self-reinforcing assumption that the economy today would behave like it did yesterday, and tomorrow like it did today. Such computations became a guide for how the economy should behave and a formula for profitable business. Despite the crisis in 2007–9, the notion that smart people could control economic aggregates never got challenged. The expectation was that they could make the crisis a blip in the economic records, a temporary diversion from the trend. A few years after the Great Recession erupted, it was believed, the economy would soon again run like a Swiss train. But it did not.

The growth of globalization

Globalization's variant ideologies were not just articles of faith; they had real substance. Trade and investment had invariably grown since the end of World War II. Their speed of growth, it seemed, could only accelerate. And for a couple of decades, the profusion of economic freedom powered unrelenting globalization and corporate readiness to profit from it. Two other forces defined globalization's acceleration.

First, new markets opened up and entered the world economy. The story of trade growth in emerging markets is thrilling, but the age of globalization was not just about events after 1978 and China's first tentative steps toward a market economy. The era begins before BRICs (Brazil, India, Russia, and China), NICs (newly industrialized countries), or Asian Tigers (Hong Kong, Singapore, South Korea, Taiwan) stepped into the international market. For a long time, it was a pretty narrow affair, centered on trade and investment between countries to the east and the west of the Atlantic Ocean. Trade jumped during the 1970s and, if trade data are adjusted for inflation, grew faster than in the 1980s.

Second, there was a sharp cut in the cost of transportation and other real trade costs because of new technology, especially the shipping container. While it began in the mid-1960s, the containerization of international trade had spread widely ten years later and exposed larger firms to new patterns of production and competition.[13] Containerization did not just cut the headline cost of shipping, it locked products up in safer boxes, freeing – not completely, but substantially – trade from pilferage, damage, and theft. New York dockers had previously joked that they got paid 20 dollars a day "plus all the Scotch you can carry home," but containerization put an end to those fringe benefits and led to such a productivity shock that a unit of dock labor moved from handling 1.7 tons per hour in pre-containerization 1965 to 30 tons per hour in post-containerization 1970–1.[14]

Both these factors paved the way for the real boom of globalization in the 1990s, following a new wave of technology and liberalization that reduced barriers to market integration. The Cold War had ended and people in what was previously called the Second World gravitated toward the capitalist democracies of the West. Reforms in China and India opened them up to far deeper linkages to the world economy. A new global trade agreement turned the rather obscure GATT, the General Agreement on Tariffs and Trade, into the World Trade Organization (WTO) and established new international market rules. A continental North American Free Trade Agreement reduced barriers to trade between the US, Canada, and Mexico. Europe gave birth to its Single Market and sleepy economies on the continent and in northern Europe were shaken to life by far greater exposure to competition after product markets had been deregulated.

Soaring globalization can be seen in the growth of trade and investment. Global trade began to expand much faster than the global GDP – and FDI continued to expand faster than trade. Through the 1990s, the volume of merchandise trade grew by 6.5 percent, up from growth of less than 4 percent in the 1980s, and more than three times as fast as global GDP.[15] Trade growth slowed down in the first decade of the new century, recording a 4.3 percent expansion rate, and once the Great Recession started the deceleration continued. Standing behind the fast growth had been, first and foremost, the expansion of emerging markets as sources and destinations of trade, especially China's move into the global economy. The country's share of global exports doubled between 1990 and 1996. And then it doubled again between 1996 and 2001, and doubled yet again between 2001 and 2006. Since 2006 it has grown by just 50 percent.[16] For China and other countries, the development was extraordinary. In 2014, China's GDP per capita was 13 times higher than in 1990, when measured in purchasing power.[17]

Globalization spawned big changes in the corporate world. For companies that wanted to maintain their market positions, it became almost impossible not to join the bandwagon of globalization. It is no wonder that "globalize or die" became that generation's corporate theme song. A former head of the OECD even made use of Darwin to drive home his point that the only choice for companies and countries was to "globalise or fossilise."[18] Globalization, then, was an almost existential call.

Moreover, globalization was also a good strategy to raise profitability for Western companies, and that naturally explains why companies readily embraced it. Throughout the Western world, the era of globalization raised corporate profits and, particularly in its second half that ended with the 2008 crisis, the return on capital. Naturally, profits did not rise equally across companies and countries: political and economic institutions, and their differences between countries, were critical for the performance of both companies and countries during globalization. While Western profit margins generally show a pattern of mean reversion, a move to the average over time,[19] the corporate sector in many Western countries has shown high levels of profitability in the past decades (see Figure 5.1). Countries like Germany, the United Kingdom and the United States even had significant trend improvements in corporate profit margins.

There are several explanations behind the movement of profit margins over the past decades. Obviously, some important ones relate to broader macroeconomic conditions and how well political leaders adjusted policies to the tune of globalization. In the middle of that thicketed territory, however, stands the simple observation that a country's history and industrial structure defined the propensity to prosper from globalization. Successful companies usually came from countries with a pedigree of international commerce and a long history of enterprises making their way in the world. Importantly, they also had an industrial structure, and policies

Source: US Bureau of Economic Analysis; UK Office for National Statistics; Federal Statistics Germany.
Figure 5.1 Profit margins in the US, the UK, and Germany

supporting that structure, which matched the patterns of demand that emerged during the era of globalization and growth in emerging markets. Equally important, they had an industrial structure that could internalize the cost advantages offered by foreign labor entering the market – and the new cost-efficient inputs they produced.

Take Germany, the industrial powerhouse of Europe, as an example of a successful industrial globalizer. The country's corporate sector enjoyed a clear rise in profit margins from the early 1990s up to the crisis. From the mid-1990s, Germany's margin dropped, partly as a consequence of the country's inflexible labor market. Labor costs exploded after the German reunification when East Germans got salaries and benefits close to West Germans, despite a big gap in productivity. Germany's nonfinancial corporate sector reduced its profit margins to levels comparable to those in other European countries like France. It had moved between 30 and 35 percent as share of gross value added. However, from the late 1990s up to the start of the West's financial crisis the country's profit margin steadily rose and peaked around 40 percent in 2008, far above the rate in several other continental European countries.[20]

For sure, Germany's corporate sector did not prosper because of growth in domestic demand. German demand growth has been muted throughout the period, partly because of the "demographic preference" for saving as the population grew older. The country's high taxes on consumption and ossified services sector have also given consumers good reasons to deposit their money rather than spending it. Private consumption growth either shadowed or trailed the rates in other European countries and, for a while, Germany was referred to as the "sick man of the euro."[21]

Corporate Germany recovered to healthy levels of profits through labor market reforms and globalization, which accelerated in the same period up to the crisis. Its export sector has grown extraordinarily fast and the country has grown its surplus from trade for a decade and a half. However, Germany also raised its imports of inputs as German companies connected themselves to the arteries of regional or global value chains. German economist Hans-Werner Sinn portrayed this new German economy as a "bazaar economy,"[22] a shift in the balance between the export sector and the domestic sector, and rapid growth in the country's import of inputs.[23]

Compare Germany with France, an economy that prospered less from globalization, especially the new opportunities for exports and for globalizing production structures in order to internalize the cost advantages of importing inputs. Like German firms, French companies internationalized throughout the postwar period, both through investment and greater trade exposure. However, the interesting story of globalization is hidden in relatives rather than absolutes, in this case how resources are reallocated in the economy in response to increasing global competition. The difference between Germany and France reflects a broader context of industrial structure, the general degree of competitiveness economy-wide, and how political authorities respond to globalization. Simply put, companies internationalized in different ways and the actual composition determined the scale and scope of global expansion, and the benefits received by companies and countries.[24]

While German firms emerged after World War II in an industrial context that generally put few restrictions on companies, France grew protective of technology and successive governments favored a strategy of indigenous creation of technology and core corporate assets. French dirigisme, its state interference in the economy, accelerated in the late 1960s after the publication of an incredibly influential book, Jean-Jacques Servan-Schreiber's Le Défi américain (The American Challenge), often seen as a call to arms against US technological and corporate superiority, but what should rather be read as an admiration for American corporate prowess.[25]

Servan-Schreiber's thesis about a "confrontation of civilizations ... in the battlefield of technology, science, and management" was an invitation to make defensive political interpretations. And generations of French politicians have ever since been alert to the troop movements on the battlefield of global competition. They received the thesis as an invitation for greater economic interference, but the biggest influence was not a general wave of protectionism.[26] The cold-water tap of protectionism certainly cooled economic dynamism, but the lasting influence was the hot-water governmental embrace of French ownership advantages, especially the technology, R&D services, and management of French blue-chip firms. Yet France's protection of the core value-generating assets of companies proved counterproductive. It gradually eroded France's corporate readiness to import key resource advantages from other countries, and eventually, French firms' competitiveness abroad.[27]

The French business sector continues to rank low in its orientation to global expansion. The Swiss IMD Business School, for example, recently found in a survey of attitudes to globalization conducted across 59 countries that French executives had the most negative attitudes.[28] Neither the French industrial exporting sector nor its input-importing sector expanded globally along the pattern of German companies. While its services sector was more successful, French industry gradually weakened its competitiveness because it did not or could not reap the gains from globalization. The expansion that did occur was also less responsive to global demand – especially demand in those parts of the emerging world that swelled at breakneck rates, like China. The French companies that were successful often operated across Europe.

Other countries in Europe like Italy and Spain share France's experience of a modest pace of global expansion. Their exposure to foreign competition increased, but their footprint in Asia has not been particularly strong, partly because there was no natural alliance between their industrial structures, especially their export supply, and Asia's offer of imports and exports. In 2013, for instance, Germany represented 45 percent of the European Union's total exports to China, more than the next three countries (the UK, France, and the Netherlands) combined.[29]

Therefore, in countries with a tradition of outward-oriented expansion and a corresponding industrial structure, the corporate sector could expand through exposure to emerging markets. They could scale up production on current levels of investment, contest new geographic markets, and cut costs by importing inputs from lower-cost countries. Germany, the United States, and other globalizers had companies with a strong profile in those industries that grew faster than others, especially capital and investment goods, ICT, and business services. Importantly, they also had companies with prior experience in international expansion and developed the particular types of organizations and skillsets required to move quickly into growing markets, especially during the peak of emerging market growth. In the United States, new companies in the field of information technology like Intel, Microsoft, and Google quickly seized the opportunities offered by international markets, and became global firms almost instantly.

From scale to scope – from the first to the second generation of globalization

Global expansion motivated companies to adopt visions of corporate success connected with the planning machine and its "technostructure." Emerging over several decades, it was the organizational reflex to new market opportunities in different parts of the world. For a variety of reasons, size was an advantage in global competition and the race to break into nascent markets. It was also a key factor for success in the globalization of production, trimming the marginal cost of production by using the cost advantages of other parts of the world. Corporate size, to quote Galbraith, had an "unabashed alliance" with industrial planning, and still does.[30]

Obviously, scale orientation is one of the great economic benefits of globalization, pushing down consumer prices and raising welfare. It is equally apparent that globalization's scale preference favored large companies more than small or medium-sized companies. Globalization, when defined as trade and investment, largely became an affair for big business. A study of US trade, for instance, showed that in the year 2000, the top percent of US exporters represented a bit more than 80 percent of total US exports. A good part of the trade – about 50 percent in the case of US imports – was actually trade within the large firms rather than trade between a company and an unaffiliated partner.[31] United Nations data likewise show that multinationals represent 80 percent of all world trade.[32] European countries, most of which share land borders with several countries, usually have greater dispersion of trade, but the differences are not that great. In France, for instance, two-thirds of all imports are attributed to a very small group of companies that trade and take part in business group networks.[33]

As globalization progressed, the advantage for large corporations grew bigger – and more so in capital-intensive sectors and markets that are complex. Natural "barriers" to global competition also escalated and reduced the space for new entrepreneurs breaking into markets to compete with incumbents. In a way, the fixed costs of markets and market entry (costs not dependent on volumes of production) went up when global competitiveness required a presence in an ever growing number of international markets. Harder still, the cost of downstream competition became fiendishly high for many entrepreneurs, facing diverse distribution systems due to differences in language, legislation, local competition, infrastructure, and customs.

Globalization then changed face and began to affect companies in a different way. The new pattern of competition that emerged when corporate supply and value chains globalized and fragmented made it far more difficult to compete unless a company had access to production networks that could produce cost-effective inputs and logistics that ensured access to inputs at the right time and in the right place.

Global success, then as now, demands that a company constantly optimizes its organization and production processes, with a view to cutting costs, and generally structures its organization to manage differences in countries and regions. For a producer unable to be at the constantly expanding productivity frontier, orientation toward global markets was a risk rather than an opportunity. Global orientation required skills that enabled firms to exploit both the horizontal and vertical advantages offered by globalization. Smaller firms could connect to the artery of globalization through various networks of production – by becoming one of many suppliers of inputs to a company closer to the end customer. At the top of that network reigned a company with the skills, capital, and market position necessary to manage and defend the organization of multiple and fragmented production networks.

The entry ticket to the group of companies privileged to capture the advantage of globalization became less an issue of what a company brought to the market and more about market position and operational efficiency. The key to success was not so much the technological ingenuity or capacity for innovation of a company, or its disposition to contest markets with new products, but rather its organizational talent in managing a complex network of producers and commanding better control of the market. Globalization demanded technocrats, not entrepreneurs.

The growth of production networks in particular shaped the character of globalization. Competition moved from countries to firms and ushered in new business structures to defend and exploit core ownership advantages. While it was not a novel idea in the late 1980s or early 1990s to begin contracting out parts of the supply chain to affiliated partners, the scale and sophistication of the fragmented networks that evolved from the early 1990s changed the texture of corporate globalization. For centuries, trade had broadly conformed to the standard wine-for-cloth thesis developed by David Ricardo in the early nineteenth century. Countries exchanged final goods with each other. Various endowments and advantages of countries (absolute or comparative) largely defined the actual composition of that trade. In this version of globalization, concentration of production was stronger than fragmentation, and specialization broadly followed the pattern of geographic concentration.

Trade economist Richard Baldwin has defined two distinct phases of international trade expansion, each with a different profile: globalization's first and second unbundling of production.[34] The first unbundling – the end of the need to make goods close to their customers – from the steam engine in 1820 to the mid-1980s, a period with ups and downs, was based on a reduction in trade costs. Tariffs went down and it increasingly got cheaper to ship a product produced in one factory to another country.

The second unbundling – the end of the need to keep most manufacturing stages close to each other – reduced transmission costs more than it cut trade costs, especially after the spread of information technology that allowed for greater efficiency in the internal organization of fragmented production. Falling transmission costs allowed companies to radically expand their use of externally sourced production and combine it in a way that was more responsive to markets. Moreover, companies could integrate important units by other means than trade. As the digitalization of the economy expanded, many firms quickly seized opportunities for new forms of integration within companies as well as between markets. Today, their digital flows generate a higher value added than all their goods in trade.[35]

The second stage of globalization was different from the first in that the geography of production and competition changed: in the first era there was mercantilist competition between products, while the second era unleashed competition in production stages and between input producers (of both tangibles and intangibles such as knowledge).[36] In the first generation of globalization, companies profited by a Henry Ford type of specialization: production fragmented and sequenced along the conveyor belt, yet still remained under a single roof. In the second generation, the specialization of production moved out of firms and adjusted itself to advantages of the market rather than those of the firm.

Companies responded fast to new opportunities. Big companies grew even bigger, in terms of staff, sales, and capitalization. However, the qualitative shift was even more pronounced and produced larger changes for corporate strategy, competition, and innovation. The global company "decentered" production through new types of supply and value chains that used proximity and cost advantages in subtler ways than before.[37] Companies began to trade not just in parts and components, but different tasks.[38] Value chains were "sliced up," as Paul Krugman put it in a famous essay,[39] and pushed volumes of trade even higher as companies become ever more reliant on imports within the firm, or imports from affiliates tied intimately to the company through increasingly sophisticated production networks.[40]

The emerging fragmentation remodeled – not completely, but substantially – the way a company produced and created value. Proximity still matters in splintered production networks with high degrees of outsourcing, but the profile moved away from the classic perception of trade between producer and consumer.[41] First fragmentation pushed up intrafirm trade between parent and affiliate, and second, it spawned "arms-length" interfirm trade based on the new contract system of production.[42] While there is often a trade-off between intrafirm trade and contracted interfirm trade, they are both united in their effect on the reorganization and fragmentation of production.[43] They both embody the deeper division of labor that emerged during globalization's second unbundling.

The foreign trade content of production increased rapidly as a consequence of this new form of economic integration. In the production of a typical German car, for example, foreign value added increased from

21 percent in 1995 to 34 percent in 2008.[44] A more famous example, from the really fragmented electronics sector, is Apple's music player, the iPod.[45] While an iPod – just like an iPhone – is "made in China," only about 2 percent of the value added of an iPod is captured by China. In other words, 98 percent of the value of this particular export is generated abroad. The United States – where Apple has its headquarters and invests in marketing, design, R&D, and more – takes between one-third and one-half of the iPod value added.

This is a familiar situation for many countries. East Asia's magnificent rise in trade, for example, is closely tied to trade in global production networks, but the richer they have grown, the more important it has become to capture a larger part of the value-added content of traded goods.[46] In Europe, too, the rise of cross-border production networks has transformed production and trade. Germany, for instance, is linked up with several countries in Europe through what has been called the "German-Central European supply chain."[47] Exports to Germany from Central European countries in the cluster exceeded their exports to other countries in the region, and a rapidly growing share of those exports had significant German value-added content.[48] In that way German firms were trading intensively, back and forth, with Czech or Slovak firms and affiliates. The national origin of that volume of trade came less and less to match the value added of the trade.[49]

In today's global economy, the old mercantilist view of trade is outdated, other than in political rhetoric, and the volume of trade – or the trade balance – no longer gives a reliable measure of gains from trade, if it ever did. Competition is not between companies of different national origins using local comparative advantages, but between firms that run fragmented operations across the world with just-in-time operations, requiring little inventory but a great sensitivity for time, distance, marketing, and logistics.[50]

Clearly, globalization's second unbundling has been stronger in the goods sector than in services. Globalized and fragmented supply chains are predominantly a phenomenon in the manufacturing industry. Trade in services remains much smaller than trade in goods, and a substantial part of services production is not exposed to international competition in the same way as in goods sectors. Restrictions on trade in services are still substantial.

Services sectors have changed, though. As value chains have globalized, services have generally become more globalized. This is partly because a good part of the growth in trade in some services is linked to trade in goods. Economists, not a profession known for linguistic talent, call it the "servicification" or the "servitization" of the goods trade.[51] For example, a quarter of the export value of a car consists of service inputs.[52] There are also services sectors that have witnessed both global and contestable competition in a direct way. Telecom network services have been a contested market, and partly remain so even if network incumbents have become less innovative and the market saturated. Retail, airline travel, and financial services have clearly seen big changes over the past 30 years, too, and sometimes the change has happened through a combination of globalization and Schumpeterian innovation. Regardless of how it happened, the increased role of competition has made food retailing, air travel, and bank services cheaper and more accessible.

The landmark changes in these markets are getting a bit old now. In Europe, many of the changes happened in the 1990s and spurred growth in competition, productivity and income then, but less so in the past ten years. Interestingly, new competition and innovation have not changed market orders and hierarchies as much as imagined. Take our native country – Sweden. The "big four" among the banks are basically the same ones as 30 years ago. The difference between, say, 1990 and today is that banks have merged and obtained a bigger share of the market. The food retail market has seen new competitors like Lidl, but the market remains dominated by the three groups that dominated it before the market opened up. The mobile subscription market is still dominated by the three players that dominated it 20 years ago (although one has been acquired by a foreign owner).

In fact, the services sector appears to be pretty similar to the goods sector as far as globalization's effect on contestable competition is concerned. It may not manifest as fragmented supply chains, but corporate behavior in services sectors has changed as services companies followed the general outward orientation of the economy. The globalization of services also has a second face. In this version of globalization, companies have reinforced habits that, while still raising efficiency and the diffusion of technology, have distanced them and markets from big innovation and contestable competition. This is the paradox of globalization: it has raised the efficiency of economies while concurrently reducing the space for contestable innovation.

Globalization has moved the boundaries between firm and market

In order to understand second-generation globalization and how it could spur efficiency rather than contestable innovation, and generally create markets with managed competition, we need to go back to the basics of industrial organization, and especially Ronald Coase. As companies grew bigger, global, and fragmented they changed their habits but not their character. They still operate, for want of a better word, on "the Coasean principle," the software code of corporate behavior that we introduced in the previous chapter

The beauty of globalization was that it cut market transaction costs – and, as a consequence, allowed for a reorganization of production. That change also created new conditions for how companies balance internal and external transaction costs. Companies could contract away a larger part of production because falling trade and transmission costs also cut market transaction costs. What is more, they could now define and bundle their core assets in new ways, and change their strategies for how to make money. Globalization, then, helped companies to "marketize" their supply and value chains, and benefit from taking selected parts of them out of their own organizations. Multinationals became the logistic hubs they are today.

But the changing conditions for companies choosing between "make or buy" are just one aspect of how globalization influenced companies and capitalism. Equally important was how companies employed the energy and focus that was no longer needed to ensure that production previously kept in-house was competitive. Multinationals started to change the way they defined their firm boundaries, and put a lot more emphasis on those parts of the production process that operate in areas where market transaction costs remained high.[53] Falling competitive pressures on the supply of inputs, components, knowledge, data, and other central parts of making a product made large and global companies focus more attention on their market positions and their defense.

When the boundaries of firms were redrawn it became far more important for firms to get better control of their downstream customers. While companies fragmented upstream, most of them put stronger management on their downstream. The best crop of executives managed to set the firm's boundaries in a way that both captured the dynamism of the market and effectively reduced downstream market competition, or competition in its end-customer market. In that way, they "agglomerated" markets functionally. Major streams of competition swarmed under the large companies that were close to the end market. These companies had proximity to the market and, through the management of the supply chain, parental control over upstream production. Ever more production resources in the world moved in the direction of the large and global companies that had scale, networks, and market acumen, and that gave them even stronger positions. Many of them now became the "integrator" of markets and production.

Some went even farther in that direction and almost stopped being companies. They behaved as if they were the market, as if controlling access to end markets became the business model in itself. The skilled companies could set their firm's boundaries close to the market boundary and reduce the risk of radically new competition from others than the incumbents.

Competition undoubtedly intensified as production fragmented, and most of the firms that have managed to escape contestable competition most effectively would rightly say there is fierce competition in their markets. But competition is not a singular thing; it comes in different shapes and forms, and affects markets in different ways. The outcome of competition always has a context. While there has been growing competition between existing products – and a substantial part of it has been connected to competing production networks – it is less obvious that corporate attempts to contest markets also have intensified during globalization's second unbundling. The initial phase of new market entry *did* provoke more contestability. But as globalization changed character, modern competition typically came to be defined by controlled or managed competition *within* long, multiple, and fragmented supply chains. That process helped to increase scale and other benefits. Yet given other market conditions, especially the rising fixed costs of market entry, vertical integration hardly promoted contestability of established markets close to the end customers. On the contrary, as entry costs to end markets increased significantly with globalization and supply-chain competition, competitive ambitions seem, perhaps surprisingly, to have turned farther away from the ideal scenario of constant competition moving markets and prices toward the marginal costs of production.

Drawing on the contestable market school of thought – William Baumol's idea of competition as a contest between incumbent firms – the patterns of competition emerging under the second-generation globalization period increasingly resembled so-called oligopolistic and monopolistic competition.[54] It may sound counterintuitive, but it is close to what actually happened on many markets. They became more concentrated as competitive strategies focused on market position and ownership advantages.

However, the imagery of legal monopolies – that is, old utility services like postal and telecom services – or Soviet-style bureaucratic colossi does not apply here. Neither does Marx's monopolistic theory of capitalism – his view that capitalism leads to "a constantly diminishing number of the magnates of capital, who usurp and monopolize all advantages."[55] Marx raised several good questions about capitalism, but got neither companies nor markets right. Oligopolistic competition and monopolistic competition are something else.

In fact, monopolistic competition is not about classic monopolies at all. It is in many ways the opposite of legal monopolies because it is defined by low entry and exit barriers to the market and features many different producers. In this market structure "competing" companies are not directly competing in the same market space. They are not selling identical products and they deliberately differentiate their products to make them less substitutable. Pepsi and Coca-Cola, for instance, have no problem competing with each other, but they protect themselves from the type of competition that would make them direct substitutes – for example, they do not invite customers to switch between the sodas through a reduction in the relative prices between them. Hence, competitors can structure the market in favor of incumbents by engaging in a certain type of competition. And the paradox is that the bigger the market gets, and the more they converge their prices, the more difficult it will be for a new rival to contest the market with a substitutable and almost identical product.

By way of contrast, oligopolistic markets have high entry barriers and only a few competitors, and they are usually large companies too. They compete, but tend to follow each other – both in products and prices. Undoubtedly they use lobbying and market power to keep entry barriers high to avoid others contesting the market. Like markets with monopolistic competition, more competition can lead to fewer central market players in oligopolistic markets.

Both approaches, while abstract, define quite well two key features of the type of competition that grew stronger under globalization's second phase. Firms could gain greater control over the market by moving competition toward the monopolistic or oligopolistic versions. While pushing up the entry barriers to the market, leading to fewer competitors, many global firms have magnified their value by tightening the firm's boundary closer to core ownership assets: the assets that determine the company's value and capacity for internationalization (e.g., technology, intellectual property, brand, R&D services, parental production process control, and so on). Assets not central to value creation could be spun off as long as they could be controlled. Likewise, through a higher degree of specialization, companies could make products less substitutable. Many companies that managed globalization successfully convinced markets that their products were either difficult to substitute with other products on the market, or that the substitutes were costly to use as it would require a wholesale switch to a different platform of products. That habit of competition has a longer history, but globalization reinforced it.

As a consequence, markets moved toward an even greater role for the big companies. The effective rate of market concentration in several markets went up. For example, between 1997 and 2012, two years when the US Census Bureau measured sector concentration, the market shares of the biggest companies increased in 10 out of 13 sectors (see Table 5.1). That is a somewhat imprecise way to measure competition and concentration, but more granular approaches lead to the same conclusion. Take agriculture and financial services, two very different sectors. In US agriculture, the four biggest firms increased their market share in virtually all agricultural submarkets between 1972 and 2002.[56] In finance, the loan market share of the ten biggest banks increased from 30 to 50 percent between 1980 and 2010.[57] In other sectors too – such as mobile subscriptions and transport – the trend has been the same or similar.[58]

Industry	Change in revenue share earned by top 50 firms, in percentage points
Transportation and warehousing	11.4
Retail trade	11.2
Finance and insurance	9.9
Wholesale trade	7.3
Real estate rental and leasing	5.4
Utilities	4.6
Educational services	3.1
Professional, scientific and technical services	2.6
Administrative support	1.6
Accommodation and food services	0.1
Other services, non-public administration	-1.9
Arts, entertainment and recreation	-2.2
Health care and assistance	-1.6

Generally, the influence that big companies have on an economy has risen sharply, especially after the wave of mergers and acquisitions from the 1990s onward. According to data from the US Bureau of Economic Analysis, Fortune 500 companies doubled their share of the US economy between 1955, when Fortune launched its stock index, and 2014.[59] This trend has continued. Both America and Europe have seen a broad wave of industry consolidation, with several M&As between leading firms. Competition authorities in Europe have several times been concerned about, and sometimes blocked, M&As when they could lead to a reduction of key market actors from four to three. The planned acquisition by UPS of the Dutch logistics firm TNT was rejected on such grounds, and it is frequently employed as an argument against further consolidation in the telecom sector. However, these concerns follow on the heels of consolidation that has already taken place. In many industries, the large firms are much more influential than they were 10 or 20 years ago.

It is true that increasing concentration does not have to be an economic concern. Greater concentration can also generate benefits, provided there is still competition. Generally, those economies where large firms are an important part of the total of economic activity tend to be rich economies. In Europe, for instance, there is a difference between higher- and lower-income countries. Countries like Finland, France, Germany, and the UK are more dependent on larger enterprises (with a workforce in excess of 250 people) than Italy, Portugal, and Spain.[60] As we have discussed previously, large firms are closer to the productivity frontier. They help to import new technology and better production processes, partly because they are anchored in international markets to a far greater degree than small firms. Their FDI is a vehicle for raising productivity and prosperity in many parts of the world.

Ronald Coase's simple idea helps us to understand how concentration in recent decades has gone up – and progressively reduced the space for market experimentation and contestability. As market transaction costs were reduced, firms narrowed their ownership advantages and put a lot more effort into raising the boundaries around them and their assets. Globalization offered smart global companies a chance to, first, reinforce the role played by their size and market reach in competition. As they got larger and had presence in most markets, it became more difficult to compete with them. Second, the same firms then tightened their control over markets by focusing far more on protecting market position and exploiting their core value-generating assets. Companies were not going to fail because their in-house, repetitive, low-value input production did not match that of their competitors. While there could be substantial competition in the lower trenches of the supply chain, the higher end of the value chain could increasingly be shielded from contestable competition.

Competition is now defined much more endogenously than before, by firm or network behavior, than exogenously, by markets. New market entrants today will often have great problems circumventing the big firms and their production networks. A start-up based on a new drug, chemical, battery, turbine technology, or toothbrush for that matter, will have to invest far more today than 20 years ago in order to get into the market and reach scale. It is not just that the price of entry has gone up, but that production is so tightly knitted and efficient that it is difficult to contest the market without stepping into one of the production networks. The more firms have tightened their boundaries, the more they have had to focus on repelling boarders and preventing intruders. Most of the expenses of a firm have had to go in that "Coasean" direction of defending market position, including innovation resources. Those expenses largely became annexed to the broader corporate strategy of exploiting and defending corporate boundaries. Even if the process was seldom articulated in this way, many companies reallocated resources to defend the natural (or nonpolicy) barriers against competition created by market transaction costs and their firm boundaries. In that way, the industrial structure of the big firms and their networks increasingly came to define the process of innovation and adaptation.

Firms' boundaries are central to understanding how companies innovate and compete. Take the example of telecom giant Ericsson. Today, it is a world-leading producer of telecom network infrastructure and services, but up to the early 2000s it competed in the mobile devices market. At the prestigious CeBIT fair in Hanover in 2000, Ericsson made a big splash with a cool new product it had developed, called the Cordless Web Screen (initially the Cordless Screen Phone).[61] People seemed impressed, and it was thought of as "the next big thing." The developers were excited but not exactly sure what to call it. They were sure, however, that they were sitting on a potential gold mine, as the market for this "screen phone" was estimated at US$100 billion. Yet that estimate turned out to be conservative. The Cordless Web Screen was, of course, a tablet – and some media called it a webpad. Ten years ahead of its time, it used Bluetooth to connect with the internet and a pointer for the screen. Pictures of it show a remarkable resemblance to Apple's later blockbuster, the iPad. Ericsson's developers also thought that customers would use the Web Screen as an iPad is used today.

Why did Apple, and not Ericsson, contest the mobile device market with a tablet? There are surely a multitude of explanations such as bad timing, poor design, and insufficient marketing. But Ericsson largely made a decision that followed the Coasean playbook. Other companies also failed to seize the tablet market – Nokia and Honeywell were basically sitting on the same product, and they did not have great market success with their tablets either. And the showing of its Cordless Web Screen came at an inopportune moment. Ericsson needed to narrow its firm's boundary, partly because it was financially stressed after the dot-com bubble fizzled, and could not afford to support its entire product range. Moreover, it had been badly affected by supply shortages of components for its mobile products, and needed to lessen its exposure to supply-chain risks. In order to grow the company, it also needed to reduce peripheral products that were not connected to its main business: network infrastructure and services. Ericsson therefore hived off its Web Screen and other mobile devices into a partnership with Sony with the ambition to grow both companies' share of the mobile phone market, not to build a new market for tablets.

No one knows what would have happened if Ericsson had run with its tablet. Perhaps it would have been successful; perhaps it would have failed, as Ericsson clearly struggled to make it big in other consumer device markets. Arguably, Ericsson made what appears to be a rational decision about its firm's boundaries and how its resources for innovation should be allocated. Given its market position and incumbency advantage in mobile networks, it had to reallocate corporate innovation resources away from a wild orchard of devices to a concentrated and consolidated part of the market where it could manage competition in a better way. Ericsson needed to specialize – and once it did, it generated efficiency gains for itself as well as for the broader mobile economy.

Ericsson's evolution is not unique. Economic efficiency through specialization and narrowed firm boundaries is a central factor behind the shape and direction of globalization. The great contribution of globalization to the welfare of society was its ability to improve efficiency and productivity through that process. In most advanced economies, multinational firms represent the productivity frontier[62] because they are more productive than home-market firms, partly because they are better at incorporating technological change, created indigenously in the firm through their R&D operations or absorbed through adaptation or imitation.[63] Equally important, multinational firms host workforces and management with an ability to transmit skills and knowledge that is usually better than in home-market firms.[64] For instance, once the German-Central European supply chain had reached sufficient scale, the participating catch-up economies could more easily improve their performance because they could access technology, skills, and organizational advantages in German firms. Consequently, they performed better than their peers; they had faster productivity growth than other countries in the same region.[65]

Ericsson is also a good example of globalization's second unbundling and how it accelerated the growth of vertical specialization. While the initial phase of globalization spurred horizontal expansion, it was vertical specialization that powered its second generation and became a powerful force behind larger efficiency gains in the economy.[66] Vertical specialization has evolved in a manner in which the parent firm of a network has been not just in general control, but particularly in control of the active ingredients of value creation, especially technology, capital, R&D, and market position.[67] It is an "integrator" of inputs from external sources – the "Art Vandelay logistics operation" if you like – but its position is entirely dependent on its size and ability to control the market in which it competes.[68] The parent of the multinational firm has increasingly special-ized in providing these core services and values. Capital- or skills-intensive parts of production are thus less "marketized" and fragmented in supply chains. In the event they are contracted out, they are subject to much more control.

Globalization, specialization, and sunk costs

Advanced forms of economic specialization are a tribute to capitalism. Specialization is also an important source of economic growth and has powered rising prosperity ever since the birth of the modern economy. However, specialization is not a universal habit that can be taken off the shelf of management consultancies to work its wonders in all economic contexts. The actual shape of specialization and its effect on the economy are influenced by economic organizations – from the individual to the firm to countries. Importantly, specialization of production can, and often does, increase the sunk costs of a firm: the costs that cannot be recouped. And for companies that have specialized through R&D and innovation, the past investments in these areas are today sunk costs that often guide corporate decisions about investment in future innovation. While the rational economic approach to an obsolete technology is to drop it, a good part of the real world remains tied to the sunk costs incurred: they are the costs that guide current and future directions.[69] Indeed, sunk costs can (and often do) slow down the diffusion of new technology and the appetite for invest-ment in innovation.

The effect of sunk costs on any economic system can be exemplified by the reluctance of governments and companies to invest in nonfossil energy to battle climate change. Much of the technology needed to move Western societies away from their dependency on fossil-fuel based energy already exists today – including in the transportation sector. Yet the world remains dependent on oil and gas, and will for quite some time. A key explanation is that decision-makers in policy and business are allowed to disregard some environmental costs, which makes investment in some renewable energy financially daring as their economic advantage is not captured in the price comparison. Sunk costs, however, are equally important. Those who have already sunk capital into a system based on fossil fuels – like those who own a car running on fossil fuels – have an incentive to postpone the energy transformation in order to avoid a capital loss, and to invest in incremental specialization of their sunk capital. It may not always be the only incentive they have, but it adds a new complexity of capital and costs to technology. Scientists and inventors can develop a green energy technology but if it does not follow the structure of sunk capital it will take long time for real market change to happen.

The combination of specialization and sunk costs is important. While the political economy of specialization is often misunderstood, the presence of sunk costs is routinely ignored. In the era of corporate globalism, specialization advanced to such a degree that it resembled a sunk cost. Helped by globalization, new technology, and the allocation of labor and capital, companies explored new opportunities to specialize in a way that raised the return on assets. That specialization did not happen spontaneously but was manifested in various forms of economic organizations that structured production in accordance with globalization and technology. Furthermore, it was backed up by massive investments in capital – physical, human, and intellectual – that worked with the dynamic of economic specialization. Specialization does not have an entry in a corporate balance sheet, but a significant part of the assets of a firm is defined by the particular version of specialization it has tried to exploit.

Specialized organizations are often better than less specialized organizations at accommodating *incremental* technological change and the results of investment in research and development with that profile. However, when inventions and discoveries challenge the profile of specialization and the boundaries of the prevailing economic organization, specialization often turns into a cost. When that happens – as in the case of Nokia and Microsoft – specialization can actually become a factor of resistance to any innovation that disrupts and charts a different future than the one a firm has invested in.

There is a similar logic for individuals. Take education, or human capital, as an example. Rising levels of education largely mean a higher degree of specialization. A physician, for instance, goes to medical school and after half a decade or so, he or she has obtained a basic medical education. Then begins a period of greater specialization, represented by greater investment in human capital, and perhaps 20 or so years later the same person is a specialist in treating pancreatic cancer or another diagnosis that requires highly specialized skills to treat. The greater the degree of specialization, the more that human capital and its surrounding economic organization will be skilled at adjusting to new knowledge that conforms to their invested capital.

However, if new knowledge invalidates a good part of the invested capital, both human capital and the invested capital in the economic organization supporting specialized human capital, there is a greater resistance to adjustment because it would entail a capital loss. For those who have invested in the prevailing form of specialization, the cost of destroying that capital may be far too high, or be *perceived* to be so, to allow for adjustment, let alone rapid change. This is partly why so many professions have lobbied for occupational licenses. Specialization, then, can act as a barrier to pushing individuals and companies toward a more productive path. It can prevent economies from growing on the back of innovations that shift capital and labor in new directions.

Take the case of Fredrik and Bjorn (yes, the authors) and their families. We have both lived through two decades of booming globalization and digitalization. Both changes have made our lives richer, freer and happier – and that is no small matter, at least not for us, because what they did in essence was to help Fredrik to become more Fredrik, and Bjorn to become more Bjorn. However, neither globalization nor digitalization pressed Fredrik and Bjorn to chart new directions shifting them off their path of specialization. In that, our generation is different from our grandparents and their experience of technological change. The big changes in technology and economic organization they lived through pushed them onto a different and more productive path. Transport innovations allowed them to move and get jobs outside family farms and household economies. Medical innovations helped them to work with fewer health disruptions. Changes in households, partly through the innovation of home appliances, helped our grandmothers to take jobs and earn their own salaries. The large productivity gains occurred because innovations did not make previous generations specialize on the basis of their existing path. New technologies did not make housewives better housewives – they made them employable labor and allowed many women to gain an identity outside the boundaries of the home.

Academic progress, it has been jokingly said, starts with funerals, because only then will old knowledge fully retire and make space for new knowledge. There is a similar logic in the mechanics of specialization. Specialization is capital, and invested capital does not change direction without friction. Therefore, corporate specialization is sometimes a blessing and sometimes a curse – and it helps to explain why corporate strategies in innovation and R&D conform to firm boundaries and why companies do not invest much in substantial innovation charting a new direction for a particular market, away from the core assets of the firm. It also explains why innovation in the past decades has not done much for the productivity of Western economies. Incumbent firms have incrementally improved their products *but* they have plowed their controlled territory to such a degree that invaders cannot get in easily. Invading innovators might have created new markets, but that is an extremely challenging enterprise that requires capital support of a kind that most potential invaders cannot raise. If radical innovation cannot connect to the artery of the existing economic organization, the pace of change will be slow and limited, if it comes at all.

The high degree of specialization in today's economy both spurs incremental innovation and slows down radical innovation. It may sound paradoxical to those who think that globalization has reinforced all forms of competition between companies. It is not a point of criticism, against either globalization or specialization, but an observation of how specialization is a factor of resistance to moving labor and capital easily to the innovation frontier – or to expanding that frontier. Specialization has exacerbated the role of sunk costs for the larger corporate world. The predictable response by many big companies has been to effectively shrink the significance of big innovation and investment in it. Moreover, talented companies have managed to make the firm's boundary a market boundary by raising the costs of market entry and focusing strategic investments so that they are aligned with entry barriers to the companies' protected territory.[70]

This view does not sit comfortably with much of the thinking about innovation and specialization in the corporate world. And the prevailing philosophy among business professors draws inspiration from Joseph Schumpeter's view of short-run market power as the key to R&D investments and big innovation. That side of the argument thinks large companies should spend more (relative to size) than other firms on R&D because they have the organizations to process new technology and defend the property rights of innovation. Furthermore, big companies have their own internal capital markets that are better at directing investment to innovation than external capital markets.

However, that conventional wisdom has had a hard time proving itself in real economic life and data. There is no compelling evidence that large companies have higher budgets or greater appetite for innovation relative to their size, but there is plenty of evidence pointing in the opposite direction. At least some have woken up to the fact that the old dinosaur theory of innovation does not stand up – and that incumbents instead face growing innovation costs. African innovator and entrepreneur Bright Simons has an apt summary in the *Harvard Business Review* of the new landscape of innovation: "Technical complexity, social risk management (including lower tolerance for unintended consequences), diminishing returns, and talent challenges have all combined to raise the cost threshold of break-through innovation, even as downstream the costs of proliferation – reproducing, replicating, diffusing, disseminating, and indeed hacking innovation – have decreased."[71] Big companies know this by heart. They learned to navigate this landscape of innovation a long time ago – and thus lost their "Schumpeterian" dispositions, at least as far as innovation invest-ments are concerned. Modern research shows that large and diversified corporations have problems directing investment from less to more value-creating targets, including innovation.[72] Likewise, large and diversified companies tend to have organizations that impede big and novel innova-tion, partly because internal capital markets do not work to the advantage of such innovation.[73]

Another explanation, harking back to Friedrich Hayek's view of the decentralized nature of knowledge,[74] points to the practice within large firms of centralizing R&D services and confining them to their firm boundaries.[75] With a fragmented supply chain, companies close to the end consumers have been pushing input innovation costs down the chain – but, in that process, they have lost proximity to upstream innovation. Most experience shows that R&D needs to be decentralized and closer to actual products (and their markets) in order to generate novel and profitable results, but the sunk costs of markets actually give protection against rivals that can copy innovation.[76] Therefore, decentralization runs counter to the objectives of the planners within big companies who desire control and prefer innovation to stay within the firm's boundary.

The mentality of the planning machine – with its appetite for managerialism – was easily integrated with globalization. It is also the centerpiece of Western business schools, spreading the global company creed throughout corporateville. Global companies consolidated markets and directed the flow of the market and new ideas toward them. As they grew bigger, the multinationals needed more top-down control and management, and many firms turned into bureaucratic colossi as they put more emphasis on monitoring firm and network behavior. It required a particular type of manager skilled at making the logistics and finance of global companies work seamlessly. With their organizational talents these companies learned how to quickly move into new markets and exploit globalization's opportunities. Yet the growth of this "technostructure" of managerial capitalism had a cost – and that cost was the loss of innovative and entrepreneurial talent. Consequently, companies grew to incorporate a command-and-control identity that was necessary to manage their complex structures. The typical multinational company today is an enormously sophisticated platform for logistics and communication, with managerial skills – from top to bottom – that would have made the masters of centrally planned economies envious, including Stafford Beer.

Large firms are very good at both defending and extending ownership advantages and making them respond to scale and globalization. In a way, a good part of corporate globalism in the past decades has been to exploit ownership advantages in capital, technology and R&D. In most cases, that required greater central control, and progressively that control promoted capitalist planning mentalities but demoted instincts for contestable and game-changing innovation. This behavioral change fitted the globalist worldview. Corporate planners became part of the Greenspan–Rubin cosmos through their edifying belief in rationalism and their predilection for turning uncertainties into calculable and manageable risks. That worldview sanctioned managerialism, and for the most part, the corporate planning machines made economies more prosperous. They certainly made us all more specialized, but they also swung the direction of capitalism away from innovation.

6

THE RETURN OF THE REGULATORS

Laws are like sausages, it is better not to see them being made.

Otto von Bismarck

I've always felt the nine most terrifying words in the English language are: I'm from the Government, and I'm here to help.

Ronald Reagan in a news conference[1]

The mentality of managerialism is increasingly guiding the way elected politicians make decisions about innovation and regulatory policy. The political leaders on the left and the right that have managed the capitalist system in the past four decades have united in a preference for market stability and innovation predictability. They espouse a belief in economic regulations that make innovation politically manageable. In that way, they also make regulation a key determinant for what innovation will happen and how far it will disrupt markets. That policy has a longer history, but its consequence in the past decades has been that ambitions to contest markets have been increasingly tempered by regulation. All too often, innovation now goes with the flow of regulation.

It was not always like this. In the 1980s and 1990s, economic and business regulations became less restrictive and reforms created far better conditions for changing markets by various forms of innovation. Several sectors such as telecoms and construction have greatly benefited from the gradual removal of product-market regulations and other barriers to competition. The greater ease with which companies could enter and exit those sectors spurred economic dynamism and reinforced the evolution of greater international competition after World War II. Importantly, economic deregulation improved the capacity of companies to diffuse innovations between markets.

Yet the trend of reduced economic regulation did not prove lasting, either in America or Europe. It is an illusion that Western economies are deregulated. Take the example of Thibaud Simphal and Pierre-Dimitri Gore-Coty. In June 2015 they were hauled into a police station and later indicted for helping travelers reach their destinations in Paris. Anyone who has searched for a taxi at a Paris train station, or anywhere else for that matter, knows how frustrating this task can be. The waiting time for a taxi can sometimes be measured in hours. Those who are lucky enough to get a licensed fare will not leave the taxi without feeling robbed. And if you have ever wondered why Parisian taxis have to be expensive and give poor service, there is an obvious answer. The taxi market is regulated to keep it that way by maintaining a huge shortage of licensed drivers.

This is not a new problem. Parisian authorities put a cap of 14,000 on the number of licensed taxis in 1937, and despite the massive rise in citizens, tourists and business visitors moving around Paris every day, the number of licensed taxis has only grown by another 2,000 or so.[2] As in many other big cities, the shortage of taxi licenses has created a thriving secondhand market. To acquire one in the City of Lights costs around 180,000 euros, suggests the OECD. The price rises steeply if you prefer a sunnier city on the Riviera like Nice, where it hits 300,000 euros.[3]

All of this might suggest that Messrs Simphal and Gore-Coty would be welcomed also by local authorities for finding a new way to help people travel across the city. Had they been the usual nonlicensed cabbies, trawling in the shadows for clients, they would still be in business rather than in court. But they are not underground operators. They manage the French arm of an energetic, some would say brash, app-based company offering transport and car-sharing services in most parts of the metropolitan world. And the company is not trying to hide its ambition to disrupt the Paris taxi sector. But it has been forced to take a crash course in the political and legal grammar of innovation, because it has faced mounting opposition from competitors, trade unions and authorities. Its opponents are calling for it to be either forced out of business or regulated to make it behave and operate just like every other taxi firm it competes with.

As you might have guessed, the company in question is Uber – the San Francisco-based transport network company offering services via an app. UberPop, its peer-to-peer car-sharing service using unlicensed drivers, closed in France following the arrest and all the protests against it. Trade unions had taken strike action in protest against Uber, and some of them became violent. They burnt tires and aggressively harassed Uber drivers and their passengers. Parisian police authorities had previously tried to slow the company's expansion by ruling that taxis could not turn up sooner than 15 minutes after the car had been booked. The move was directed against Uber, which offered a faster service than incumbents. France also introduced a new transport law in 2014 ruling that only licensed taxi companies were allowed to show the real-time location of a car on a map; an innovation that first gained Uber prominence among the taxi-riding community. A new squad of 70 officers was tasked to police the law.[4]

Problems such as these are not confined to Paris. In Brussels local authorities have treated the rise of Uber as a threat to the established market order, sided with the regions cartelized taxi companies, and invested to help other firms imitate Uber's app technology. A commercial court in Brussels banned the company's car-sharing service in 2014 and imposed a fine of up to 10,000 euros every time it got caught. The ban was lifted not long after the first court decision, however. National and regional governments in Belgium, embarrassed by the episode, promised to change the regulation to allow for car-sharing services. Speed is no virtue in politics, though, and the new law is not likely anytime soon. Meanwhile, a court introduced yet another ban in the autumn of 2015, coincidentally during a week of heavy demonstrations from other taxi firms.[5] Car-shares had to go underground again – and, by the end of the year, the city authority's loathing of the company led the mayor to pressure a local charity to cancel its cooperation with Uber to deliver Christmas donations to the needy.[6]

In Germany the company has fought a heavier battle against authorities. Other taxi firms and the trade unions had been pounding Uber cars and in early 2015 a court in Frankfurt ruled to ban UberPop, threatening it with a fine of up to 250,000 euros if the law is violated.[7] Other German city authorities have followed Frankfurt's lead, and countries like Italy, Spain and the Netherlands have also banned the peer-to-peer service, all citing violations of commercial licenses as reason to expel it from the market. In Johannesburg, São Paolo, New York and other metropolitan cities in the world, the company faces similar charges. Mayor Bill de Blasio in New York tried to rehash an old type of regulation, restricting the growth of car-riding services like Uber, Sidecar and Lyft to 1 percent a year, seemingly copying the thinking behind the taxi regulation in New York that has capped the number of yellow cab medallions.[8] In Miami, these companies are banned.

There is a larger story about regulation embedded in these examples. Anchored among existing structures of incumbents, regulation all too often helps to saturate or cement markets. While many existing firms complain about the effects of regulations, they know how to manage business under regulation and, if they are skilled operators, they can turn government interventions in their favor. In the extreme form, the relation between regulator and business mutates into crony capitalism. "In much of the world," writes economist Luigi Zingales, "the best way to make lots of money is not to come up with brilliant ideas and work hard at implementing them but, instead, to cultivate a government ally."[9]

Surveying the battlefields of political lobbying, this rings true. It is not a distant thought that cronyism is an important part of Western economies – and perhaps it has been for a long while. In the United States alone, annual subsidies to firms amount to more than $70 billion.[10] And taxpayer handouts are not the most profitable privilege or rent that a firm can get from the political system. That prize goes to regulation, leading to a far greater redistribution of money between firms, and from consumers to firms. Brussels and Washington DC, the two lobbying capitals of the West, have in recent years seen the fastest growth in income per capita in their respective countries and regions. This is not surprising. If regulation has become ever more important for business activity, lobbyists will be greatly rewarded for their work.

Regulation and political romanticism

Uber's experience tells us a lot about regulation and innovation, and how political perceptions of innovation have lost touch with the reality. "Is Uber a threat to democracy?" asked a former head of the United Nations Development Programme, seemingly without understanding the absurdity of the question.[11] The point he was trying to make, however, is an old one: when Uber steps into a market it destroys incumbents and compels its competitors to either step up and face competition or see their staff become unemployed. That is neither lamentable nor a threat to democracy, but the essence of innovation and dynamic capitalism: it helps to destroy less productive behavior, either by provoking more competitive behavior or relegating uncompetitive companies to history.

The political opposition to Uber reveals a banal but rarely observed point about regulation: regulated markets do not sit comfortably with innovation and an ambition to contest them. And Uber's story is a telling example of how regulation – intentionally or not – preserves a particular form of market behavior and puts up barriers to contestable innovation. That is all too often true even with the benign form of regulation. For example, regulation tends to increase the barrier to entry for the simple reason that the cost of regulation per employee or unit of sales is higher for a new entrant than an incumbent firm. Both economic and social regulations have that effect. A survey by the OECD, for instance, estimated the annual regulatory administration cost per employee to be about nine times higher for a company with fewer than 20 staff than for a company with a workforce of 50–499.[12]

Less benign regulation preserves an existing market order by protecting investors and labor from competition, including competition from innovation. Such regulations do not have to damage competition intentionally because regulation is often designed to address the economy as we know it, not how it may evolve in future. Moreover, regulations generally follow "the logic of collective action" sketched by the economist Mancur Olson. Never mind the cost of regulation, Olson argued in an influential book, if the costs are diffused and the benefits concentrated on a small group, the political process of regulation regularly leads to more rather than less regulation.[13] And more to our point, it will almost invariably benefit incumbents at the expense of future competitors.

Markets distorted by regulation turn innovation into a political choice rather than a commercial or market choice. Innovation goes with the flow of regulation rather than the logic of commerce and technology. Those companies that dare to defy that political compact of innovation all too often end up in trouble. Perhaps they do not get their market approval fast enough; perhaps they get a new regulation thrown at them. Uncertainty about whether an innovation can be marketed or not drives up the cost of innovation – and forces innovators to invest in political lobbying.

Occasionally, companies can defeat political and regulatory resistance. Uber managed to stop, at least temporarily, a New York City regulation against their expansion by hiring political strategist David Plouffe and mounting a huge digital campaign against city regulators. However, the time and money it takes to sweet talk regulatory powers are often punitive, especially as the outcome of lobbying is at best uncertain when there are incumbents fighting on the other side. Investors and innovators therefore go for safer alternatives. After all, if it is necessary to hire the likes of Plouffe, a mastermind of President Obama's legendary 2008 presidential campaign, to create the policy space to innovate markets, most companies will not bother.

Interestingly, this view of regulation as an obstacle to contestable innovation and contestable competition runs counter to the conventional

wisdom of a pending innovation blitz in Western economies. Both technological optimists and pessimists seem to share the view that radical and
contestable innovation will be approved under existing regulations, allowing
for a fast process of market disruption. And that fits the paradigm of the
planning machine, especially its technological determinism and disregard
for those factors that determine whether an invention can be turned into
market-renewing innovation. In this view, regulators and politicians will
embrace the new innovation, regardless of its impact on competition,
and allow timely and undisrupted access to consumers. Markets will thus
flourish naturally on the back of innovation – and the speed at which
innovation can ripple through various markets will not get arrested by
policy barriers to entry. Even if there may be some initial resistance, the
paradigm of the planning machine holds that technology will inevitably
trump politics. In the battle between innovation and existing policy or
market hierarchies, innovation will always win.

It is a romantic view of politics – and that bee has stung a good part of
the tech commentariat. The notion that politics runs on the spirit of
bettering the welfare of humankind is not without merit. Much as sausage-
making in day-to-day politics, if you recall the introductory quote by
Bismarck, appears short-sighted and cynical, things do tend to get better in
the long run. Or to paraphrase Winston Churchill: politicians tend to do
the right thing once they have exhausted the alternatives. Therefore, if we
take a long view, technology does tend to take primacy over politics. And
the same conclusion largely holds for knowledge. The basic plot, if you
allow a simplification, in much of the intellectual history of the world
centers around the battle between new discoveries and old dogma, and the
former tends to win over the latter – not immediately, not in the short run,
perhaps not even in the medium term. But in the long run new discoveries
often do win.

However, in the long run, as John Maynard Keynes noted, we are all
dead. Political romanticism better suits a historian of ideas than a scholar
of contemporary politics and economics. The judgment about the Danes in
1066 and All That, the humorous version of English history, also applies to
economic policy: you cannot be both "right and very romantic."[14] Innovation
delayed is innovation denied. When opportunities to change markets with
the help of a particular innovation are barred, they may not return as
new opportunities in the future. There is no predetermined way for markets
and innovations to evolve, but it should be obvious that politics and regulation stand in the way of innovation. Despite all the talk about the need to
foster innovation, regulators and the political sector are not embracing

innovation unconditionally, and the political process of getting from an invention to the market is often dreadfully long.

An alternative vision of politics would rather emphasize the arbitrariness of regulation and the unpredictability of innovation succeeding if it challenges the established regulatory order. Think of Tiberius, the Roman emperor. A famous war general, not known for his cheerful persona, Tiberius collected a huge fortune after his military campaigns in Europe. His preferred store of value was gold. One day, when a goldsmith courted the emperor to display his new innovation – aluminum – which he had discovered through a complicated chemical process, Tiberius did not exactly appreciate the good opportunity to invest in what two thousand years later would become one of the world's most important metals. Instead, he feared that this new shiny, silver-like metal would debase the value of gold. "Therefore," Pliny the Elder recalled in his *Naturalis Historia* "instead of giving the goldsmith the regard expected, he ordered him to be beheaded."[15]

Politics moves in mysterious ways and, through history, politicians and regulators have slowed rather than accelerated innovation and radical changes of markets. "Fear of creative destruction is often at the root of the opposition to inclusive economic and political institutions," observe Daron Acemoglu and James Robinson in their great study of *Why Nations Fail*.[16] Innovators may no longer be decapitated when they bring new technology to market, but rulers still have that spirit of resistance in them.

When Amazon's Jeff Bezos, for example, unveiled the company's new "flying vehicle," the new drone prototype for delivering packages, it took less than a week for US authorities to ground it because there was no commercial legislation covering drones. The Federal Aviation Administration had already begun working on rules for commercial drone aircraft, but they were behind schedule. Amazon was granted a special exemption a year later, but by then it had already moved on to another advanced drone device.[17]

Innovation around mobile technology provides yet another example. The buzz of modern tech investors is that "mobile is eating the world," and undoubtedly there is much going on as internet use moves from the laptop to the smartphone. But it has hardly been a speedy development and far too few of the admirers of current technological change ask why it has taken so long for mobile technology to get to its current position. After all, the first mobile phone call was made in 1973.[18] Perhaps blinded by all the new and cool apps, they have forgotten that mobile technology was actively slowed down in many countries because of government resistance. Several governments banned mobiles for a long time because they ran up against opposition from the local fixed landline monopolies. Our native country,

Sweden, today tops the league table of the most connected country in the world, but when we were growing up in the 1980s, it was against the law to have a cordless telephone. In fact, all phones – yes, all devices – were for a long time the property of the state telecommunication monopoly. People were fined if they owned one.

Tesla, Elon Musk's electric car company, has effectively been kicked out of some US states because it runs a direct-to-consumer sales model. New Jersey, for instance, withdrew Tesla's license for dealer-free car sales in 2014, forcing it to go through a franchise if it wanted to sell cars in the Garden State.[19] Likewise Airbnb, the online platform for individuals to rent out their homes, has effectively been banned in cities like Barcelona and Santa Monica.[20] Other city authorities, such as in Berlin and New York, impose regulations – old or new – that seriously constrain homeowners from renting out beds or entire home on sites like Airbnb.[21] All too often innovators need to err on the wrong side of regulation if they aim to contest markets.

The time and money of regulation

If regulatory resistance to innovation is strong in business sectors that are comparatively less regulated like car sales and online services, imagine then the effects of regulation in energy, pharmaceuticals, neuroscience, medical technology, and other sectors with more complicated regulations. Investor Peter Thiel has contrasted two different regulatory worlds and how the different regulatory approaches feed different innovative outcomes. In the "world of bits" regulation has for some time had a "light touch," while "the world of atoms" has been burdened by the heavy hand of regulation. The difference helps to explain why in the past decades there has been so much more innovation in software than in physical things. People rightly appreciate the advances in modern software technology but seldom question why the speed of technological change is so much faster in this sector compared to others. After all, a good part of the new technological development in "the world of bits" has little economic payoff, and a lot of it is frankly junk. Economist Alex Tabarrok asked pointedly: "Yo is a smartphone app. MelaFind is a medical device. Yo sends one meaningless message: 'Yo!' MelaFind tells you: 'biopsy this and don't biopsy that.' MelaFind saves lives. Yo does not. Guess which firm found it easier to put their product in consumers hands? Oy."[22]

A smartphone app sending a meaningless message needs no regulation at all. A medical device is different. But, as innovator Joseph Gulfo chronicles in his Kafka-like story about MelaFind and getting the product approved for the market, the regulatory burdens placed on an innovator deter innovation.[23] It is not surprising, therefore, that Western economies have problems pushing the innovation frontier or raising poor growth levels of productivity. We get a lot more gadgets and technologies that do not make our habits more productive, but fewer of the radical innovations needed to disrupt economies and create more competition and economic renewal.

Perhaps that is why many of the new innovations that have happened in the past decade or so have influenced our leisure time more than they have increased the professional capacity of labor. The blossoming app world, for instance, seems to hold greater promise for what we do in our private time than what happens to our work productivity. Unlike the period when household appliances were rapidly introduced, many new technologies used during our private time now are not freeing people up to focus on a professional career or to be more productive at work.

Economist John Kay tenders a similar view, but with a different twist. "Technological advances of the past decade," he argues "seem to have increased the efficiency of households, rather than the efficiency of businesses, to an unusual extent."[24] Regulation partly explains that trend. It is not difficult to see why regulation is an important factor in determining the areas, or the direction of, innovation. Regulation influences how corporate boards and financiers make decisions about innovation investment, and if there is a risk of bumping into regulations that can crush a promising new technology, the investment will hardly be made in the first place.

Such natural reactions also explain patterns of innovation inside sectors that have seen the biggest change in recent times. Investors and innovators in the digital space talk about an "offshore" pattern of innovation: it moves into products where there are fewer regulatory risks against the commercialization of a new technology. "If someone with a brilliant idea on online advertising in Germany calls me up, I end the conversation immediately. I am not that stupid," says a San Francisco Bay Area venture capitalist with a focus on Europe – and knowledge about the odd way Germany regulates online advertising.[25]

As the example of MelaFind showed, regulations in the field of healthcare have a strong impact on not just the direction of innovation but also the speed of diffusion. That has not escaped other investors and entrepreneurs. Google's Sergey Brin, for instance, noted about the healthcare sector: "It's just a painful business to be in ... the regulatory burden in the US is so high that I think it would dissuade a lot of entrepreneurs."[26]

One can understand why. Just take the cost, and sometimes time, required to get a new drug or medical device through the approval process of the Food and Drug Administration (FDA) in the United States, or its regulatory cousins in other parts of the world. Costs have gone up almost continuously – and far faster than the inflation rate. Scholars at the Tufts Center for the Study of Drug Development found some years ago that the cost of developing a new FDA-approved drug went up by 13 times between 1975 and 2005.[27] The cost of developing an average drug in the mid-2000s was around $1.3 billion.

Others contest that number, arguing that it is actually higher, if not far higher. More recently, scholars at the Tufts Center have argued that the average cost of developing an approved prescription drug has gone up to about $2.6 billion.[28] Science writer Matthew Herper, studying 15 years of corporate R&D spending in the pharmaceutical sector and comparing it to their drug approvals, contends that the figure is substantially higher, in excess of $4 billion.[29]

Multiple factors explain the rise in cost. One factor is the increasing cost of developing new medicines for complex diagnoses. Another factor is the rise in the cost of regulation, for example the cost of clinical trials demanded by regulatory authorities. Scholar Avik Roy, for instance, argues that the R&D costs associated with Phase III clinical trials have gone up significantly and represent about 90 percent of the total R&D costs for the typically approved drug.[30] That cost has surged because there is far more information required to be submitted to the FDA.

The earlier Tufts study showed that between 1999 and 2005, the length of a clinical trial process increased by 70 percent and the clinical staff burden by 67 percent.[31] In more recent years, other studies argue, it is not the time required for an FDA approval that has pushed up costs, but the size and complexity of clinical trials. Roy argues that the problem in the system of FDA approvals is not only because of changes in regulatory behavior related to Phase III clinical trials, but because the regulatory system cannot work efficiently with new drugs that are not treating acute diseases. The current approach, with less emphasis on conditional approvals, leads to a market where far too few drugs can be commercially motivated – and where only big companies can afford the financial risks of taking a drug through a Phase III clinical trial. Pharmaceutical firms have responded to that development, and some have done it by cutting R&D and reallocating resources to buying smaller companies with novel drugs that have passed the first regulatory hurdles. Narrowing their firms' boundaries, these companies have specialized in knowing the ins and outs of regulatory systems.

The study of the cost and complexity of regulation is not an exact science, and the cost of taking a new drug to the market may be higher or lower than the figures cited above. More certain, however, is that investors and companies consider that there is an increasing complexity to bringing a new drug to the market, and that investments in innovation are depressed by the increasing cost. It affects not just Big Pharma but, perhaps more importantly, private equity investors in the medical space and, as Roy argues, smaller innovative firms that cannot afford to expose themselves to the risks involved in a process that takes time and heavy resources. It also impacts generic firms that cannot get their approvals quickly enough, making it even more difficult to have competition in the off-patent drug market.

Innovation in medical devices confronts similar problems. The time it takes to get such an innovation to market – and, therefore, the wait before diffusion – has increased. The process of getting market approval is generally longer in the United States than in Europe. But to gain *effective* access to Europe's healthcare market – to be able to actually sell the product – also requires going through an extremely time-consuming process to get government approvals for reimbursement in many different countries and regions. Undoubtedly new devices, or medicines, need to prove their effectiveness for consumers in a different way than other goods and services. But the time the regulatory approval processes take is remarkably long and affects innovation and its aim to push positive adaptation onto economies.

A study in the *New England Journal of Medicine* comparing the "time to market" for devices going through both a market approval process *and* a reimbursement approval process has a sobering message, especially for Europe's patients.[32] For the United States, the process for the average medical technology is around 21 months. In Germany, however, the same process takes more than 70 months when both market and reimbursement approvals are considered. For a product like the Stratos implantable pacemaker, the time to market in the US between the date of the application to the FDA and the date of the reimbursement decision was 14 months. The same process in France took almost 40 months – and Italian authorities needed 70 months to clear the product for effective market access. The first submission for approval of the product in Italy happened five years before the first submission in the United States. Yet patients in America could get access to it earlier than patients in Italy.

Patients suffer in the end. If technology trumps politics, it certainly does not happen overnight. And in our view, this is part of the real innovation problem facing the West. While many regulations emerge for good reasons, the spirits of politics and innovation are not really in tune with each other, nor with the idea of a pending acceleration in disruptive technological change. Most of the time, regulatory systems as we know them are still decelerators rather than accelerators of innovation. They undermine the case for corporate innovation by fanning regulatory uncertainty and increasing the time lags in bringing innovations to market. It is simply impossible to motivate investments in innovation if the process of regulatory approval can delay market entry for years. For investors that have poured capital into such innovation projects, it is like getting trapped in Death Valley. And today, investors have a far better understanding of where these risks are, and act long before they get close to that territory. The way they act, however, far too often entails evading plans for contestable innovation and investment for that purpose.

An era of deregulation and diffusion

Regulation and deregulation are no different in this regard: they both change the direction of innovation and business planning. Twenty years of partial market deregulation in America and Europe lifted growth – and directed much competitive energy in businesses toward those markets that got freer. This trend was real – both for policy and business – and indicators of product market regulation (PMR) show a clear direction in the developed part of the world. Economic and business regulations are generally less of a barrier to market entry today than 40 years ago. For the developed world, restrictions on prices are much less significant today than in the past. Licensing requirements for entering markets are less obstructive for competition, and there are fewer markets that are exclusively under the control of a legal monopoly. Barriers to trade and investment have fallen, making it easier today than at any time in postwar history to take a good to market in another part of the world (services are a different story). If we consider the general levels of product market regulation on their own it should be easier today than at any time in history to bring innovation to global markets.

This is good news. Markets that have changed because of product market deregulation have become far more dynamic than before and deliver more value to customers. Take the example of the Memphis International Airport in Tennessee, and changes in airline traffic. Memphis is hardly a center for international passenger traffic; it serves only a fraction of the annual passenger traffic of airports like Dallas/Fort Worth International Airport and O'Hare International Airport in Chicago. But those who do get there should skip the airport shopping and take a look at the northern part of the airport, which is the center for Federal Express, or FedEx, and

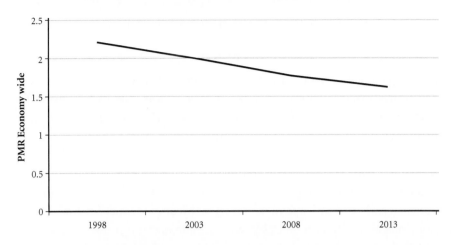

Note: Product market regulations are measured on a scale from 0 to 6, where a lower score indicates less restriction on product market competition. The average for each observation is based on the membership of the OECD at that point. As the OECD has expanded and come to include countries that joined with PMRs higher than the average of older members, the figure does not do full justice to the trend of PMR reform in the latter group.

Source: OECD, "Indicators of Product Market Regulation," at http://www.oecd.org/eco/growth/ indicatorsofproductmarketregulationhomepage.htm#indicators; averages calculated by the authors.

Figure 6.1 Indicators of product market regulation (economy wide), OECD average

its "superhub" for national and international cargo services. In an operation covering 15 million square feet, an impressive "matrix" for sorting packages, and 179 jet aircraft gates, 1.5 million packages pass through FedEx's Memphis base every day.[33]

In many ways, the story of FedEx and air cargo services competition and innovation is a story about regulation. Cargo services are today a central part of national and international commerce, and their importance only grows as more people shop online and need fast and reliable transport of their purchases. But for many decades the entire air cargo sector struggled to expand volumes and get into the big markets of postal and transport services. In the United States, the big break came in 1977 when many of the regulations on air cargo services were removed. Prior to the deregulation, the entire sector had been depressed by a pallet of regulations aimed at keeping it that way by insulating the market from competition.

The Civil Aeronautics Board (CAB) in the US kept a tight control of the market. "In the twenty years prior to deregulation," write two economists, "the CAB refused to certify the entry of any new cargo carriers or the expansion of existing ones into new routes and limited the size of planes allowed for air cargo hauls."[34] Undoubtedly an odd way to regulate a market, but that is how it often was before the era of deregulation started. As a consequence of the regulations, air cargo companies like FedEx could not expand into bigger planes that would bring volumes up and variable costs down. Nor could it plan its business in accordance with actual demand, and companies using air cargo services could not locate themselves in places that were far from the approved routes. For those in the business, the upside was that the regulations strangled competition.

Deregulation, however, led to a rapidly expanding market – and made it far more open to innovation and general changes in the transportation market. This was a boon for the economy. Logistics is a general purpose industry and its own improvements have direct consequences for innovation and competition in other sectors. The logistics revolution in the 1980s was critical for the growth of lean production, an important process innovation that required just-in-time delivery of many source products and components. It provided companies with many new opportunities for where to start or grow businesses, and how they could reach consumers.

Market deregulation helped to accelerate the diffusion of new technologies, making it easier for a company to take an innovation to market and for a user to adopt it.[35] Moreover, changes in product market regulation reduced the capacity of companies to use market power such as first-mover advantage to limit innovation competition or to block markets to new entrants.[36] Even in markets that have become more concentrated in recent phases of globalization, the spirit of competition brought by deregulation has been maintained and continues to limit the role of first-mover advantage.

The flip side of the coin is that the rate of knowledge obsolescence – how fast new knowledge or an innovative product becomes obsolete – has increased rapidly as well, meaning that the capacity of companies to naturally dominate markets on the back of past innovation has weakened. Economists measuring the pace of knowledge obsolescence, often by studying the time it takes for a patent to lose citation power (how often a patent is cited in other patent applications), have found that in the early twentieth century, the annual rate of knowledge obsolescence stood at 2–3 percent.[37] By the late 1980s it had risen to 10–12 percent, and it has continued in that direction in the past decades. This development coincides with a rapid rise in the number of patents filed and granted, and it gives an indication of the flow of new knowledge: the higher the rate of knowledge obsolescence, the greater the diffusion of new knowledge. Knowledge would not become obsolete if new knowledge did not manifest itself in the market. Market reforms have helped to retire knowledge much faster.

Economist Edwin Mansfield, a scholar of knowledge diffusion, found in a 1985 study of industrial technology that 70 percent of product innovations were known and understood by competitors 12 months after the innovation.[38] That process now works much faster. In later studies, several economists have found the economic lifetime of patents to be much shorter than their duration. Jean Lanjouw, for example, concluded in a study that over half of computer patents, whether commercialized or not, are worthless within ten years of their application date.[39] This rate of obsolescence also applies to the computer market generally. The depreciation rate of ICT capital is fast.

William Baumol, the erudite economist and painter, has shown how quickly products that are highly dependent on innovations can become obsolete. For example, by the time a new computer model appears in retail stores, production of it has ceased. The manufacturer is already planning how to take a newer model to market.[40] A broad cross-country study across two centuries by economists Diego Comin and Bart Hobijn recently found that, while it took an average of 45 years for a new technology to get adopted, more recent technologies have been embraced much quicker.[41] The time lag between invention and adoption in the sample was 120 years for steam and motor-powered ships, about 40 years for cars, and less than 20 years for the personal computer.

These examples are indicative of the type of economy that has emerged in the past 40 years and how the new partial openness of markets in the Western economies contributed to a special pattern of competition and economic renewal. The diffusion rate increased and a good part of international business strategy was built on capturing business opportunities in a world that invariably moved quicker.

Deregulation and the reallocation of business

It is less obvious, however, that market reforms spurred innovation beyond diffusion, and that they provided for sufficiently good conditions to ensure the regular contestability of markets.[42] In several ways, they clearly did, as the story of FedEx shows. The telecom liberalization in the past decades also testifies to how product market deregulation established a far better institutional context for the sector to spur constant innovation (although with a varying degree of economic impact). Deregulation created a wave of market contestability, predominantly by exposing old incumbents and markets to outside competition. However, the surge in productivity growth and improved sectoral performance that emerged after some markets had

been deregulated petered off after a while. The boost in economic performance from changes in market or industrial organization was partly
temporary.

Past deregulation still has a positive effect on the efficiency of markets,
but it has not changed them to the degree that they are open to regular
contestability. The evidence marshalled in previous chapters shows that
diffusion has spurred gradual market change and incremental innovation.
Deregulation helped businesses to connect markets, geographically and functionally, and reap greater scale and specialization benefits. That delivered
clear economic gains, but they have also been subject to diminishing returns.

Changes in economic organization can impose universal changes upon
an economy, but it is more common that they give producers and consumers
incentives to reallocate their labor, capital, and spending power. And this is
also what happened in the past decades as a consequence of market reforms.
The broad wave of deregulation did not affect all sectors equally. The actual
flow of the economy carried the hallmark of regulation rather than reflecting
natural changes among consumers and producers. Reforms generally motivated companies to focus their energy on horizontal expansion and vertical
specialization. Or to use the mathematical image of Peter Thiel: companies
were not incentivized to move from "zero to one" – to bring something new
to the market – but to go "from 1 to n" – to expand volumes on the product
and resource base they already possessed.[43] Together with the shift in
economic structure – from industry to services – product market reforms
reoriented the way companies compete and how much importance they
place on contestable innovation.

Such business patterns can also be seen at the macroeconomic level.
Take this example of how globalization reallocated sources of production
and growth. In 1995, the retail price of a flat-screen TV in Germany
roughly equaled the cost of a hip replacement (or, to be more precise, the
reimbursement rate for a hip replacement). Fast forward ten years and
there was a remarkable change in the relative prices between a flat-screen
TV and a hip replacement. Germans could actually get six flat-screen TVs
for the cost of a hip replacement. Add another five years and they got ten.
Still, the total amount that consumers spent on flat-screen TVs, or other
electronics on a similar price-deflation trend, went up faster than the
amount spent on hip replacements.

This is a good example of the so-called "Baumol's disease" – the astute
observation by William Baumol that labor costs in low-productivity sectors
(often services) rise faster than productivity because they follow salary
growth in high-productivity sectors. However, there is also another dynamic

at play. The prices of flat-screen TVs have dropped because of relative changes in competition and productivity as a consequence of the unequal coverage of market deregulation. To go back to the example, the cost of a hip replacement has also gone up because the healthcare services in Germany have not been exposed to the same forces. It is impossible to escape the fact that the change in relative prices between flat-screens and hip replacements reflects the way these markets have performed because of regulatory reform, or the absence thereof. Essentially, one sector is tradable, the other is not, and their relative performances in price, productivity and production are defined by their two different economic organizations.

That difference is important, especially for the West, where economies are ever more reliant on services generally and non-tradable services particularly. As these are locked into patterns of low competition, high fixed barriers to entry, and stagnant productivity growth, they weigh entire economies down, including sectors that are more dynamic and open to competition. The most tradable sectors are the ones that have seen the fastest growth in productivity, especially in the growth and productivity spurt that followed on the heels of market reform.

Today's structures of competition are in many ways rather fixed. Competition continues to deliver improvements, but not at the same pace as before. Yet increasingly fixed structures of competition also affect the diffusion rates of the economies, perhaps even in those sectors where conventional wisdom holds that adoption of technology happens very fast.

Take internet and online services as an example. Headline numbers support the thesis that innovation now happens faster – that people actually get access to products and use them at an ever faster speed. Two Oxford economists, for instance, have suggested that Angry Birds – the popular app game – achieved in 35 days what it took the telephone 75 years to do: reach 50 million users.[44] Even if something more useful for the economy than Angry Birds is compared, the story is basically the same: everything is just getting faster and faster. It took 38 years for the radio to reach 50 million users, and when television was invented later it needed 18 years to exceed that many users. The internet, however, needed just four years. A Forbes writer popularized the theme of accelerating diffusion by observing, provocatively, that WhatsApp, the cross-platform messenger service, achieved in six years what Christianity needed 19 centuries to accomplish: to get more than 600 million adherents.[45]

While there is much that speaks for the narrative of accelerating diffusion, at least in the digital sector, memes like these are nevertheless misleading and hide the actual speed of diffusion in the economy. For real and important innovation to ripple through an economy and get high rates of adoption, it usually takes time. The bigger the economic effect of an innovation, the more old capital needs to be retired to make space for the new technology and capital. With declining levels of investment, the diffusion of new innovation has not necessarily accelerated in the past decade or had a greater economic impact than in the past. The more advanced companies and economies have become, particularly because of strong specialization, the higher the hurdle to get an innovation adopted.

Innovation sometimes gets arrested because markets and companies are highly efficient. Alexander Gerschenkron once argued that economically backward societies could industrialize faster than others because they had less sunk capital standing in the way of innovation.[46] A similar dynamic sometimes defines modern markets, making countries that are less competitive and have less accumulated capital better at adopting new technologies quicker. Mobile banking in Africa is one such example: the penetration of mobile banking in Africa is higher than in any other region in the world because traditional forms of banking in Africa were less developed, less competitive, and less prone to defense by incumbent capital.[47]

It is therefore to be expected that important breakthrough innovations today will take time to spread through economies with sunk capital. In fact, it is doubtful that the Oxford economists are right that the internet really spread like wildfire.[48] While it sounds impressive for the internet to have achieved in less than a handful of years what it took almost 40 years for the radio to achieve, such comparisons hide the fact that new technologies should reach a certain volume faster because there are many more consumers today because population and prosperity increased quite substantially between the introduction of the radio and the arrival of the internet. Controlling for differences in population, some even make the case that it has taken longer for the internet to spread compared to radio and television.[49]

Perhaps that is also a doubtful conclusion. There is no exact way of measuring the speed of technological adoption. Many online services have been spreading fast in recent years. While they do it with assistance from past market reforms that have made it easier to step into some markets, the reality is that much of the digital development of the last two decades has moved into areas that are less regulated. And, one can add, where the economic impact of technological change has not been all that impressive. There remain significant barriers not just to innovation, but to the process of diffusing innovation through adaptation and imitation. If the era of deregulation did not reduce those barriers, imagine then their consequences when regulatory interference has started to grow again.

After the deregulation wave

The economic reform era in the West ended at around the millennium. Market reforms no longer power the economy in the way they did in the 1980s and 1990s. In fact, market reforms have not just stalled but regulators have in several ways returned to old regulatory habits. The economic impact of regulation is increasing and that is not just because economic regulations are becoming more restrictive again. Industrial policy is back in vogue and Western countries sprinkle money over particular sectors, often with the expressed intention of giving them a direct competitive advantage over their foreign competitors. Other forms of regulation are becoming far more detailed and prescribe a certain behavior, adding new regulatory costs and deterring entrepreneurship just by the sheer volume of regulations that a business need to absorb. In the United States – that mythological example of laissez-faire capitalism – states are banning people from selling home-baked bread.[50] Almost 900 measures restricting foreign trade were imposed in the US between 2008 and 2015.[51]

Regulation is back in fashion and Figure 6.2 shows this trend for selected Western countries by using data on regulatory performance in the Fraser Institute's ranking of economic freedom in the world. Economic regulations concerning credit, labor, and business were reduced or elimi-nated in most of these countries from the late 1970s up to the early

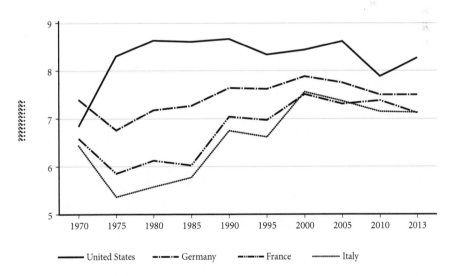

Note: Index rates are for component 5, "Regulation," in the total index. The higher the index score, the greater the regulatory freedom.

Source: Gwartney, Lawson, and Hall, "Economic Freedom of the World: 2015 Annual Report."

Figure 6.2 Index of regulatory freedom in selected Western economies

2000s – leading to a higher index rate – but in the past 10–15 years, regulations have again become more stringent in Europe and, notwithstanding an upturn in recent years, the United States. And that trend did not come about as a result of the financial crisis and the new financial regulations that were put in place in response to it. The trend of declining regulatory freedom started several years before the crisis and covers far more areas of regulation than finance.

There is a similar trend for regulatory trade barriers, even if the data do not go back as far in time. Regulatory trade barriers are different from tariffs. Tariffs in Western economies are generally too low to influence competition. They are also bound in World Trade Organization agreements and cannot be increased without causing political friction and legal disputes. Regulatory barriers, however, can be changed with greater ease, and they are today the prime form of protection in Europe and the United States. Just as in the index of credit, labor, and business regulation, Western performance improved up to the millennium. Since then there has been an unambiguous trend in favor of greater regulatory restrictions on trade (see Figure 6.3).

Similarly, labor in Western economies is getting more protected than before. The trend is not about employment protection legislation. OECD

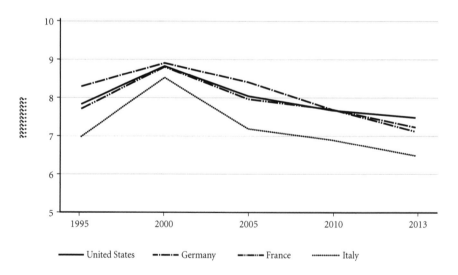

* *Note*: Index rates are for subcomponent "Regulatory trade barriers" in the total index, including nontariff barriers to trade and compliance costs of importing and exporting. The higher the index score, the greater the trade freedom.

Source: Gwartney, Lawson, and Hall, "Economic Freedom of the World: 2015 Annual Report."

Figure 6.3 Index of regulatory trade barriers to international trade in selected Western economies

statistics show that such legislation has not moved much over the past four decades. The pernicious trend in labor protection is rather the return of guilds – the increasing numbers of jobs that require occupational licenses. Figure 6.4 shows the trend for the United States. State occupational licenses have grown steadily for many decades, and a quarter of all workers in the US today need a license. If jobs that require some form of certification are added, the share goes up to almost 40 percent. Europe is no different. There are 800 occupational standards in Europe's services sector alone,[52] and if the entire economy is considered, the European Union has more than 5,000 regulated professions.[53]

But there are not that many professions that require an occupational license or a regulated standard. It is one thing for physicians or lawyers (at least some lawyers) to be required to hold a license that reflects skills. However, these professions required a license half a century ago and the growth in the past decades largely reflects an excessive desire to regulate and an increasing ambition to protect professions from competition. The West has gotten its own License Raj, India's dirigiste version of regulation.

Take these examples. Those who want to be an interior designer in Florida need to go to university for four years to be able to apply for a license. Florida has its own Board of Architecture and Interior Design that blocks the entry of interior designers from other US states. When the state legislature was debating an unsuccessful proposal to deregulate the interior design sector in 2011, it was suggested that such a reform would cause

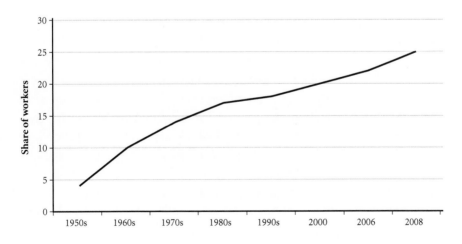

Source: White House, "Occupational Licensing: A Framework for Policymakers," p. 17.
Figure 6.4 Share of workers in the US with a state occupational license

88,000 deaths in the state because unlicensed designers would use fabrics that spread disease. Some years ago, Texas ruled that every computer repair technician should acquire a private investigator's license to continue repairing computers if they come into touch with data. Louisiana's Board of Embalmers and Funeral Directors has ordered coffin makers without a license to go out of business. To become a manicurist in Alabama, the aspirant needs first to go through 750 hours of training and take an exam. An African hair-braider in Utah with 23 years of experience had to close because the state's Barber, Cosmetologist/Barber, Esthetician, Electrologist and Nail Technician Licensing Board told her she could not practice without a license.[54]

Occupational licenses work as a market restriction against competition. They slow down diffusion because people are hindered from moving between countries or states to practice a profession.[55] They also affect innovation and how companies make plans for innovation. Because they give great flexibility to regulators to determine what is required for a license to be granted, occupational licenses drive up the barriers to innovation and often make them difficult to comprehend. That is especially true when they behave unpredictably. Just as increasing regulatory restrictions on business and trade prompts innovators and managers to reallocate their plans for investment and innovation, the proliferation of licenses and standards pushes market contestability into "off-license" sectors. On current trends, there will not be that many sectors without such requirements in a few decades.

Corporate funding, innovation, and regulation

Business regulations are on an upward trend, and more so in the area of financial regulation than anywhere else. Western economies have spent the years since the crisis raising the level of regulation in the financial sector, and as these new regulations continue to kick in, regulatory freedom will shrink further. Perhaps more regulation is what the financial sector needed, but new and old regulations have clear side effects. One of them is that they reinforce the disconnect between financial markets and the real economy. Together with tax policy and other regulations, new financial regulations make capital markets and their products more homogeneous. Regulations take capital markets further away from the business of funding long-term corporate ambitions. A greater share of capital ends up with identical investment profiles, chasing the same types of targets.

That development is not new – and it is part of the gray capitalism we portrayed in Chapter 3. The role of capital markets for corporate funding has changed over several decades, but more so in the past two decades. Modern companies of size have no problem funding themselves on capital markets, but the qualitative profile of available capital has progressively become less of a match to long-term funding. Companies are today principally funded by debt and not equity, and for a long time tax systems have made the former more advantageous to issue than the latter. Companies can still tap into sources of long-term debt funding but their capital structure has progressively moved toward shorter-term debt. And with that development, the capital-performance demands they face reflect the greater role of liquid forms of debt and owners with shorter stockholding periods.

There is a paradox in modern capital markets, and regulation partly explains it. Despite the "savings glut," or a growing surplus of capital chasing investments, companies have gradually seen their funding for long-term investments squeezed, and that is not just because investors demand better short-term returns. One of the interesting patterns of financial development in the past decades is that while leverage and balance sheets in the financial system have increased, and substantially so, long-term investment and innovation exposure in the corporate sector have declined. Investors increasingly prefer to put assets into investments with a shorter life cycle.[56] Though that is not an acknowledged reality in some branches of modern corporate finance theory, it is perfectly obvious that greater reliance on external capital funding has changed the relative prices of various investments inside companies. If it is easier to finance short-term plans than long-term plans, companies are incentivized to plan for the short term.

Politicians assisted that trend, and not just through tax advantages for substituting equity with debt. Regulations in the area of corporate governance and capital markets have increasingly tried to make investment behavior predictable. Resources have been reallocated as a consequence – and investments associated with a greater degree of uncertainty have been disadvantaged in regulations that want investments to follow a political formula. The postcrisis surge in various financial regulations has not made it better. The regulations that guide those that fund companies have become far more complicated. The Dodd-Frank Act and its cousins in the European Union and elsewhere have managed to make a fiendishly complex regulatory system for finance even more complex. History will show if all these new rules have made the financial system more stable, but it is already clear that they exacerbate the demand for predictability and reduce the willingness to be exposed to long-term volatility or uncertainty. Uncertainty simply cannot be married with financial regulations in the way they are now designed, and a business sector that is increasingly reliant on capital markets for funding inevitably has to reduce it.

Moreover, growing regulatory complexity has raised the entry barriers to capital markets. That trend has been strong for several decades because the "put option" that governments have issued to banks – "if you fail we will bail you out" – has redistributed money between different sectors of the economy and triggered excessive growth in finance.[57] But now this operates through overly prescriptive regulations and compliance procedures that demand far more risk management at every level of finance. In other words, financial regulations have pushed up the cost of capital and will continue to do so once the newer regulations kick in. Regulatory complexity also leads to a market with stronger concentration in several parts of the financial sector. Regulations make the scale benefits larger and have already reduced the market for niche actors representing a different type of asset management than the market standard.

Banks and other financial companies, hardly innocent bystanders in this development, respond to regulatory complexity by standardizing products and compelling the entire market to behave in the same way. This is also an intended consequence of regulation: regulators want substantial homogenization of the way financial actors invest and react to new information. In other words, one consequence of many financial regulations is that the structure of gray capitalism has become more firmly anchored as standardization leads to concentration and less product variation. Associated regulations, like those guiding investment funds and asset management, that have emerged in the wake of the crisis will, like complex bank regulations, perpetuate a capital market with some unfavorable consequences for the nonfinancial economy. Just like the Dodd-Frank Act, new regulations such as those governing investment managers or insurance companies and their capital management will standardize and commoditize investment. Part of that is pushing fund managers to increasingly follow general market trends and ratings from credit rating agencies, which have also been regulated in a way that promotes standardization and commoditization. Regulations dress themselves in the language of promoting competition, but the competition they seek is based on the idea of a low-margin, low-spread, high-volume, and commoditized capital market.[58]

Such capital markets, also characterized by the growing role of intermediaries, *will* affect the ability of companies to raise funds for long-term investments in innovation on standard capital markets.[59] There is a short-termism in modern finance, and the way that gray capitalism has changed both external and internal funding for innovation should concern everyone.[60] The changing patterns of investments cut the growth potential of economies. Some claim the real-life effects to be even stronger – indeed about life and death.

Take the example of cancer research and corporate innovation. A general trend across corporate medical research has been to reduce risks associated with clinical trials, especially the Phase III trials we previously discussed. Together with the long time lags between discovery and innovation, or invention and commercialization, companies are encouraged to focus their innovation investment on products that can be commercialized in the short term and that are subject to less demanding clinical trials. When these considerations are combined with uncertainties about funding, and a patent system that cannot distinguish sufficiently between innovations requiring long or short patent protection, corporate investments in cancer research have been incentivized to go for short-term opportunities and reduce the long-term risks.[61]

Ultimately, that type of capital allocation has consequences for the ability to cure people of cancer. The safe, defensive and (financially) liquid forms of cancer innovation generally relate to later-stage treatments, not to early treatments. For the war on cancer to be won, however, it is the early-stage treatments that need to improve. That will not happen unless there is far more capital ploughed into research and innovation – and diminished uncertainty about the chance to profit from innovations once they have been developed.

It would be unfair to blame the slow progress in cancer research on capital market regulations. They are, however, partly to blame for a general shift in the way companies get funding, and what they seek funding for. Together with a general climate of greater business regulation, companies have become less prone to experimentation and big innovation. For two decades the climate of regulation improved. However, that trend was not all-encompassing. In reality, the wave of deregulation was systemically important in only a few sectors. It ignored key categories such as labor reform and housing – critically important for the speed of adaptation. This partial, or incomplete, liberalization of markets helped determine the types of businesses and forms of economic growth that would dominate in the decades leading up to the financial crisis. Capitalist energy moved in the direction of those markets that were liberalized, and the emphasis on trade and current account liberalization spurred trade and specialization. Equally important, the selective coverage of liberalization changed the relative performance between sectors, and drew business activity toward the open sectors rather than the closed.

In the past 15 years, politicians have again started to favor more rather than less regulation. That trend is not about to reverse. Nor is it only about economic regulation. In the same period of time, there has been a remarkable growth of a completely different set of regulations – noneconomic regulations. They are proliferating and are holding innovation strategies back as much as economic regulations, if not more. It is to this issue that we turn next.

7

KILLING FRONTIER INNOVATION WITH REGULATORY COMPLEXITY AND UNCERTAINTY

It is difficult to make our material condition better by the best laws, but it is easy enough to ruin it by bad laws.

Theodore Roosevelt, speech at Providence, Rhode Island

This time it was neither too hot nor too cold. It was just right.

The Story of Goldilocks and the Three Bears

It has been billed as an example of democracy triumphing over sinister corporate interests. In June 2015, the European Parliament finally closed a much-debated regulatory loophole that had allowed companies to continue using cadmium in their production. Cadmium is a transitional metal used, for instance, in illumination and display lighting, but it is toxic. In fact, it is carcinogenic, causing many workers that have been exposed to the chemical element to develop cadmium lung cancer. Therefore, its use has been heavily restricted and it seemed at the time of the vote that the European deputies considered it their mission to complete the protection of health and the environment. And the result speaks for itself. The European Parliament voted 618 to 33 to reject a proposal to continue exempting certain uses of cadmium from the restriction.[1]

Yet was it really such an epic battle for the health and the environment? While some companies wanted the exemption prolonged, others – with competing products on offer – wanted it closed. Neither was the outcome of the vote necessarily the friendly option for health and the environment as the main substitutes are not safer. Surprisingly, the result of the European

Parliament's vote was not an end to the exemption. In fact, the statement from the European Parliament itself underlined that cadmium would not be banned, even if it voted to close the exemption. Instead, a new safety assessment of cadmium would be done, with the preferred result that it should be banned.

It is a confusing way of making regulation, especially as the European Commission had already asked a group of environmental and engineering experts for a safety assessment before proposing a vote on the extension of the exemption. And they had in fact recommended an extension, with the proviso that it should be for a limited period of time, in anticipation of a competitive and cadmium-free material becoming available in the next few years.[2] In effect, parliamentarians rejected one scientific assessment and called for another, without exactly knowing what was wrong with the first one, except for the conclusion. Brussels' lobbyists, however, appreciated the result because the vote fired the opening shot for yet another lobbying battle.

The cadmium example carries a larger story about how the regulatory sausage makers increasingly create regulatory uncertainty – and, as we later will see, undermines innovation. Time is of essence in any business, but more so for those who are about to launch new innovations. In this cadmium case, companies using the chemical under the current exemption will not know for another couple of years whether their products can be put on the market or not. It may come across as a small, isolated and perfectly innocent; something that will only be a minor item – if an item at all – when companies make decision about innovation. But that is the wrong conclusion, both in this case and regulations in general. Regulations are often well intentioned and not products of malice. Most of them are not draconian in intent or effect. However, when combined they create a complex landscape that fans uncertainty and damages investment in innovation.

However, many regulations that have emerged over the past decade or so have bred complexity rather than simplicity, and therefore had disproportionate consequences. They are often "precautionary regulations" or regulations that are based on ambiguous objectives. It is not exactly clear what such a regulation intends to achieve, nor can the consequences be predicted. Those affected by it cannot understand what behavior it prescripts. As the regulatory process that led to such a regulation often is non-transparent it is difficult to use the process as a guide to the exact intention of the regulation. Precautionary regulations are not economic regulations because they deal with regulatory instruments other than the classic economic ones.

They often manifest the spirit of precaution in various forms of social regulations such as environmental and consumer safety.

Uncertainty is the main problem with complex regulations. They can be structured in different ways and recent trends in regulation have preferred confusion rather than clarification. They affect innovation because they compel companies to innovate in a way that pleases an increasingly risk-averse and precautionary society. They have created a permission-based culture of innovation. Regulation is not neutral between existing and future products. It places a wedge between efforts to improve on current products and putting vastly different products and services on to the market. Regulation has become a known unknown – and, by extension, made it a disruptive force in the innovation process.

Business has responded by predictably. They have either cut down on innovation expenditures or reallocated them in a way that fit with new regulatory petitions. Complex regulation has reinforced the growth of the managerialist mentality in corporate management – and subordinated the appetite for radical innovation. Just like grey owners and company managers, regulators prefer companies that are predictable and innovate in accordance with political formula. In their view, innovation should not be too hot or too cold – but just right, if you remember the Goldilocks principle. But that is not how innovation works. When the costs and risks of regulations get too high for companies, or when regulatory processes just take too long time, they naturally move in other directions, hoping to avoid the long arm of excessive regulations.

The precautionary principle at work

Precautionary regulations often make regulations complex – and innovation risks larger – because they are by definition ambiguous in their intent. They do not address known problems – but unknown problems, or problems that may occur. That is a regulatory climate that erodes the spirit of innovation. Take the example of chemicals. According to an impact study undertaken by the EU, one of its landmark reforms on chemicals – mandating the registration, testing and authorization of all chemicals in use – has diverted funds from innovation, increased the time to market for new chemical innovation, and generally created a decade-plus long period of regulatory uncertainty.[3] The EU chemical industry goes further and claims that the regulation was not only misconceived but that it drained the sector of innovative competitiveness by shifting production away from Europe to other parts of the world.

That assertion may or may not be accurate, but what is clear is that regulatory complexity and uncertainty followed hard on the heels of the introduction of the precautionary principle in EU regulation. Such a principle is impossible to marry with the ambition of promoting an industrial culture of innovation and experimentation. "The reflex is to first look at a new product's risks as opposed to its benefits," making "technological progress almost impossible," says one industry leader.[4] The precautionary principle shifts the burden of proof by demanding that it is up to a producer to show that a product is not causing harm. Harvard professor Cass Sunstein calls it "literally paralyzing."[5] Science writer Ronald Bailey has sum it up: "Anything new is guilty until proven innocent."[6]

Proving a negative is not just a philosophical challenge. The precautionary principle prompts a regulatory culture that is unpredictable and often non-transparent. It is difficult to know what needs to be done in order to be on the safe side of a regulation and approval processes. It takes time and it costs money. When regulations are ambiguous regulators are often handed flexibility on how to determine whether a product is cleared or not. The precautionary principle erases the scientific ethos that should guide regulatory conduct, and adds significant costs to innovation.

Nanomaterials is another example. Nanotechnology is a promising technology, especially for Europe and its big industrial enterprises. However, European authorities have not figured out a way to regulate it, and claims that while "nanomaterials are not per se dangerous" the risk that they may be dangerous prevents them from granting general approval for them.[7] Again, that may seem perfectly innocent, until the consequences for nanotechnological innovation are considered. Such a regulatory approach means that all individual materials have to go through a case-by-case authorization process. Every time a new nanomaterial is invented or applied, new regulation will have to be written.

Such regulatory discretion creates additional uncertainty because it opens up for a greater degree of politicization of the approval process, sometimes leading to stalled approvals for innovations that have been scientifically proven to not cause any harm. Just look at the case of Amflora, a blemish on the European regulatory body. The European Food Safety Authority (EFSA) approved the genetically modified potato used to produce certain potato starch in 2005, However, despite the authority clearing it from causing harm to the environment and human health, which is the legal basis for rejecting applications, the innovation did not get final market approval.[8] The applicant, the German chemical company BASF, justifiably felt it had been treated unfairly and eventually filed a complaint with the European

Court of Justice in 2008, citing that the authorities had sidestepped its own rules for how soon approvals or rejections should be made after the scientific evaluation. Pressed by the general opposition to GM crops in Europe, the European Commission did not wave the approval through but ordered another evaluation of the crop in 2009, perhaps in the hope that a new evaluation would deliver a different result or silence the opposition. EFSA cleared Amflora yet again, leading finally to a decision in 2010, five years after the application, that Amflora could be cultivated and used in Europe. It was the second decision ever of the EU to approve the cultivation of a GM crop.

In practice, however, that never happened. A few of the EU member states filed their own complaint with the courts, on the grounds that the European Commission had violated the same procedural rules for approving or rejecting an application. The member states, led by Hungary, were not arguing that the crop was dangerous, or that EFSA had failed in its multiple scientific evaluations of the crop. Hungary dug up a rule relating to the scientific basis for approving decision that could be employed to their advantage, never mind how Kafkaesque it made the process.

Since EFSA had conducted a second evaluation of Amflora, Hungary argued, the formal basis for the European Union approval should have been the *second* rather than the *first* evaluation. Never mind that both evaluations had cleared the product, in December 2013 the General Court of the EU upheld the complaint and annulled the authorization. For all practical purposes, however, the case had already ended before the court's decision. BASF had withdrawn its application for the GM crop in 2012 because of huge opposition. Packing up its entire GMO research operation, it moved out of Europe.[9]

One can understand why. The opposition to GM technology, or "Frankenfood" as some call it, was loud, powerful and backed up by vested interests. All of which, adds more weight to the case for regulations that are simple and transparent. Regulations giving substantial discretion to regulators or politicians in deciding whether a company complies or not are multipliers of uncertainty. When regulations embody the precautionary principle it is close to impossible for an innovator to know what is needed to get necessary approvals. Such regulations only tell companies to divert investments away from them. It forms part of the narrative of why regulation – despite a general trend towards reduced product market restrictions – is a growing source of friction in the cosmos of innovation and why far too many companies are afraid of experimentation.

The Amflora case is one example of how firms cut or offshore innovation resources in response to regulation and uncertainty. If we go back to the case of the cadmium, we find a similar reaction – this time also stalled entry of new technologies. Cadmium, no doubt, is hazardous, and if you live next to a plant that has been poisoning land or water with the chemical element, you may well want to call Erin Brockovich. But no regulatory authority claims it to be dangerous when used in very small quantities in isolated solid-state materials. And, important for the commercialization of nanomaterial innovations, no authority claims it to be dangerous in the production of quantum dots (QD), a promising nanomaterial now used, for instance, to produce better versions of what probably is the most watched object in the world: computer screens.

QD is an interesting technology even when you take the glossy corporate pitches with a grain of salt. It can help to produce more efficient illumination and reduce the waste of energy and light in many displays. That would generate savings in energy bills for households and offices, and creating a better work environment for those of us who stare into a screen for many hours a day. As QD displays create better image quality, taking away the blue light filter on LED screens and wasting less color than OLED displays, it adds a qualitative dimension too. But it is a technology that could be useful far beyond consumer electronics.

At the Consumer Electronics Association's annual gathering in early 2015, a QD based neon blob was put in the Nevada desert, not, as some people mused, to outshine the lighting of the Las Vegas strip, but to demonstrate that it could be seen from space.[10] Solar cells with QD, some claim, are likely to become more efficient than other photovoltaic technologies,[11] and NASA suggests its efficient use of energy could allow it to be used to power deep space explorations.[12]

The cadmium used in QD technology is coated in glass and plastics, which is why regulatory authorities have approved its use. As long as workplace practices reduce the potential exposure during production and there are electronic waste systems to take care of the cadmium (and other toxic materials) in disposed screens, the dangers of cadmium-based QDs are contained. The European Parliament, however, was not convinced. Its resolution went as far as to claim the existence of alternatives to cadmium, making it redundant in reaping the potential gains from QD. It is a bold view, to say the least, and those developing the technology did not appreciate the quality of the argument. In fact, all of the companies producing and using QD, barring one producer (that also lobbied to close the exemption), assert that cadmium is necessary in realizing light and energy savings of the nanomaterial. Adding, that the only realistic alternative to cadmium is indium, another chemical element that is hazardous.

What is the lesson of this tale? Quantum dots may or may not disrupt the electronics industry, and cadmium-based QD screens may or may not be available in Europe in the future. Yet for consumers and producers in Europe, it will take time before serious investment is made because of the looming regulatory uncertainty. And that is the takeaway. The chilling effect of regulatory uncertainty is often to slow down the process of innovation and investment in it. Uncertainty affects the time-to-market for innovators and the ability of inventors and developers to reach consumers, which is key as revenues typically fund additional innovation. Importantly, it affects consumers too as they get deprived of new technologies that could bring gains. It slows down the process of getting everyone in an economy to behave smarter and more productively.

Regulatory uncertainty adds to the commercial uncertainty of innovation. While some investors and inventors are undeterred by regulatory uncertainty, some even see opportunities from it, for most actors it translates into a cost, especially a capital cost that is associated with risk. A study by Harvard scholar Ariel Dora Stern, for instance, found that for frontier innovation in medical devices, the lengthy approval process cuts the expected lifetime revenue of an innovation by eight percent.[13] It may not sound like very much, but it can be the difference between making and breaking the commercial case for investing in an innovation.

In most companies, the board or the corporate management will block innovation processes if regulatory uncertainty is too big, or if there is a risk of serious cost in obtaining regulatory approval. Under the current regulatory regime in Europe, there is not much investment into GMOs for the simple reason that European GMO regulation is so complex that no one can say if a product can be marketed in Europe even if safety assessors say it is safe. The entire biotechnological sector is damaged when one branch of it cannot innovate. It is not just BASF that has moved research operations out of Europe and withdrawn applications for regulatory approval. Other companies in the field, like Monsanto, got the message too. Likewise, European investment into both shale gas and renewable energy are heavily depressed because the regulatory framework in many countries makes it close to impossible for a company to understand what market opportunities will exist in the future.

Conflicts between regulations

Many areas of regulation have become so fiendishly complex that they require heavy resourcing just to understand what is allowed and what is not under current regulation. But complexity is not just about design flaws. When the number of regulation grows so big that no one knows how one regulation relates to another – it regularly happens that one regulations conflicts with another, that they prescribe conflicting courses of action. Economists call this phenomenon regulatory accumulation, and defines it as "both a process and an outcome of our reactive regulatory structure."[14] In other words, as the number of approved regulations grows, they inevitably interact in ways we may not expect. And when taken together, multiple regulations can overlap or conflict, become the primary focus of company management, or even interfere with a company's willingness and ability to innovate.

A much-publicized example of regulatory conflicts – a conflict emerging from the same regulation – happened in 2013 when Europe had Germany battling France on market access for Mercedes cars. The Financial Times reported that summer that: "sales of thousands of the most prestigious Mercedes cars have been halted in France since Paris last month refused to allow the registration of four new models that include a refrigerant in their air-conditioning systems that has been banned by the EU on environmental grounds."[15] Unsurprisingly, Mercedes was up in arms over the French decision, arguing that the ban would badly hurt sales in France. They also claimed that the French government had an ulterior motive for banning the new Mercedes model. It was a protectionist act aimed at supporting France's ailing car companies. The explanation, however, was less fiery. French authorities were making the case that the EU had outlawed the air-conditioning coolant because it contained gas adding to global warming. While the exact timetable for phasing out the coolant was partly a matter of choice, it is clear that the decision was based on judicious implementation of an agreed law. German authorities, on the other hand, had not banned the coolant because the replacement was dangerously flammable. They were also basing their decision on law, and were acting equally judiciously in allowing companies to use a safer product. The question was not between right and wrong; It was between conflicting regulations.

It is not the first time that different regulations have conflicted with each other. In fact, it happens quite often. This new crop of regulations has made the regulatory framework much more prescriptive and granular. Michael Mandel and Diana G. Carew give in a study of regulatory accumulation the example of how green building codes in the United States – which total 275! – conflict with the Energy Policy and Conservation Act (EPCA) as they use different standards for energy efficient home appliances:

Two major court cases in Washington State and Albuquerque, New Mexico yielded opposite verdicts on the legality of their building codes when they set construction guidelines that related to the efficiency of appliances. In both cases, local HVAC trade associations filed suit on EPCA grounds. In Washington State in 2012, the court upheld the building codes since the language in the code did not require builders to use more efficient appliances. In Albuquerque, however, the court set an injunction on the city's green building codes in 2008, saying they were pre-empted by EPCA. A 2012 update suggests Albuquerque's green codes were completely stricken in lieu of much more relaxed general state-wide building codes.

What they describe is a largely uncontrolled accumulation of regulations – a growth that has not been as recognized as the growth in economic regulations because few monitor them. Those who do, however, generally reject the notion of the past decades as period of substantial deregulation. Between 1997 and 2012, show Patrick McLaughlin and Richard Williams, the total number of restrictions in the *Code of Federal Regulations* grew by 12 000 – per year.[16] Using text analysis, McLaughlin and Omar Al-Ubaydli show there has been an acceleration and spreading of regulations for all sectors in the economy. Remarkably, they found no sector that has experienced a decline in the number restrictions or the amount of regulation.[17]

Regulatory accumulation causes a complex regulatory landscape where it gets difficult to understand what regulations that apply, and if one regulation is compatible with another. Faced with such structures of regulation, companies think twice about innovation and business planning. They do not necessarily deter innovation, but they slow them down and reallocate innovation efforts.

If self-driving vehicles are to deliver on their potential and not just become a narrow product used for niche transport, let alone one of many promising technologies in the automotive sector that has ultimately failed,[18] authorities will have to practice restraint and change many current policies that govern markets and technologies.[19] Even if developers and media give the impression that intelligent vehicles will soon be common on Western roads, the reality is different. Crucial to the evolution of the market is the instinct of regulators, legislators and the courts. And not, as one might think, predominantly the technology or the quality of the vehicles.

The coordination required to make various regulations of such vehicles interoperable can easily fail and squander a substantial part of the promise of intelligent vehicles. In several countries, there has to be regulatory and legal innovations to circumvent the potential effects of such a basic legal institution as the assignment of liability in the event of accidents. Or to put it differently: if a driverless car crash or cause an accident, who should be blamed – the owner of the car or the producer of the car, or perhaps the company producing its software? Some companies are experimenting with different solutions, but it is a highly contentious issue. As two leading experts in transportation in the United States soberly note: "the major obstacle to motorists and firms from adopting them as soon as possible is whether the government will take prudent and expeditious approaches to help resolve important questions about assigning liability in the event of an accident, the availability of insurance, and safety regulations."[20] Prudent and expeditious approaches, however, are not the main characters of Western regulators and their political masters.

Regulatory and policy uncertainty shape investment allocation

No one can say by exactly how much regulatory uncertainty damages the propensity to invest in innovation. Economic research has been clear for a good while that policy uncertainty generally reduces economic output.[21] It is intuitive and easy to see how a high dosage of uncertainty clogs the economic arteries of corporate investment. Any business faced with policy or regulatory uncertainty will become more defensive and cautious, even if it does not necessarily lead companies to halt investment. Academic research concurs. Scholars studying the effect of uncertainty clearly show how it influences corporate investment allocation and the general willingness to invest in innovation.

Policy uncertainty is not the same as regulatory uncertainty, even if the two hang together. Policy uncertainty covers a wider range of government interventions in the economy, like taxes. Yet both depress investment – and they depress it more than most people might think. A group of scholars have quantified the effect of general policy uncertainty and concluded that about one third of the decline in capital investment during the Great Recession was due to policy uncertainty, not market uncertainty.[22] That is a startling figure considering the severity of the drop in capital investment during 2007-2009. Yet it is not difficult to see how companies in a situation like that perceive policy to be too uncertain for them to advance business investments. Policy uncertainty at the macro level alone was substantial. A significant part of the economic commentariat predicted depression-like, tit-for-tat protectionism and a regulatory tsunami to follow hard on the heels of the economic decline and the credit collapse. Such policies would directly affect business development. Add to that the "normal" growth of regulation and it is easy to see why uncertainty became the dead hand of capitalism.

The results confirm the general trend of falling investment growth discussed in chapter two and find that policy uncertainty explains why companies have built up very strong cash balances rather than investing the excess liquidity. Market uncertainty alone has been large enough to prompt executives to postpone investment and build up liquidity positions that can help companies sustain themselves during another period of credit squeezes or a temporary drop in demand and revenues. Regulatory uncertainty exacerbated the commercial propensity to hoard cash rather than turning it into investments. It was a double-whammy of uncertainty, and no doubt the corporate reaction to uncertainty is one of the reasons why the growth of investment, productivity and output has been muted.

Another group of economists from Stanford and the University of Chicago concur. To better understand the evolution of policy uncertainty they have constructed an index of it. Using index figures, they have found intimate relations between variations in policy uncertainty and economic performance. They argue, for instance, that general policy uncertainty in the past few years has choked the recovery of the U.S. economy, not least by denting gross investments by around 6 percent.[23] Given all the political chaos around fiscal policy, debt ceilings, healthcare and other issues that have paralysed Washington, the result is hardly surprising. Even if short-term trends and swings can have many causes, it is reasonable to assume uncertainty about important government bills have a substantial impact on decision making in corporate board rooms. Taking the long-term view, however, it becomes more obvious that uncertainty caused by the political system affects business plans. The index shows a long-term trend of increasing uncertainty in the United States (see chart below). Barring a decline in the 1990s, policy uncertainty has largely been growing uninterruptedly since the 1970s.

Uncertainty is not just throwing sand into the economic wheel. More damaging over time is that uncertainty changes the composition of business investment and expenditures to the disadvantage of R&D and innovation. Economists from Purdue University in the U.S., for instance, have found that uncertainty particularly depresses irreversible investments the most, and irreversible investments like innovation are usually long-term investment. Naturally, investment facing an unpredictable future is held back until there is better information about the future and the rates of profitability that can be expected, and such effects, the Purdue scholars show, are particularly strong in sectors with high sunk costs.

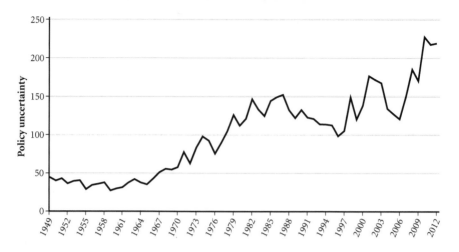

Figure 7.1 Economic policy uncertainty in the United States

We have been here before: high sunk costs affect business planning and, in this case, make companies particularly cautious about investments associated with uncertainty. It changes company behavior, especially the way a company allocates funds, and impairs the productive behavior of an entire economy.[24] Regulation plays a role for how companies allocate resources[25] – and in sectors with big potential to push the technological frontier, such as energy and healthcare, regulation is a key factor for the direction the sector takes and whether companies move fast or slow. In other words, governments can determine how the corporate sector spends it resources, and whether it will invest in high-productive or less-productive targets.

It is not just big and global firms that get affected. In fact, there are many casualties, and some of them get far more bruised by regulation than multinationals. For start-ups and small companies with the potential to develop and market new and challenging technologies, the impact of regulatory uncertainty can stop development completely. They do not have internal capital markets that can fund innovation and often have to rely entirely on outside investments. And as every small innovator that have raised capital from investors knows, it is a humbling experience to ask them for money. But when regulatory risks add to market and technology risks, the experience is humiliating rather than humbling. Outside investors usually do not have the skills to understand all the nuances of regulatory risks for a particular innovation. Even if they decide to go ahead with an investment, some damage is already done because resources have been allocated for the purpose of assessing regulatory and legal uncertainties instead of developing and marketing new innovations.

It does not have to be a black-and-white issue. Nor do all regulations damage the allocation of capital or the propensity to invest in innovation. In fact, sometimes innovation can be encouraged by regulation. Whether it is an intended or unintended consequence is debatable, but many companies, for example, have invested in innovation in order to comply with new regulations. Companies also innovate in order to circumvent regulations, and there are examples of how such innovation has disrupted markets.[26] Regulations can also set standards that reduce uncertainty about whether innovative products can be approved for the market. If regulations set a standard that is achievable, and desist draconian measures if there is not full or immediate compliance, the effect can be even more favorable.

Take the example of U.S. regulations enacted in the 1970s to lift the environmental standard of automobiles. Several scholars have found that these regulations prompted greater innovation activity among American automobile firms and that they had to shift the allocation of the R&D budget from D to R.[27] Annual changes of the style of the cars were demoted in order to channel resources to innovation that could improve the fuel-efficiency of cars. And that is a good thing; it is the right form of allocation because it stimulates real innovation.

However, there are limits to what regulation can achieve, also in this case. The effect of these regulations did not prove lasting and uncertainty played a role for the stop-go pattern of innovation. The willingness to innovate and put money into it proved temporary. Amendments to the fuel-efficiency acts were not just very costly but also impossible to reach, and least in the time frame that had been set. U.S. authorities had subsequently to delay the implementation of them, especially the move towards catalytic converter technology. And once the benchmarks had been achieved, there was a drop in innovation activity by U.S. auto firms, and they reduced the R&D shares.

This example points us to one effect of moving target regulations. Most economic research into the area shows there are discouraging effects on innovation from regulations that constantly move the goal post of what should be achieved. No doubt the effects are particularly strong when moving-target regulations are applied stringently and without necessary flexibility for firms to qualify for approval. Even worse, if the standard and the condition for compliance are ambiguous, moving-target regulations can erase the willingness to innovate altogether.[28] That is an extreme form of bad regulation, but even when moving-target regulations are open to some degree of flexibility they still create disincentives to innovate. This happens partly because they reinforce the long-term uncertainty about whether companies can eventually recoup the cost of the innovation. If a company knows that regulation will change once they have achieved the initial objective, that tends to weaken their appetite for moving into that territory, or make alternative investment opportunities appear more appealing. It certainly changes the allocation of innovation investments away from big and market-changing innovation to small and incremental innovation – from the unknown to the known. This is probably the most damaging effect of regulation because it directs corporate innovation activity away from the innovations that can raise the productivity of companies and economies.

Regulation is a delicate matter and there is a natural reason for why many regulations have gradually raised the standard. The regulatory process is also a learning process and, just like others, regulators are influenced by the constant generation of knowledge. The conclusion is not that regulators should stop regulating, but that there are particular forms of regulations that pollute the innovation environment. With an evolutionary regulatory process, it is important that regulators complex and ambiguous regulations. They need to regulate in a way that brings clarity rather than uncertainty.   ·

Greening energy by complex regulations

Regulation that deters innovation tends to be more frequent in sectors that are important for pushing the technological frontier and that could lift productivity and economic growth. The problem is not necessarily that they are exposed to more economic regulations than other sectors, even if that is the case with sectors like energy and healthcare. A bigger problem is that a surprising amount of new social regulations ticks all the boxes of the type of regulation that deters big and game-changing innovation.

That such regulations depress innovation is not just a side effect; it is partly intended. The cost of pharmaceutical innovation increases because of complex and inflexible standards for trials that presume that there is a greater priority in controlling all risks with a new medicine than providing needing patients with it. That is a political choice, not one that is determined by the medicine. Precautionary regulations often demand potential innovators in sectors like chemicals to prove a negative, and that is determined by a political presumption. Likewise, GMO innovations are effectively denied access to the European market because powerful politicians want it that way, even if the innovations actually comply with the regulation.

Unfortunately, there are no signs that regulators, and the politicians that ultimately mandate regulatory action, are about to change habit. It is rather getting worse and regulation is increasingly becoming part of industrial policy. Social regulations are now part of how Machiavellian politicians carve up the market to favor particular businesses at the expense of others. Take a sector like energy, important for both the economy and the health of the planet. It is not just constrained by complex and stringent regulations that erode their innovation desire. The same regulations are designed to distribute the gains from the market to those who are politically privileged.

A promising sector for the future like renewable energy now runs with the stream of regulation rather than commerce and technology. If markets and regulations had been less complex and ambiguous about compliance, Western economies would have been far greener. Europe's regulation of biofuels is a case in point. Ever since the early noughties, European governments and Brussels' institutions have been pushing to expand the use of renewable energy in transport.[29] Big and expensive efforts have been made to substitute fossil fuels with biofuels. Taxes on fossil fuels have increased substantially and subsidies have been sprinkled on biofuels producers to motivate them to invest and expand. However, the support did not pay off. A few years after the pioneering reforms were done European authorities had to overhaul the regulations of biofuels production and consumption, and in that drive they aimed to direct the market more firmly. However, the complexity and uncertainty that the new regulations created, and the abject attempt to use these new regulations as hand-outs to particular firms, almost broke the back of biofuels use in Europe.

Europe's regulators wanted both to raise the volume of biofuels production and the quality of the fuels, and the new regulations that emerged went for direct supply-side measures rather than weak demand incentives. Perhaps the intention was a good one but when the machinery of politics got up to speed, national politicians and Brussels' regulators did not practice restraint. Industrial ambitions also took hold of the regulatory process and what started as an idea to green Europe's energy use suddenly became part of advanced industrial policy planning. Those who spotted an opportunity to take biofuels policy hostage wanted to release competitive pressures from Europe's producers of biofuels and the feedstock (rapeseed) they predominantly use to produce the fuel. Imaginably, the first casualties of such ambitions were foreign producers of cheaper biofuels based on a different feedstock. They were already disadvantaged as both feedstock and fuels producers in Europe got direct subsidies from governments. Yet that support was not enough to make Europe's producers competitive. Nor were

the investments that the European industry had made utilized to the necessary degree for investments to be profitable. Far too little of the capital
ploughed into new refineries was operating at full capacity and the more
European industry sunk itself into high capital costs, the more competitive
foreign producers got.

The crony instinct kicked in and European producers lobbied for regulations that would stack the odds even more to their favor. Politicians,
already in cahoots with the industry and the farmers growing rapeseed,
yielded to the temptation of additional support to the green economy. They
were careful to avoid using classic beggar-thy-neighbor protectionist policies, and partly for that reason politicians created a regulation so complex
that few expected it to be noticed, let alone observed. Because trade and
protectionism are regulated in international agreements, the EU could not
just hike up tariffs and protect industries in the traditional way. Europe had
to find a regulation that covertly distorted trade and rearranged market
preferences in favor of local producers. The final result of this crooked
approach to regulation became so complex that no one really understood
how to comply with the regulation.

One of the new regulations gave prescriptive instructions for how traditional fuels should be blended with biofuels in order to get the right market
approval. However, regulators failed to harmonize all the different ways
that biofuels are produced and used for blending in Europe, and local
incumbents thus got indirect protection against competition from other
European producers. Another regulation ruled that not just the actual
biofuel but also the way it had been produced should be considered when
deciding if a fuel could be traded and used in Europe without restrictions
or disadvantages. Unsurprisingly, the complexity of the regulations wors-
ened when it was implemented. Most of the times, biofuels had to be
nationally certified, but there were competing forms of certifications, and
regulators could not agree on which one to use. While that flexibility was
initially welcome because it helped many existing producers to obtain
approvals for production and market access, it soon became a source of
regulatory uncertainty and cut markets off from each other. National
markets never faced much competition or forces of change because no one
really knew what type of biofuels that could be traded, or exactly what
certification was needed to market biofuels in another European country.
When protection-seeking producers hijacked national regulations – such
as the Spanish regulation demanding a particular geographic origin of the
feedstock used for blending traditional fuels – the market for traded
biofuels was for a while prone to collapse.

Luckily, it did not collapse – but, unluckily, nor did regulators take a pause in making life difficult for those that wanted to invest in improving the environmental quality of biofuels. A few years later it was time for yet another reform, with the ambition of regulating derivative effects of the way a biofuel has been produced. European authorities then introduced so-called indirect land-use effects in its regulation of biofuels. It was an obscure regulatory concept, to say the least, and it is still unknown what it actually infers, despite that there is a regulation about it. The notion behind it can easily be understood. If an increased production of energy crops used for biofuels leads to new land being cultivated in order to produce food crops that were substituted by the energy crop, the environmental effects of the new cultivation should form part of a judgement if the energy crop should be approved or not. It is intuitive, especially in light of the reports about possible negative environmental effects when new land is cleared for farming.

However, intuition is not a good source of regulation. Nor did the regulation answer a pretty basic question: exactly what is it that should be regulated and what should the producer of the energy crop do to comply with the regulation? Indirect land-use effects can be real, but they are neither observed nor measured in the production of the energy crop. It is not a known reality, but markets are fungible and it is impossible to determine what new cultivation that occurs because some farm land has been used for energy crops. While regulators and campaigners came up with all sorts of ideas for how to observe these effects, none of them were fair, transparent and conformed to the most basic forms of good regulatory standard. They were all, however, convoluted, speculative and impossible to pin down. Companies would never know whether their actions were compliant with the regulation or not – until they were told they are not.

The outcome was what everyone would expect. The complex and non-transparent regulations deterred investment in biofuels and innovation. While the machinery of regulation worked to support greener and better fuels, consumers in Europe got saddled with unsophisticated first-generation biofuels that was not only costly but produced few environmental gains. The natural progression of biofuels innovation did not entirely stop. Rather than investing in innovation that both could generate economic and environmental savings, European producers – and the governments that supported them – have mostly made safe and defensive choices by allocating their small investments in innovation into incremental improvements of their current output. For Europe, the innovation promise of biofuels has therefore failed by a large margin.

Complex regulation and economic growth

The consequences of complex regulation and regulatory uncertainty work the stairs from the level of the firm up to the entire economy. Ultimately, they translate into weaker productivity growth. The productivity of an entire economy depends on many factors, and some of them are beyond the control of individual companies investing in innovation. Business-related factors of productivity have shown weak performance and that there are few signs that they are about to change through innovation.[30] Regulations cannot be ignored as a source of the weak development.

Regulators deserve blame because they have made regulation excessively complex and created conditions of widespread regulatory uncertainty in some sectors. Under these conditions, companies reallocate resources from frontier to incremental innovation. Worse, they sometimes take resources away from innovation entirely, and focus only on the exploitation of existing ones. Diffusion and imitation are natural market developments and companies have grown increasingly skilled at adapting products and markets to whatever technologies that are available.[31] However, there are diminishing returns to exploiting the stock of existing innovations, and the potential growth of an economy gradually weakens when new innovation is not forcing market change as much as it should.

When regulation is either excessively stringent or too complex to understand (let alone comply with) companies naturally get cautious. That is not rocket science: everyone becomes guarded when conditions are uncertain. Such a simple observation, however, has not guided politicians and regulators in the West. They have made regulation a source of innovation risk. And that also gives us an explanation to why the pace of innovation and market change in many sectors have been so poor over the past decades. Regulators asked for it.

Economic research shows clearly that reallocation of innovation investments due to regulatory distortion have considerable consequences for economies.[32] At the macro level, it lowers general productivity growth and the capacity of economies to carry sustained high rates of economic growth. It diminishes the willingness of firms to experiment, and the resources that companies spend on experimentation.[33] Firms make their own decisions about how much risk should be associated with R&D and innovation strategies, and the uncertainty associated with regulation in frontier technology prompts companies to lower the innovation risks.

Another way to describe the same corporate response to regulatory uncertainty is that regulation has helped to anchor the managerialist mentality in the corporate sector. While the general level of regulation in Western economies is restrictive, the real problem today are regulations that exacerbate commercial innovation uncertainty and make companies less experimental and entrepreneurial. Therefore, regulation does not just influence the aggregate performance of innovation and productivity, but migrates it into the micro level of corporate selection, for instance the selection of managers and executives that are tasked to run companies, and the skills that managers and executives develop.[34] Like in every other market, the labor market for managers rewards some skills more than others, and for the past decades the skills that have rewarded managers and executives the most related less to innovation and more to corporate managerialism.

8

CAPITALISM AND ROBOTS

Dost thou faint, mighty Titan? We laugh thee to scorn.
Dost thou boast the clear knowledge thou waken'dst for man?
Then was kindled within him a thirst which outran
Those perishing waters

Percy Bysshe Shelley, *Prometheus Unbound*

Every act of creation is first an act of destruction.

Pablo Picasso

Western capitalism is not flourishing on innovation and new ideas, at least not as much as it should or could. Our problem is not one of input – or that scientists, inventors, and others have stopped exploring the future and pushing the technology frontier. With rising prosperity across the world, there are more people chasing new knowledge and developing new technologies then ever before. The problem is rather one of output: our economies no longer foster that spirit of capitalism that is necessary to propel growth into a higher trajectory. Even exceptional technologies falter when the economic habitat is inhospitable.

Still, it is technology angst, not technology frustration, that has taken hold of the Western world. The current innovation hype hosts an unnerving anticipation that Western economies are on the threshold of a fast-and-furious technological shift, which will crush jobs and income from top to bottom. Somewhat unexpectedly, that view also draws support from traditional opponents of the lump-of-labor fallacy, the popular zero-sum view that there is a fixed amount of work, a portion of which robots and intelligent machines will now steal. Tech gurus and high priests of economic liberalism like *The Economist* magazine have flirted with this historical fallacy, forecasting "huge social dislocation" as a consequence of new technology.[1]

So the pioneers of the computer and digital revolution – for decades lauded as the saviors of Western prosperity – are no longer wizards of the World Wide Web but more like the Wicked Witch of the West. Ever faster technological change was supposed to boost growth, jobs and Western competitiveness. However, economic growth has nothing but underperformed for decades. The small growth that has occurred has not brought many employment opportunities. Nor has it boosted take-home pay much. If that period was just the warm-up act for the digital revolution, should we not reduce our economic expectations even more now that the real innovation show is about to start?

Indeed, the dystopian sentiment is so strong that the tech aristocracy itself is honing the story of how new innovations will be poison for employed labor. *Après nous, le déluge!* Eric Schmidt, Google's executive chairman, contends there is a "race between computers and people."[2] He used his floor-time at a Davos summit to frighten the audience with the message that new technology can wipe out much of the employment that automation never reached. Many of his Silicon Valley peers are airing the same message. Devilishly desirable, the new intelligent robots and machines are like cocaine for Western workers. They cannot stop flipping their mobile and table screens; they cannot resist the fix. But they know it will destroy them in the end.

Prophets of the New Machine Age argue that Western economies are inevitably advancing towards an inflection point where technology will destroy employment, as we know it. Their high form of technology determinism is daunting, and had Karl Marx been alive today, he would have blushed from embarrassment for his lapses from determinist faith. They imagine a new society, or superstructure to use Marxist jargon, whose iteration is solely dependent on the growth of computing capacity, or what Marx would call the base. Technological limits of the past will be blown away; new innovators armed with algorithms unimaginably more powerful than today will relegate labor to history, or at least to unemployment. It is an economy that, if it is not innovating itself to death, will be so profoundly shocked by robots and intelligent machines that a good part of the working population will enter the dispossessed digital proletariat.

Should we prepare for a technological blitz? The troubling reality is that we should fear an innovation famine rather than an innovation feast. The thesis of a New Machine Age radically contradicts our view of stagnating economies, increasingly incapable of catering for their own future. Perhaps we are the odd men out, but to us the thesis is a utopian rather than dystopian vision of the future. Never mind the "Luddite" ring to the whole story of new technology, its vision holds optimism about the creation and diffusion of game-changing innovation. The drama it unfolds suggests that the Western economy is about to combust on innovation again – that the middle-age version of the Western capitalism can still shake things up.

Unfortunately, this vision is just like the grand idea of the planning machine. The thesis relies on a textbook version of markets and firms where there are no barriers to new technology. An invention becomes an innovation, and innovation leads to adaptation, without any friction. The passway of new technology from laboratory to market contestability is clear if not straightforward. But Western economies have gradually weakened their capacity to foster innovation and new technology in a way that impels fast diffusion and forces producers, consumers and legislators to behave much more productively. In light of Western capitalism's decline, the thesis of a pending technology blitz confounds rather than convinces.

It is hard to escape the feeling that many of the advertised technologies for the future underwhelm. No doubt, much of coming innovations in big data, the Internet of Things, machine intelligence, robotics and more should be commended, yet they fail to impress, at least our technology-frustrated generation. Perhaps this is to rain on the parade, but for someone who grew up in the wake of Apollo's moon landing, Stanley Kubrick's *2001*, and the original Star Trek series all that stuff seems a bit dull. What happened to the space race? Humans have yet to colonize Mars. Antigravity is still a dream. Teleportation of complex matters remains a theory. Doc Brown's flying car in *Back to the Future II*, took him and Marty McFly to October 21 2015, but today's world is far less exiting than the one imagined in the movie. We do not travel by flying cars, to start with. Nor do we have home fusion reactors or hover-boards. The time in the 1990s when the Star Trek's futuristic Eugenic War was supposed to end, the real world was worrying about a cloned Scottish sheep called Dolly.

Innovations are happening, but they are seldom game changing – and nor should their future iteration be seen as fixed or inevitable. New technology still has to battle against resistance in society and the economy – and it still needs successful entrepreneurs to break down those barriers and push new technology into the economy. That is not a done deal. New knowledge does not automatically translate into innovation. To see why, consider a couple of examples. We are still burning organic matter to power industries and fuel cars. French engineer August Mouchot wrote the first book on solar energy in the 1870s and a decade later John Ericsson designed a steam-engine based on solar power. William Morrison designed America's first electric car in 1890. It carried six people and travelled at a top speed of 14 miles per hour[3] – much faster than the first gasoline automobile Karl Benz drove in Germany in 1886.[4]

And why stop there? We still do not have the option of using flying cars, yet roadable aircrafts were developed in the 1930s. And why have we not found a cure against cancer? After all, it was first observed in 3000 BC and its genetic origin was discovered in the Nineteenth century. The American Cancer Society, the first organization to fight cancer, was founded in 1913. Yet, a hundred years later, we are mourning more people than ever because of the heinous disease. In a similar vein, the German doctor Alois Alzheimer discovered the disease now carrying his name in 1906. But we have yet to learn its cause, let alone how to treat it effectively.

There are no limits to how radical innovations could improve our lives and the economy. But the technological revolution that is now prophesied does not even come close in advancing them. While there is no end to the flow of apps for selfies, games, gossip or even to improve the way we kiss, (yes, app encouraging kissing your smartphone), the really cool stuff appears anything but imminent. Paul Krugman calls it "the big meh," suggesting that much of the new technology is "more fun than fundamental" and hence does not boost the economy as much as the media and tech developers claim.[5] It is easy to agree with that view. Mobile gaming, for instance, has grown much faster than industrial robotics. Whilst some observers might fret that "robots are coming," the real concern is that industrial robots are not employed more widely. When people become anxious about the rapid growth in the use of robots in the services and industrial production in the future they do not appreciate the low absolute levels that growth is starting from and that growth will need to accelerate much more if Western economies are to avoid supply disruptions. Western population is ageing and too few young people are interested in industrial jobs, leading to falling substitution rates in industry. Structural labor shortages in Europe will grow fast over the next decades. Several industrial sectors have skills shortages already today; they cannot expand because they lack staff with the right education and training.

There is a similar dissonance between expectation and reality in the transport sector. The media propels fear about intelligent vehicles and how they will make taxi and truck drivers redundant. In the real world there are ever more chauffeurs trying to get a taxi medallion. If the current trend of growing shortages of truck drivers is not arrested, the United States will have a 175 000 shortage of truckers in eight years, partly because the workforce is retiring.[6] The American Trucking Association says there is an immediate shortage of about 50 000 skilled drivers. Why this gap between the projection of technology and the market or economic reality?

Arguably, prophets of the New Machine Age get two things wrong – and this chapter will explain why. First, the relationship between man and machine is ambiguous. It has been a gradual and evolutionary process and, since the late 18th century, one that has not forced "huge social dislocation" upon society. On the contrary, periods of rapid innovation tend to be those that raise employment and labor compensation.

Secondly, the current sclerotic version of Western capitalism – including the regulations that embrace it – is not susceptible to radical innovation that contest markets. Believers in a technology blitz imagine a miraculous economy that, just like Pippi Longstocking, can suddenly lift a horse even if it does not have the physiology for it. But for the economy, innovation is far more about adaptation than creation – and the real issue of our time is not about what technologies are created but how fast companies, markets and regulations can diffuse them. Besides, no one knows what the future might hold in terms of technological breakthroughs and innovation. Therefore, projections of the future should not start with technology. The starting point should be Western economies today – and, unfortunately, they show every sign of reduced economic dynamism.

The New Machine Age

The New Machine Age – or the current technology hype – is a confluence of facts, fiction, and futuristic supposition. Revealingly, the hype rose to prominence amid the Great Recession and the sharp rise in unemployment that followed hard on its heels. Just like in other periods in history where there has been low growth and high unemployment, our time has elicited growing demands for explanation. The response has combined a fascination for new technology with fears about its consequences. Step back to the 1960s and you will find several similarities with contemporary technology discourse. The post-Second World War recovery cycle had ended and Western economic growth was slowing down. Like today the likely culprit was new technology and more specifically automation which was increasingly visible in industrial production.

Then as now, media was awash with panic inducing stories about how new technology would steal jobs. Beware of the Milwaukee-Matics, the *Life*

Magazine told its readers in 1963. Machine and computer development have reached "the point of no return for everybody" and next to the article were placed gloomy pictures showing the casualties of this innovation. 18 workingmen were standing in front of the Milwaukee-Matic, with the innovative machine ominously towering behind them. The machine, said *Life Magazine*, was capable of doing the work of 18 men. The future for industrial labor seemed ever more gruesome as there was no end to how much manufacturing could be transferred to the Milwaukee-Matic and other machines like it. A union member bitterly observed, "without a shorter work week, 60 percent of our members will be out of a job."[7]

Academics exacerbated the anxiety with a steady stream of dismal predictions. Economists, sociologist and psychologists amongst others sent jitters through society with predictions that life in the age of automation would be filled with unemployment, loneliness and meaningless. Although not everyone was fueling the panic, predictions of a bleak future were shared by many. Political leaders worried that with the seemingly unlimited productive capabilities of the new machines being developed, it would not be the same amount of demand for labor in the future. Richard Bellman, mathematician and father of dynamic programming, concluded in 1964 that technology advances thus far implied that it would only take two percent of the working population to produce what was needed for the American population. The British economist John Maynard Keynes had previously expressed the same sentiment, arguing that technological development would result in the abundance of leisure time as Westerners would only have to work fifteen hours a week.[8] Bellman went much further and predicted that his two percent scenario would happen within 25 years from the time of writing, and would be more likely to occur within 10 years.[9] Futurist Herman Kahn – the founder of the Hudson Institute, and famous for inspiring the character of *Dr. Strangelove* – belonged to a moderate group who estimated that Western economies would move to a four-day workweek and thirteen weeks of holiday.[10]

It was all perceived to be very serious, especially as the age featured its own version of the "average-is-over" thesis, contending that everyone with just "average" performance would be demoted to permanently low economic expectation. Nobelist George Thomson expressed the sentiments in a book from the late 1950s, when asking, "what is to happen to the really definitely stupid man," or even those of "barely average intelligence."[11] President Lyndon B. Johnson was so concerned that he appointed a Blue Ribbon Commission on automation and innovation. A group of independent scholars, calling themselves the Ad Hoc Committee, feared the "triple revolution" and the arrival of a new "cybernation" with its Promethean thirst for automation. Potentially, it was argued, automation could destroy the industrial fabric of the United States and cause mass unemployment a la the Great Depression.[12]

However, the majority of these fears turned out to be unfounded – and by the end of the decade, when the economy had improved and fears had abated, no one remembered what the panic had been about. Automation, like previous technological shifts, destroyed jobs – but it also created new ones, much safer and better-paid jobs at that. An automation blitz never occurred, the process took several decades as technology had to adjust to the composition of markets, companies and several other aspects than only the labor-substitution capacity of machines. Just as in the industrial revolution, automation did not win merely by showing up. It progressively improved and adjusted to the economic, social and institutional conditions for innovation.

Contemporary prophets of the New Machine Age make the same mistake. They judge the speed and quality of future innovation on what technological creation they see today, not on how the economy works. They labor under the notion that new technology works like instant coffee; just drop some innovation powder in hot water, stir, and – hoppla – the economy has perked up!

Intriguingly, they also seem to share the key economic gospels of previous eras of technology fascination and fear. *First*, they are occupied with the character and properties of technology – and assume that new technology will have an easy passage into the economy as long as the rational of technology is good enough (however that is defined). *Second*, and part of that same process, they assume that markets and structures of competition are naturally embracive of new technology – and that there is a good deal of economic dynamism that drives forward the forces of creative destruction with barely any friction or interruptions. *Third*, and last, they worry that employment opportunities will be destroyed in the wake of new innovations – upsetting the cycle of labor adaptation and relocation.

While there are differences in the quality of the arguments that are made – and some believers in the technology blitz have come up with thought-provoking and astute observations – they all share the economic gospels of the New Machine Age. They ignore two key features about fast and radical innovation. For new technology to power fast-and-furious innovation there has to be, *first*, entrepreneurship and, *second*, a general economic dynamism that is open to contestable competition. In contemporary Western economies both entrepreneurship and openness to contestability are in the decline and depress the capacity of the economy to foster and transact new technology.

Companies, entrepreneurs and complexity

While it is easy to be impressed by what modern science labs and tech innovators create, the chief lesson from economic history is that the economic benefit of new technology has less to do with them. As we have shown, the economic power of innovation comes mainly from its adoption, not from its creation. And adoption of technology requires resources for investment, entrepreneurship, and dynamic markets. The Western economy has moved in the wrong direction on all three accounts.

For technology to be adopted extensively, someone has to channel it from the inventor to the market. And that someone usually has to increase investment and capital expenditure for the invention to reach an audience. For Voice over IP (VoIP) to become the preferred technology of telephony, there has to be significant investments in high-speed telecommunication infrastructure for instance. The same logic also applies to human capital. If, for instance, a new surgical method for a cancer treatment is invented, there has to be investments in re-training of the surgeons and nurses before it can benefit patients. Or to take an example from the global warming debate: the problem with the struggle to reduce man-made greenhouse gases is not that scientists lack the knowledge and technology to radically cut emissions. But, rather the limits of capital – reductions of carbon emissions are slowed down because of costs and capital limits to quickly substitute old capital with new.

Therefore, no matter how genius they appear, do not expect ideas, technologies or innovations to make it big only by showing up. Even if factors like sunk costs do not hold companies back, nothing materializes into applied products or services without great effort – and a bit of luck. Innovation success is not a quick fix, or something that is parachuted externally into companies. The way companies and markets work, and the extent to which companies can muster their resources for that purpose, determine the success or failure of an innovation. Entrepreneurs control their own performance, but they cannot control unpredictable markets. Business failures would be a matter of choice if they did. Innovation based only on its own technological or corporate merits does not have the power to break into markets. Markets are far too complex for that to happen.

Take Google glasses as an example. The air over the San Francisco Bay area vibrated with anticipation when news circulated that Google Glass was due to be released. The optical head-mounted display was like the Ericsson's Cordless Web Screen that had been invented fifteen years earlier – "the next big thing." And if you have tried a pair, you know they are pretty cool. Google went much further than Ericsson ever did when they started to sell the glasses in May 2014. Yet, Google still failed and production was halted less than a year after release for the simple reason that sales were not good enough.

In the aftermath of this public mishap, Astro Teller – the head of Google X laboratories – explained that the company had failed by ". . . not making clear to everyone else that what was out was really just a prototype of the smart glassware, and too much bad publicity was really what killed Google Glass."[13] Failure happens – every day – and premature scaling is a common recipe for failure. But this was Google, a company with near limitless resources for planning and preparation. It is media savvy and its market reach is second to none leaving many to question how the company could have allowed such a publicized failure.

It was not the first time a Google project went sour for reasons that appeared obvious. Project Loon, for instance, was an idea to deliver Internet services via balloons floating close to space. It failed because the balloons could not stay afloat long enough due to leakages. A peek into the history books reveals that leakages have been a familiar problem to the ballooning community for over hundred years, if not longer. One spectacular incident occurred in 1897 when Swedish adventurer S. A. Andrée and his crew failed to cross the North Pole in a hydrogen balloon because of this problem. Had it not, they would have been pioneers of balloon journeys across the Pole. Now they were probably killed by polar bears as they were trying to make it back home by foot, but that is another story. Google X staff fortunately did not have to worry about grumpy bears and they were still around to draw the right conclusions from the failure. To Astro Teller the leaking balloons were a good experiment and a lesson in trial-and-error process of innovation and business development. "Sometimes the most interesting failures," he concluded, "are the ones that you don't expect. Particularly, when they are something that you think will be the easiest part of the project and it turns out to be the hardest part of the project instead."[14] Tech failures are just one of the problems faced by new innovations.

New technologies have to fight for a place in the market. Take electronic payment and wallets as an example – a market and a technology that many oddly consider not to be very complex. With the introduction of digital payment technologies, the electronic wallet was initially considered a fundamental challenge to the payment market. Credit card companies and other established firms, using the old payment system, were thought to face a difficult future, or perhaps no future at all. The old guard had supposedly little resistance to offer when new and smarter ways to pay were suddenly introduced. The leather wallet was a thing of the past; the only thing consumers needed was a smart phone. Yet the incumbent payment companies are still here – and they are not about to become a footnote in economic history. It rather seems their future is pretty bright.

The reason is market complexity. Credit card companies that came into existence in the 1940s and 1950s developed their businesses in a tough environment of conservative users and merchants, dealing with old habits, security, emotions and different payment cultures. They were forced from the start to create business models that delivered value, and those models extended far beyond the use of the plastic cards. Plastic cards is an innovation introduced by American Express in 1959, which made payment more convenient. And that is how the sector has grown – by creating value in addition to immediate money transactions for people and storeowners. A company stepping into this world, armed with only a technology, will not get far.

The first universal electronic wallet was introduced in 2000.[15] The use of electronic wallets is likely to increase, but to generate a lot of value, electronic wallet companies will have to become much more than their technology or else remain satisfied with being technology suppliers. Many e-payment newcomers are now working with the established market structure for that reason. Asked why, Will Wang Graylin, the CEO of LoopPay, a digital wallet company focusing on the interface between merchants and credit card firms, explained to *MIT Technology Review*: "Think about the infrastructure and how long it took to create that. It is very difficult to change merchant behavior."[16] No one knows how this market will evolve, but markets, competition, and consumer behavior – not only the technology itself – will determine its future success.

The same is true for another promising technology that can be applied to the payments market: blockchain or mutual distributed ledger technology (like bitcoin). The market clearly sees a big potential in blockchain technology. It could reduce the costs and risks in transactions, and create a far better system for information sharing in financial markets. Some has billed it as a greater technological leap than the Internet for capital markets. Perhaps it will be, but the hype around the technology is premature and the expectation of big market changes is an aspiration. A study from 2016 of how market actors work with this ledger technology concludes that "the understanding of the technology lags well behind the hype." The technology, the authors argue, face the problem of "excess inertia"[17], because the users of the technology are locked in to existing market structures. And they point to a common feature in the resistance to new technology: "private profit incentives are not strong enough for individual firms to adopt a more efficient standard or technology, even when adoption would reduce costs for the industry as a whole."[18]

What all these examples show is that there is no such thing as a superior technology that effortlessly sweeps through markets. What is required, however, is plenty of hard work, repeated processes of trial and error, and the temperance needed to not let errors get under the skin. For Google, leaking balloons and unhappy glass customers should feed back into the next generation of balloons and glasses – or other completely different projects. Google, like others, will certainly fail in future – and hopefully they will – because failure is part of the innovation process. Without failures, nothing really new would be innovated. Aviation security, it is said, is "written in blood." Likewise, the history of innovation is full of wrecked business attempts.

Markets are becoming increasingly complex because of vertical and horizontal specialization and a confluence of perpetual trial-and-error processes and generations of technologies, traditions and customer values. Value chains are increasingly sliced up into smaller parts, and today fortified turrets of firms stand in close ranks protecting their market territories and firm boundaries. New technologies that span over several territories, boundaries and areas of specialization become a sluggish affair because the newcomer has to fight each turret to establish a foothold. Sunk costs bring additional layers of complexity that stands in the way of contestable innovation. Some find it appealing to look for simplifications – and the less someone knows about a market and business value, the easier it appears. This is where the analysis from the proponents of the New Machine Age often goes wrong. They simplify too much and ignore the actual realities of how markets are structured and where companies generate value. Their inclination is rather to focus only on what is seen at the surface of markets. They compare technologies as if they existed in a vacuum. But technologies that fail or succeed in the end do so because of economics.

That is not a new phenomenon. Societies have always had the tendency to overlook business and market complexity, and perhaps it has something to do with impatience, or the habit of favoring the quick and easy answers over the long and difficult ones. But there is another factor at play as well, at least in the gospels of the New Machine Age: the strange habit of taking the views from innovators and entrepreneurs as the final judgements about whether their new technology will make it or not. There are some things, author Hjalmar Soderberg once wrote, you have to be an expert in order not to understand, and there is a similar logic with innovators and their technology. Those who are too close to the technology are at risk of getting carried away. And as everyone that has been part of building businesses knows, entrepreneurship thrives on passion but the same sentiment often also stands in the way of sober market analysis. Entrepreneurs in general exaggerate their technological achievements and tend to simplify business obstacles. When asked about their innovation, they promote it as much as they can and sometimes convince unsuspecting listeners that they have come farther than they actually have. The flip side of passion is that it makes entrepreneurs biased and often blind to the shortcomings of their products and business models. Just like in other love affairs, everything looks different in corporateville when emotions run high. Most of all, passion makes them blind to market complexity and the gap between innovation and a market-adapted product.

Do not get us wrong – the passion of entrepreneurs is exactly why societies should appreciate and encourage them. Entrepreneurs are usually unaware of their intemperance as they tend to be head over heels in love with the products they promote or the company they run. If they were not, few new companies would make it past their first birthday. Passion is why they sacrifice time with family and friends or neglect private interests and put their money and reputation on the line.

When technologies reach markets for the first time they are seldom *that* good because markets are never *that* simplistic. Consequently, business planning for how new products should develop gets complicated – at best. Stanford business professor George Foster, arguing against the simplistic view of market success, contends that the "hockey-stick world," where growth takes a sudden turn upwards like the shape of a hockey stick, "is a fantasy." In the real world, start-ups go through "a lot of jarring ups and downs, more like a high-speed game of snakes and ladders." He should know because he has analysed 158 000 early companies, and almost two thirds of them experienced one or more consecutive years of decline in the third to fifth year of existence.[19] Behind those numbers hides an army of entrepreneurs battling with market complexity every single day.

Take driverless cars. Listening to the current hype may make you want to own and drive one soon. But, the technological development of driverless cars has been going on for decades and from a market perspective, the world has not come particularly far. Industry analysts believe it will take many years for the necessary infrastructure to be in place before they become commonplace. Not more than 20 percent of the cars sold in 2015 had embedded connectivity solutions. Business advisory AlixPartners, for instance, think "Nationwide autonomous driving infrastructures may not be available before 2035."[20] And that forecast assumes thorny liability issues will have been addressed by then, allowing markets without substantial legal barriers to develop.

The world economy would be a far better place if intelligent vehicles or other radical innovations would speed up. Instant innovation is a good desire, but it makes a bad partner for understanding how markets – or capitalism writ large – work today. The gospels of the New Machine Age ignore that reality and almost take for granted that there is an easy passage from the tech laboratory to the market. They appreciate entrepreneurs and their passion, but they do not capture the complexity of entrepreneurship and markets. Markets are difficult to read, let alone manoeuvre, even for skilled entrepreneurs. Markets are embracive and exclusive at the same time. They are fluid yet stable. They are never one-dimensional but always changing. Thus innovation can never succeed just by showing up.

Capitalism and economic dynamism

A modern economy, begins Nobelist Edmund Phelps in his odyssey of flourishing societies, is "not a present-day economy but rather an economy with a considerable degree of dynamism – that is, the will and the capacity and aspiration to innovate."[21] How do Western economies fare according to that standard? Arguably, the West is moving backwards rather than forwards. No doubt there is innovation and dynamism in the economy. But the capitalist spirit of contesting markets has weakened, and even if there is big innovation in some sectors, the general degree of innovation and dynamism has been cooling for a couple of decades. Managerialists occupy the central posts of business and politics, and they are on a quest to make markets less rather than more dynamic. Consequently, the economic payoff from the innovation that is generated is less than it should be.

Western economies have become middle age. When firms get older they tend to stick to the technologies they have for as long as they can. Methods, applications and some technologies are gradually modernized, but in a controlled and limited way. Neither the "capacity" nor the "aspiration" to increase innovation and speed up change improves when a company grows older. It logically follows, then, that if the total pool of companies in any economy increases in average age, the economy congeals. It is a simplification, of course, but compared to markets with a younger population of companies, the middle-aged economy looks rigid. New firms bring new ideas and innovation; older and saturated firms generally do not.

If Western economies were now under a technology blitz it would be visible in the data. For instance, we would likely see a high firm entry-and-exit rate. It is not just that new companies would enter at a higher rate, but also that older companies would exit because middle or old-aged companies make bad revolutionaries. However, the data tells a completely different story. In the United States, for example, firm entry-and-exit rates have been on a declining trend since the end of the 1970s, if not longer (see Figure 8.1). While there have been deviations from the trend, the direction of travel is undoubtedly clear and, frankly, proof of a dramatic change in American capitalism. The proportion of new firms entering the American economy has steadily abated, from a level of approximately 16 percent, to slightly over ten percent today.

Firm exit rates show a similar pattern. Firms are not leaving, or being forced out of business, at the same rate as they used to. From the end of the 1970s to 2012 – with a short spike during the Great Recession – firm exits are going down.[22] Markets are getting older too when companies age. The proportion of "mature firms," defined as companies that are eleven years and older, has increased dramatically. Half of all firms in the US in 2012 were eleven years or older compared to only one third of all firms in 1987.[23] This is the face of middle-aged economies – and it is hardly material to support the thesis of growing economic dynamism.

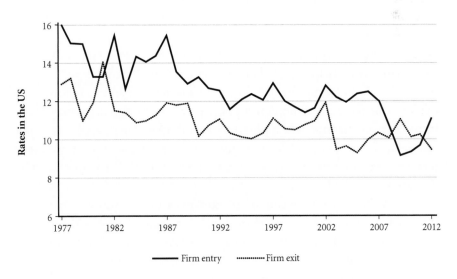

Source: United States Census Bureau and Hathaway and Litan, "Declining business dynamism in the United States."

Figure 8.1 Firm entry and exit rates in the United States, 1977–2012

Diminishing turnover rates are an unhealthy sign because, aside from bringing new technologies, it is new firms that challenge incumbents, and – usually – create better-paid jobs. Their value for the economy is shown through increasing productivity growth. But as Western economies mature, people tend to stay hired in old firms. While that might be appealing to some, especially if job satisfaction is good, it is a recipe for a society distancing itself from a dynamic economy. Old firms hired about 80 percent of the total US workforce in 2012 compared to 65 percent in 1987.[24] Over the same period, the share of US people employed by start-ups in the private sector almost halved.[25]

Entrepreneurship is also on an ageing trend. In 1989, almost eleven percent of young households (thirty and younger) owned shares in private companies; in 2013 that number was down to less than four percent. In 1996, people between 20 and 30 launched approximately 35 percent of all start-ups in America; in 2014 they only launched 18 percent of them.[26]

Start-ups and young ownership is the capitalist version of the canary in the coalmine, warning miners of toxic air. Naturally, young companies and entrepreneurs only stand for a small part of the economy, but they are sensitive and responsive to trends. Unfortunately, the situation is likely to get worse. A study from Babson College, for instance, confirms that the United States is on a downward trend. About 24 percent of people between the ages of 25 and 34 said fear of failure kept them from aiming at entrepreneurial stardom in 2001. Today, that share has risen to almost 41 percent.[27]

Out of the pool of existing companies, a smaller share of them can be classified as high-growth firms. Around three percent of all firms qualified as high-growth companies in 1994-1997, but between 2008 and 2011 that share had been cut by half.[28] True, the latter period came amid a crisis-recovery cycle and it may be that declining business dynamism followed on the heels of the general downturn. However, that is not the lesson from history: crises, for sure, tend to hit output and corporate size, but they also create good opportunities for new firms with the capacity to grow. New fortunes are often minted in times of crises. However, that was not the pattern during the Great Recession.

Nor is the negative trend of market dynamism confined to young start-ups or high-growth firms in the US. It is a generic problem in Western economies. The share of start-up firms, observes the OECD, generally declined from 2001 until 2011.[29] Out of the eighteen countries studied, all but two had "declining start–up rates." That evidence does not sit comfortably with the gospels of the New Machine Age. If new entrepreneurs are increasingly less frequent almost everywhere in the West – and especially in the United States, traditionally the heart of the Western innovative economy – where is that illusive revolutionary technology hiding?

One possible answer could be that it is inside established firms. Economies can still be dynamic if change occurs within older companies. It goes against much of what economic history tells us about dynamism and companies, but perhaps times have changed to the favor of the middle-aged firms. Unfortunately, that proposition seems incorrect as well when looking at the trends in job creation and destruction. Studying the data from the US Bureau of Labor Statistics (see Figure 8.2), the trend is moving in the wrong direction. Rates of job creation and destruction have been going south for more than two decades – and that trend applies to most sectors. There was a surge in job creation during the second half of the 1990s, as a result of the ICT boom. But when it ended, the figures for job creation returned to the long-term trend. Taking the West farther into the territory of economic lethargy.

A counter argument used by some is that the falling level of dynamism in the capitalist economy is because certain sectors have been shielded from it, especially those that are pushing the innovation frontier. It is easy to understand the logic of that argument and how it is reflected in economic history. Simply, some sectors tend to be more dynamic than others. Moreover, today's frontier sectors represent a smaller part of the general

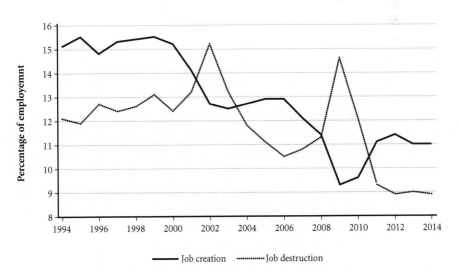

Source: Bureau of Labor Statistics, Business Employment Dynamics Database
Figure 8.2 Job Creation and Destruction Rates, Total Private Sector
(1992:Q3-2014:Q4)

economy (e.g. ICT) and they may therefore not be fully appreciated when they are hidden in big, aggregate, and economy-wide data that averages down the effect of one sector.

However, that argument fails to convince. The direct contribution by one sector to the economy will always be limited because most sectors are small. More importantly, frontier sectors should represent general-purpose technologies, goods and services – and their main contribution to the health of the economy should be shown by their indirect contribution to investment, productivity and growth. Take a company like Facebook. Its main impact on the economy is not that it improves the level of investment and productivity growth in its sector. It is far too small for that effect to happen. Facebook's chief contribution to the economy is that it improves economic behavior in other sectors.

There is even more conclusive evidence against the hypothesis of discriminate dynamism. Investment in ICT equipment when measured as share of GDP has been on the decline since the beginning of the millennium. In other words, a smaller share of GDP is invested in typical ICT goods today compared to 15 years ago. Investment expenditures on software have largely been flat since 1995. While there are differences between real and nominal expenditures, which we will turn to soon, the trend of declining and flat investment in ICT hardware and software, respectively, is difficult to marry with the thesis of the New Machine Age. Digital services are not about equipment, but they require new and better hardware, and there is a need for more of it if better software is to be quickly diffused in the economy. And when looking at the data, the investment peak occurs at the same time as the role of ICT manufacturing value-added for the total manufacturing in the US economy reaches its apex – and, importantly, when the annual decline in ICT prices slows down. ICT goods still get cheaper every year, but that is not a significant trend anymore.[30]

Moreover, the slowdown in dynamism also happened within high technology companies. Business dynamism in the high-tech sectors or technology firms increased at the time of the ICT spurt in the 1990s, but then it reverted to trend – a steady decline in turnover rates of new companies in the high-tech sector. What is more, according to a study by the Kauffman Foundation, "business dynamism, as measured by the pace of job reallocation, has declined in the high-tech sector in the post-2002 period" with the pace of decline exceeding "that of the overall economy."[31] One can think of several explanations, but the sheer fact that the technology sector has become less dynamic than other sectors generally in the American economy directly contradicts the notion of a current or pending innovation revolution.

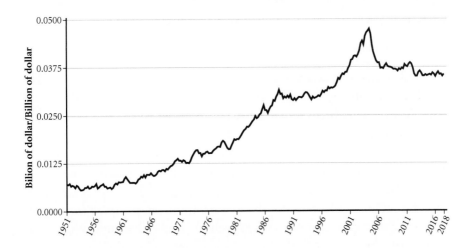

Source: Federal Reserve Bank of St. Louis.
Figure 8.3 Investment in information technology slow down

That is a disappointing conclusion for believers in the New Machine Age. Indicators of economic and business dynamism suggest the US economy is on a downward trend. Europe is doing even worse. Yet technology firms should be the odd men out, and not because their average performance is below par. If the hypothesis of a New Machine Age is correct, they should show a trend similar to the 1990s – a period when technology firms were clearly supporting a general economic upswing rather than representing a barren economy heading south.

What is wrong – the map or the reality?

Big claims require big evidence. And what should make people doubt rather than accept the promise of fast-and-furious innovation is that it is thin on actual confirmation. In fact, stripped of its technology determinism, anecdotes from the lab-floor of technology, and the general fascination for what computers and algorithms can do in the future, the proponents of the New Machine Age do not have much to offer. There is a plurality of spurious economic claims about what is happening in today's economy, but few of them are backed up with hard data. So if you wade through the gospels looking for the big evidence, you are excused for thinking, that "there is no there there," to use the prose of Gertrude Stein.

Unsurprisingly, believers in the pending innovation revolution disagrees with our portrait of a Western economy low on energy. Some might agree that in general economic and business dynamism are on the decline – and may even admit that the long-term trend of general market contestability has been on the decline. But, that is as far as most go. And to dispute evidence and data about weak economic dynamism they claim that current methodologies to measure the growth of productivity, prices and GDP fail to capture technological shifts generally and the current innovation spurt specifically. Consequently, the real economy is driven by innovation more than is suggested by economic data. It is statistics, not the real economy, which shows the innovation illusion. There is a problem with the map, not the reality. National accounts are rather like Potemkin villages – they hide the reality.

This argument comes in three different instalments. *First*, recent economic data covers a period when cyclical effects have hidden the structural shifts taking place in the Western economy. *Second*, there is a growing disconnect between recorded data in national accounts and the real improvements of products that new technology has created. In that way, the real or social value of innovation is higher than the recorded market value of the same innovation, and the gap between them has grown recently. In short, *Grand Theft Auto V*, the popular video game, is better than *Grand Theft Auto IV*, even if they were both retailed at the same nominal price.[32] That improvement, however, is not captured in the national accounts, and in a world where real improvements are often free for customers, basic concepts about productivity are grossly distorted. And with increasing digitization of economies, the distortion increases. *Third*, the decoupling of productivity and labor income proves the transformational change of technology and the unequal distributional effects of technological gains means there are larger economic effects that national accounts fail to record.

The first argument can easily be dismissed. Regardless of the direction that US or European productivity growth has taken in the past decade, it has not been cyclical. In reality the cyclical effects on total factor productivity have substantially weakened over time to become acyclical and labor productivity has been countercyclical – going up in recessions.[33]

Technology optimists such as economists Erik Brynjolfson and Andrew McAffe would disagree. In their otherwise important book *The Second Machine Age*, they claim "parts of the recent slowdown simply reflects the Great Recession and its aftermath."[34] They argue that US productivity growth "in the decade following the year 2000 exceeded even the high growth rates of the roaring 1990s, which in turn was higher than 1970s or 1980s growth rates had been."[35]

These propositions do not stand up to scrutiny. Since 1970 there has been one productivity spurt, but otherwise there has been a downward trend. Robert Gordon dates the productivity spurt to the period between 1996 and 2004, and other experts on US productivity agree. It thus ended before the credit boom and bust that took place between 2005 and 2010.[36] Consequently, the US economy was showing a declining trend in productivity growth before the Great Recession, and the pattern after 2010 was no different from that before the crisis. Noted productivity expert John Fernald concludes, "by the mid-2000s, the low hanging fruit of IT-based innovation had been plucked."[37] It follows that the data simply does not show the suggested pattern of productivity growth – a continuous, decade-by-decade rise since the 1970s.

The second argument – about a growing disconnect between recorded and actual improvements – is more intriguing. There are real and known deficiencies in GDP statistics and Charles Bean documented several of them in his 2016 *Independent Review of UK Economic Statistics*. It is obvious that, first, there is a gap between the market and social values of innovation. Economists call this "price index bias" – and it implies that there should be an upward revaluation of real GDP if all the consumer surplus that innovation brings are accounted for. And, secondly, it is only natural that backward looking data-collection like that for real GDP always need to catch up to account for perpetually changing business models. So the issue is not whether there is a problem in measuring innovation; that debate was settled a long time ago. The real debate should be about whether the problem has increased or decreased over time, despite the regular improvements made in price indexes by statistical authorities.

Unfortunately, those who make the claim of growing mismeasurement of innovation do not have much conclusive evidence supporting their thesis. When asked to present the evidence, their language become ambiguous and obscure references are employed to support vague conclusions.[38] Some suggests qualitative methodologies to measure real GDP and productivity, and some of them are useful as indicators of technological change and innovation. For instance, a popular reference in the literature has been that most people would prefer to be treated with today's healthcare than the healthcare in 1980, even if real GDP data would not support the view that healthcare has improved between then and now.[39] Likewise, most people would prefer to use a computer produced in 2015 rather than 2005, because the former is much better, even if the higher quality has not caused the price to go up. However, comparisons like these are misleading. Most people would naturally choose today's rather than 1980's healthcare, but it is highly questionable that mismeasurement between those times were larger than between 1945 and 1980, the prior 35-year period.

Others go further and make claims that basically imply measuring something else than progress in value added, for instance incorporating social and environmental impacts that were never the focus of the GDP measure. Nor is GDP a measure of general economic well-being; it is impossible to one statistic that can reflect all factors that determine well-being. New technologies can emerge without leading to innovation – and innovation can emerge without improving value added. The modern Internet economy gives many people a chance for a better life because they can work from anywhere they like, but that does not necessarily make them more productive. We can use apps to track physical exercise and measure sleep, but these and other apps are for many users good examples of Krugman's thesis of technologies that are "more fun than fundamental." Social media makes life richer and happier for some, but any serious claim that it generates more economic value than gets measured need also to come up with a measurement of potential negative effects, e.g. how social media can steal time from work. Those who prefer measures of productivity based on the amount of data generated need to answer a basic question: is more data always better than less data? If not, how should we judge what growth in data intensity that leads to greater market value added and what does not? The longer a measure distance itself from market GDP, the more it will face problems where the solution often depends on individual preferences and a person's politics.

There are economic observations that strongly contradicts the argument that the data economy leads to greater mismeasurement than in the past. If current technological change would create more productivity than observed, it is difficult to see how innovation-based productivity growth would not lead to a growth in labor productivity. Yet labor productivity, as documented in chapter 2, has been on a similar downward trend as TFP.

Furthermore, the productivity slowdown has been universal for Western economies and shows next to no variation in the slowdown when compared to ICT intensity in the economy. Furthermore, productivity differences between states in America cannot be explained by ICT intensity.[40] If there were a significant mismeasurement problem, there would naturally be a correlation between productivity slowdowns and ICT intensity, but there is not. Revealingly, that conclusion also holds for comparisons between the developed economies that have experienced a productivity slowdown.[41]

Moreover, if it was true that recorded economic output was significantly below the actual value, there would be at least one sector where that relationship did not hold – the sector that produces and services all the digital hard and software. That sector, at least, should have shown an incremental growth in their real revenues and thus providing support for the mismeasurement thesis. However, it is difficult to find evidence supporting that view. The growth in revenues and productivity of this sector is simply too small to account for even a fraction of the mismeasurement.[42]

It is often suggested that the huge drop in the prices of software is a good example of quality improvements not being registered in the national accounts.[43] That is partly true, even if changes in price indexes have enabled statistical authorities to capture product enhancements not reflected in the retail price. Yet the biggest drop in software prices occurred between 1985 and 2000, with barely any movement in prices over the past fifteen years.[44] Such observations lend support to the thesis of a roaring 1990s rather than a pending data revolution, and that is true for much of the other evidence used by supporters of the New Machine Age.[45]

Take the example of Facebook or other online media and entertainment services that have grown over the past decade. What is the real GDP value of Facebook, and does it correspond with its recorded value of advertisement revenues? Put like that, it is obvious that the consumer surplus of Facebook exceeds the recorded value. But it is also a misleading proposition. The real consumer surplus of services with declining prices, or that are free for the consumer, hardly boosts economic growth even if more experimental accounting is used. Online entertainment and information services that have become free, suggests a study, would raise US economic growth over a limited period of time by 0.019 percent per year if a greater part of the consumer surplus was accounted for.[46]

However, it is highly questionable if such measures really are merited. Online entertainment and information may in some ways be classified as "free," but in other ways they are accounted for in traditional economic statistics. The average household in the West pays for it through broadband, network, and television subscriptions – and expenditures on such services have gone up substantially. While it is free to watch some movies on the Internet, the new HBO series or the blockbuster movie do not come for free, in fact, they are charged for at far higher prices than before the entry of mass online entertainment. The fact that a lot of entertainment and information is free at marginal cost is because the marginal value of those services is pretty low. It is a standard lessons of microeconomics that marginal cost equals marginal value – and new digital services are better than offline services to exploit the relation between costs and value for consumers, especially at the margin.

Present criticism of GDP standards often resembles the idea some twenty years ago about a "new economy" that would change the way the economy works. Like the belief in the new economy, there are charges of GDP mismeasurement that confuse definitions of GDP and value-added creation in the economy. Some of it goes back to corporate valuation: high valuation of companies is a sign of markets understanding the real value generation of, say, free online services that statistical authorities are not capturing. However, despite high corporate valuations, many technology firms obviously struggle to develop sustainable business models. Take Amazon for instance. It accrued earnings in the last twenty years of two billion US dollars in comparison to General Electric that earned 15 billion US dollars in 2015 alone. Still Amazon had a higher market cap beginning of 2016, with a price/earnings ratio of 1000.[47] Amazon has been a pioneer among Internet companies and has a stronger business model compared to most younger firms. Many of them, including so-called unicorns – not yet publicly listed companies valued to over one billion US dollar – are still very far from balancing operating costs and revenues. Some lose money for every new customer they attract. Instead of sales revenues and earnings, they depend on regular outside cash injections to stay afloat. That throws doubt on the idea of "free" services, but also raises questions about companies lacking customers willing to pay for what they do. If that is the case, do they still bring great innovations and customer value that should be recorded in GDP data?

The question has no straightforward answer. Companies can of course deliver real economic progress without making money. Some deliberately run negative earnings to expand quickly; others may bring consumer and social value that have not yet been understood. However, high digital corporation valuations are often not evidence for strong business models in the making, or that the world has yet to grasp the full generation of value by the company. Such valuations rather reflect smart structures of financing. Equity investors are in the business of buying and selling company shares. And the price of a share is the result of both internal and external factors – such as capital market trends, regulatory frameworks, and substitute goods. To safeguard investments from changing dynamics of markets, investors naturally protect themselves. Later investors (referring to investment stages) routinely use liquidation preferences to guarantee returns even if future liquidation valuations disappoint. Layers upon layers of liquidation preferences are virtually norm and it help drive company valuation by allowing for investors to accept higher valuations. If expectations are not met, investors are still protected and get their money back before founders and employers. And it all looks good from the outside; it shows business strength and attracts employees, customers, partners and new investors. But many times it is a house of cards.

While it is true that traditional economic indicators do not capture the full value of innovation, it is neither a novel insight nor one where it is easy to determine if the problem has grown or not. It has been the case since the dawn of innovation that a share of the consumer surplus has not been captured in the price. That is true for electricity, automobiles, household technology, medicines and more. Electric lighting enabled people to use the dark hours of the day to do such things as reading. Still today, the introduction of electricity revolutionizes life for schoolchildren in rural Africa, but the social value or consumer surplus of that change is not captured in GDP statistics. The automobile gave people more freedom – and, indirectly, reduced horse manure on the streets, a consumer surplus that was never paid for. There is good reason to believe, that the mismeasurement of productivity has declined over the ages simply because innovation in the past had greater social impact than innovation today and that the amount of unpaid household work – where a good part of the unrecorded consumer surplus emerged – has been greatly reduced. Perhaps it is difficult for some to dispense with the notion that online media, entertainment and the app world are revolutionary services but if they are compared to the innovations that have radically increases life expectancy over the past century or so, it is easier to see how many innovations in the past have had a far greater social value.

Like so much else in the gospels of the New Machine Age, the criticism about productivity, real GDP and consumer surplus suffers from blindness to other periods in history than our current time. It is as if the period of innovation is a recent phenomenon, something that emerged with the Internet. No doubt there are many new digital products that make our lives freer and happier, but it has been a central feature of GDP statistics ever since they were first assembled that they have not captured all positive social contributions of innovation. It is misleading to claim that mismeasurement explains the long-term decline in the Western economy. Asked if the current productivity puzzle of low output and high employment in United Kingdom has anything to do with growth underestimation, Charles Bean responded that he is "pretty confident it won't explain it away. My guess is it is a small part of it."[48] The emergence of the Internet was a radical and game-changing event. It will continue to generate new value added in the future – and, hopefully, make lives happier. But previous generations have been through similar periods in life and many of them probably had a far greater impact on their lives than the Internet had on ours.

Technology and income – are they decoupling?

The third instalment of the argument requires delving into the relationship between productivity and income. Harking back to Marx's "reserve army of the unemployed" – the theory that real wages cannot grow or follow productivity[49] – some pundits now claim that while productivity has increased, jobs and wages have not, or that the age-old correlation between productivity and wages has turned against the interest of labor. The decoupling thesis is an old myth that has refused to go away. It tends to emerge when unemployment is exceptionally high – and now, when merged with the thesis of an innovation revolution, it has raised the fear of technological unemployment to new heights.

The modern version of decoupling is specious, to say the least. It requires a big leap of imagination to claim that the corporate sector has been thriving on shrinking or slow-growing labor income over the past decades. While there is a post-crisis trend of unusually high profit margins in some countries, the long-term trend for the US, the UK, France, Italy, Belgium and other advanced economies is stable, prone to mean reversion, and not exactly ammunition for the Marxian view of capital using and abusing labor.[50] Even in Germany, where profits margins have accelerated remarkably fast in the decade leading up to 2005, there has lately been a correcting return to mean.

However, the decoupling thesis, or variants thereof, has received serious support. Brooking's Bill Galston, for instance, has argued that "(t)he Great Decoupling of wages and benefits from productivity, the biggest economic story of the past 40 years, shows no sign of ending."[51] In *The Second Machine Age*, economists Erik Brynjolfsson and Andrew McAffe argue that median hourly wages have only increased by 0.1 percent annually from 1973 to 2011 at the same time as productivity increased by 1.56 percent annually.[52] In the *Rise of the Robots*, Martin Ford uses a similar observation to argue: productivity gains are not matched by workers gains in terms of jobs and pay. The Economic Policy Institute, a think tank in Washington, DC, has aggregated the differences between productivity and pay, and claims that, while productivity in the United States grew by almost 75 percent between 1973 and 2010, hourly compensation for workers only increased by slightly more than 9 percent.[53]

The debate on the other side of the pond is no different: in most advanced European economies, too, labor compensation is said to have moved away from productivity growth in a way that hurts labor. And for both America and Europe, the debate stretches into the issue of employment. If the debate itself is an indicator of how views are shifting, there seems to be growing support for the proposition that productivity growth destroys jobs. If productivity increases, the argument goes, there is less need for labor. The hypothesis is pretty intuitive. After all, many industries have for decades downsized their labor force while the volume of output has multiplied with the help of robots and automation.

Intuition, however, is a poor source of information. While the relation between productivity and employment is "ambivalent"[54], to quote three leading economists, it does not lend support to the view that employment is depressed by productivity growth. Importantly, total employment in an economy changes with business cycles and reflects stronger forces in the economy than productivity growth, like how demand is influenced by fiscal and monetary policy. For instance, the US lost seven million jobs between 2007 and 2009, and there was productivity growth in the economy during these two years, but few, if any, would tender the view that there is a causal relation between the loss in jobs and productivity during these years.

This may seem like an extreme example, but the thrust of serious analysis suggests that productivity growth does not decrease demand for labor and that the relationship between productivity and unemployment is trivial. Productivity growth, however, changes the composition of labor. Naturally, productivity growth and innovation can lead to capital substituting for labor, and it is generally acknowledged that economies have technological unemployment. Yet such employment tends to be short term. Productivity growth creates more output and unless there are serious distortions in the economy it leads to a greater demand sucking up unutilized labor, and in the aggregate productivity and employment tend to follow each other. At that level, there is no total economy trade-off between labor and productivity, even if companies and industries can face that choice.[55]

A study by the McKinsey Global Institute, a *chiffrephile* agent in the world of management consultants, brings home that point about short and long term effects. They looked at the relation between productivity and employment and found a strong correlation between productivity and employment in the United States between 1929 and 2009. Moreover, they could also show that the negative effects on employment that sometime occur when productivity growth speeds up is short term and fades away over the long term.[56] For instance, if that 80-year period is divided up and analysed annually, productivity and employment grew together in 69 percent of the time while employment went down at a time of productivity growth in 21 percent of those eighty years. However, if the same data is analysed on a rolling ten-year basis, there is close to full correlation between productivity and employment growth.

But what about the decoupling story: is that thesis more convincing? No, is the simple answer. Many people offering their thoughts on the subject seem to lament slow or slowing growth of labor compensation and greater wage inequality within economies.[57] Yet it is harder to confirm (or reject) the decoupling thesis for the simple reason that there have been so many changes in total labor compensation and, more generally, in how labor markets work. Standard indicators grossly misrepresent labor income and how it relates to productivity. Studying only the development of wages, productivity or gross output especially ignores the fact that employment remuneration has become much more dispersed and differentiated since 1970. Nominal wages are still the main plank of remuneration, but it is not the only one. That was true also in the past, but the way worker compensation has evolved over the past decades makes it critical to get the total picture of compensation before comparing labor compensation growth with productivity growth.

"Wages tells you almost nothing," says Wells Fargo chief economist John Silvia.[58] If all employer compensations to labor are considered – from higher social security payments to longer holiday and childcare support – the result is different from just take-home pay. Almost one third of worker compensation in the US is made up of benefits. While wages increased by 2 percent from 2004 until today, benefits increased by 16 percent over the same period.[59] Cross the Atlantic and you will find benefits and taxes also play a significant role in total labor compensation. Labor is heavily taxed in Europe and if the development of taxes is not included in analysis of labor and capital income shares, an all too common error, the income of capital gets miscalculated. If governments tax labor more than before it simply means that the government, not capital, is taking a bigger share of the piece. It does not stop there. Pay of skilled-workers increased faster than blue-collar workers, so any comparison between the past and now has to account for growing wage inequality.

Where do all these observations take us? Harvard economist Robert Lawrence has measured net (not gross) output per hour and adjusted compensation with the same deflator, to allow for comparisons over time, and comes to a sobering conclusion for the United States. (Figure 8.4 tracks a similar development of net income and the full compensation, or real product compensation, to labor). All things taken together, the gap between productivity and compensation growth between 1970 and 2000 generally is not a great decoupling drama. There is a decoupling but, unsurprisingly, it

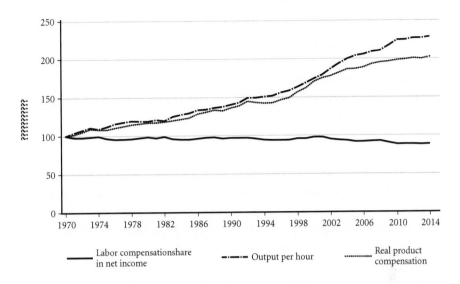

Source: Bureau of Labor Statistics and US Bureau of Economic Analysis
Figure 8.4 Output per hour, real product compensation and labor compensation share in income

emerged recently and is concentrated in the noughties, and especially the post-2008 period.[60] That result confirms what previous research has shown. Similarly, when using other approaches to income inequality, such as household income structured on age and cohort, it shows that household income followed the expected track up to the 2000s but then deteriorated.[61]

A different version of the argument suggests that labor's share of total income has fallen, and, as a consequence, labor compensation has not kept pace with productivity, however muted the latter has been. When this form of decoupling is associated with the past decade rather than previous ones, it prompts people to suggest that the villains are robots and machines, or the falling relative cost of investment goods, to be more precise.[62] Perhaps there is something to that story that is true, or will be in the future[63], but there is not a longer trend neither in the US nor across advanced economies. The differences that exist between countries in the functional income distribution rather suggest that there are other and more important factors at play.

In Germany, for example, there is evidence of a fall in the labor-income share, but there are several local factors that explain that trend. Germany went through a reunification in the early 1990s that had profound effects on the labor market.[64] Eastern laborers were not as productive as Western laborers and when wages were not allowed to manifest the full effects of the productivity differential they got depressed.

By way of contrast, Harvard's Martin Feldstein shows in a study that in the US nonfarm sector – operating under quite different conditions from Germany after the reunification – there was hardly any difference in labor-income share between 1970 and 2006, provided both output and income are deflated uniformly.[65] Generally, it is unlikely, as some has suggested, that technological innovation is causing decoupling.[66] For countries that have experienced a significant structural shift in the pattern of investment toward ICT, it is highly likely that part of the explanation for the falling share of labor income can be found in the definition of capital used i.e. using gross rather than net values of capital. This is important because ICT investments depreciates faster than other investments, and if there is a relative shift towards higher ICT intensity in investments it basically implies that neither the labor nor the capital income share have gone up. It just means that a greater share of output needs to be spent on maintaining the level of possible production.[67]

Robert Lawrence points to a set of explanations to why there has been a slight decoupling, and suggests that the story is not just about a capital substitution for labor for the simple reason that capital-labor ratios actually have fallen in sectors showing the biggest decline in labor income shares. He finds in a study that three sectors explain about two thirds of the falling labor-income share in the United States manufacturing sector, and in all three sectors new technology tends to augment labor rather than capital. In other words, the marginal product of labor has gone up faster than the marginal product of capital.[68]

All countries are different, and the actual development of wages, wage inequality and the productivity-wage correlation depends critically on institutions and what economic behavior they promote.[69] For an economy like the United Kingdom – with a relatively big service sector and relatively flexible wages – there is an intimate relation between productivity and wage growth, and it has not changed much recently either. Like in the US, there are observations about falling hourly pay for some workers, but ever since the early 1970s, shows a study by LSE economists John van Reenen and Joao Paolo Pessoa, there is no decoupling drama.[70]

Like Bob Lawrence's study on decoupling in the United States, van Reenen and Pessoa use the same deflator for both productivity and wages, and give due attention to the difference that exists between gross and net results. Furthermore, they also take account of employer compensations in order to get a more realistic picture of the relation between labor and capital. Income equality has gone up, and average wage is higher than median wage as various forms of labor have changed their relative price over the past forty years. Accommodating for the full effect of the dispersed and unequal compensation growth is necessary in order to understand if compensation *generally* follows the growth of productivity. One cannot just look at one category of labor – say, blue-collar workers – and from that narrow perspective conclude that labor has been taking a hit because the compensation of that particular category has not grown as much as productivity.

Other countries in Europe are different from the United Kingdom in many aspects important to the labor market and the pricing of labor, but their income distribution also show a stable relation over time. In a country like Sweden for instance, wage flexibility has been much smaller given the centralized system for wage bargaining between employers and trade unions. Furthermore, for a long time, the system espoused a policy that was less sensitive to variations in skills and productivity between sectors or professions, and, at least for a while, there was consensus about holding wage growth down. Right or wrong, the wage-moderation strategy was pursued in order to stimulate investments to catch up to frontier economies. Moreover, with higher growth of production taxes than in other countries over the past decades, it is even more critical to take account of the full labor cost in order to understand the relation between compensation and productivity. When all that is done, it turns out that the labor-income share in Sweden has largely been stable over a long period with no sign of increased volatility. While income inequality has accelerated rapidly[71], the Swedish government's National Institute of Economic Research shows that the real cost of labor follows productivity intimately.[72] So the previous conclusion holds for Sweden as well: no drama.

What is dramatic, however, is the long term effects of lower productivity growth. White House economists, comparing various effects on pay from different sources of growth, suggest that if productivity growth between 1973 and 2013 had been the same as productivity growth prior to 1973, incomes would have been 58 percent (or 30 000 USD) higher in the United States.[73] By contrast, if income equality had stayed the same, incomes today would "only" be 18 percent (or 9 000 USD) higher.[74]

History is history and the future may be different. While data can show some deviations in this or that direction, the decoupling trend of the past years in the United States may accelerate. If it does, however, it is unlikely to be because fast productivity growth is going to benefit capital more than labor. In economies with reduced capacities for productivity growth where corporate behavior distances the economy from sources of productivity growth, there are other factors that will push the labor income share to fall. In the short as well as the long run, there should not be any doubt that productivity growth is workers best friend, and that per-capita growth throughout history follows productivity growth.

Jobs and technology

"There's nothing like a recession to throw economists into a despondent mood," Joel Mokyr writes, and the same can be said about today's non-economists as well.[75] Labor markets have been affected by the Great Recession and unemployment remains high in many countries. But the economies woes of the West have caused many to argue that the New Machine Age is already here and destroys jobs like the grim reaper or Lord Voldemort. Several sectors, it is said, are now exposed to "big bang disruption" or "devastating innovation."

There has always been a fear that new technology will destroy jobs, or that it will be bad for other reasons. Think of Italian inventor Guglielmo Marconi, who at the end of the nineteenth century approaching the Ministry for Post and Telegraphs to request funding for his newly invented wireless audio transmission. He did not get any money, nor was he simply turned down. The Ministry referred him to an insanity asylum. But he was neither crazy nor wrong. In 1909 Marconi received a Nobel Prize in physics for "wireless telegraphy." Marconi's peers did not get a much better treatment. Alexander Graham Bell incurred the wrath of the New York Times, which slammed Bell's telephone invention as the destroyer of the private life. Kept unchecked, the New York Times argued, "we will soon be nothing but transparent heaps of jelly to each other."

Perhaps that is an extreme example. The New Machine Age may not unleash such forces that would make us all heaps of jelly, but there is an expectation that it will push a good part of labor into the economic netherworld. Almost 50 percent of the total US employment could potentially disappear within two decades conclude Carl Benedict Frey and Michael Osborne in a study of 702 occupations that could be affected by new technologies. The danger of becoming a computer road-kill depends on the nature of your work, and if you are a rental clerk and telemarketer, you are in for a rough ride, unless you are a computer of course. There is a race, the authors claim, between workers and technology, and "for workers to win the race, however, they will have to acquire creative and social skills."[76]

Such skills, however, have been important for employability for a long time and the labor market has changed profoundly over a long period of time. Entire professions have been eliminated, but new ones have also arrived. It is striking that the dynamic character of labor markets are not considered in many analyses of how technology affects jobs and professions. The rising affluence that new technology generates also lead to demand for other jobs than those that are lost. Nor are there estimates about future demand tested against the recent trend of employment in studied professions, or the current match between supply and demand. Results from such analyses are pretty boring and do not catch the imagination of journalists looking for a good story. No story is as good as a bad story. It is better, then, to aim for simplistic forms of futurism.

Executives are to blame, too. Take the example of Foxconn. In 2011 its Chief Executive Officer, Terry Gou, announced they were aiming for one million robots instead of one million workers. This was not just any Asian manufacturing executive swaging; it was the boss of the largest electronics manufacturer and the tenth largest employer in the world. Its 1.2 million workers assemble products for Apple, Sony, Nokia, Motorola and others – its market capitalization at the time of writing was 44.6 billion US dollars. And the example of Foxconn became the smoking gun for believers in the New Machine Age. It was the proof of how robots would conquer the market and make human labor redundant. Mass unemployment seemed inevitable. What is more, some used the example as imagery of the Chinese manufacturing sector, poisoning the climate with record levels of carbon emissions but not with the legitimate excuse of raising welfare through industrialization. Martin Ford's prediction seemed prescient: "the greatest risk is that we could face a 'perfect storm' – a situation where technological unemployment and environmental impact unfold roughly in parallel, reinforcing and perhaps even amplifying each other."[77]

Gou was serious about Foxconn's future in the world of robots. Foxconn had developed a "Foxbot" in 2007, and the shift followed the transition of China's economy into the higher echelons of the value chain. "I think in the future," Gou said, "young people won't do this kind of work, and won't enter the factories."[78] In early 2015, Gou was still on the offensive, claiming that 70 percent of assembly line choirs would be automated within three years.[79] The conquest of robots was now just a matter of time. Or was it?

Later, Gou's story changed. In fact, after his bold announcement Foxconn had not installed more than 50 000 "automated employees" well into 2015. In the summer of 2015, Gou suddenly retracted his claim and blamed the media for having misunderstood the original announcement. Robots, he now claimed, would substitute only 30 percent of the Foxconn manpower – and it would happen in five, not three, years. Moreover, firing workers was no longer on the agenda. The change "doesn't mean our manpower will be eliminated," Gou stated, but that the substitution would be accompanied by normal intra-corporate career progression, as "30 percent of manpower will be upgraded to higher-grade work."[80]

The jury is still out on Foxconn, but the story about its robotization is revealing. It is not a horror story, an example of robots and automated production forcing labor into the wilderness. Like so much else, the reality of Foxconn's operation is one of man and machine working together, and that the robot substituting labor is part of a larger process in which labor moves up the value-added chain and into higher-paid work. In fact, the suggestion that robots would cause a "huge social dislocation is in a way true, but not in the way it was intended. Robots may in fact be part of the solution than the problem.

Robots increase productivity and create jobs. For every industrial robot introduced between 3 and 5 jobs are created, according to an industry study, and if indirect jobs are added that number notches up.[81] That is probably an exaggeration, but we do not have to rely on industry studies as there is plenty of research pointing in the same direction. For example, economists George Graetz and Guy Michaels found that industrial robots increased growth rates, wages and total factor productivity after having studied the impact of utilizing robots in 17 countries between 1993 and 2007. The economic growth effect of robots was 0.37 percent on average, which equals about ten percent of all GDP growth in that period. While they found some evidence that robots reduced the hours worked by both low and semi-skilled labor, there was no significant effect on the total number of working hours.[82]

President Obama famously erred on the wrong side of the economics of robots and machines in 2011 when he blamed American joblessness on automation. He used the bank teller as an example of a retreating profession as a result of automated teller machines (ATM).[83] This seems plausible. After all, handing out money following a strict protocol does not sound that complicated, automation of such tasks makes sense, even if the obvious effect is job losses. There is only one problem with the story: Obama was wrong. The introduction of ATMs did not reduce teller jobs according to data going back to the 1970s.[84]

In fact, there are more teller jobs today than before ATM's were introduced *en masse*. It is better to argue that there is a problem for the economy that bank teller jobs still exist, because the alternative use of those resources could deliver better growth for the US economy. But many consumers are conservative – and the general rise in the demand of bank tellers, automated or not, means that even if some demand shifts to the machine, there can still be a growing demand for human tellers.

This is one example of how technology does not reduce jobs, and there are many more. The composition of work changes with technology, but usually in a slow and incremental way. And labor markets change also happens for many other reasons. New technology is always embedded in greater patterns of social and economic behavior. If those patterns do not change as a consequence of innovation, it means the economic payoff from it is pretty low. But even if it does change, the new equilibrium is not static. People are fickle, and therefore markets and demand change constantly.

Consider for a moment barbers. Cutting hair is one of the oldest guilds and perhaps not the first you might think of when it comes to technological change. But technology together with other factors has made the history of barbers anything but dull. Alexander the Great, for instance, promoted the barber profession when ordering cleanly shaved ranks to prevent the Persian enemy from dragging his soldiers off their horses during battle. During Palaeolithic times, hairdressers were seen as managers of the human soul because the soul was believed to fester in growing hair.

After the passing of the Roman Empire, the guild moved into a long slow down. But the luck of barbers turned when Pope Innocent III inhibited priests from surgeries. A good move, one would think, as the clergy is not known for medical knowledge. However, no other profession had better knowledge than men of religion, and by an odd coincidence barbers now became surgeons, as they knew how to handle a blade. Medical doctors eventually emerged, and considered themselves the rightful monopolists of medical tasks. Barbers were outcompeted and forced to limit themselves to matters of the hair[85]. But the vocation later returned to prominence. The wig-fashion sweeping through the European bourgeoisie promoted barbers again, and it became a highly celebrated profession.

The odd and unpredictable travel of barbers through the economic history of the world has not ended. The trade has been professionalized – but it has also spread. Saloons began to mix women and men, and the expansion of the fashion industry pushed them even more. At one point, their future seemed bleak as new do-it-yourself technology implied a radical innovation change for the industry. To the tunes of "the best a man can get," gadgets like the electrical hair trimmer and razor blades, marketed in a carpet-bombing style, revolutionized the sector. However, it did not do much for the entire barber profession as they moved up the value chain and away from daily shaves. The profession adapted and made use of new technology. Now, however, beard trimming is big business again for barbers.

They can charge top dollars, not for saving men heading for battle, but for trimming or rather sculpting a French Fork or maybe a Copstash Standard, before finishing of the trimming experience with a beard massage in cocoa butter.

Professions transform and change – and it is a slow process happening every day. Still, high-tech employment anxiety returns in a cyclical fashion and with a fairly recent financial crisis – prolonged by inadequate policy responses – it is not surprising that there are fears about other, and more permanent, forces preventing job-creation or from getting pay rises. Like in past crises, the fear permeates and projects itself on the allegedly defenseless creatures of the lower classes, unable to acquire the education or gain the intelligence necessary to compete in a new world. And this time too there is a shade of *faux* egalitarianism in all of this.

Digital literacy is today widespread in mature Western societies – and is a requirement also for most jobs that do not require a college degree. The computerization and digitalization of leisure is in many ways stronger in the middle classes than in high-income families. While Mr. and Mrs. Harvard worry that their kids do not read books often enough and have illiberal rules for how many minutes per day a ten-year-old can spend with the Xbox or the iPad, the sons and daughters of Mr. and Mrs. College Dropout typically face fewer parental phobias about the invasion of technology in their leisure time.

The Tiger Mom that bans iPads and refuses invitations to pyjama parties for her children, and rather impresses upon them a future as a Latin scholar or concert pianist, is a source of inspiration – or anger – for members of the Yale Club but not Yale's Catering Service. Anyone with a child at a pre-school or school with mixed family backgrounds will soon notice that children are generally much smarter than they were before and that the children who are more adaptive to computers and machines do not necessarily come from families with the best university diplomas or highest salaries.

Computerization has not changed the positive effects of innovation. As in the past, new technology will substitute jobs. There is always technological unemployment. But substituting manpower with tech-power is a process that eventuates even if it sometimes takes time. New jobs are created to manage and develop new technology, to spread it in the economy, and to serve new demand that comes from the new value added created by the technology.

There are economists that have been awarded Nobel Prizes for such observations. Yet it is all about pretty basic human and economic behavior

– and, as we have noted, it is not necessary to use a magnifying glass to find the relation between technology and income in economic statistics. James Joyce discovered it in poor and dirty 19th century Dublin and observed in *Ulysses* the simple logic of technology and jobs: "A pointsman's back straightened itself upright suddenly against a tramway standard by Mr Bloom's window. Couldn't they invent something automatic so that the wheel itself much handier? Well but that fellow would lose his job then? Well but then another fellow would get a job making the new invention?"[86] And when income goes up; demand follows. Consumer-preferences also adapt to changing incomes. Suddenly consumers spend money on services like day-care for dogs, or cocoa butter for the spoil of bristles. As people become richer they consume goods and services in a way that also resists the logic of technology. Consider the example of disc jockeys. Why are they still around? The technology to substitute them already exists – by making a playlist on Spotify or iTunes, if you want to do it on the cheap, or by software that beat-mixes the tunes and pretty much does what a DJ would do. But yet there are far more DJs today than before, and many of them charge the price of a minor rock star to come and play a set at your party. They not only play music, they sort out what is cool and create music themselves. While the tech-determinist prediction would be that new technology should make DJs redundant, or that it would "hang the DJ," if you prefer lyrics from the Smiths, people today are prepared to spend more money on a musical service provided by a human than provided by a machine.

Jobs have always changed according to developing needs – and sometimes in the strangest of directions. Take the history of sourdough production for instance. Fermented sourdough was invented in Egypt in 1500 BC, and later used by the Romans and spread in Europe. Sourdough production is labor-intensive and when modern bread production was introduced, using cultivated yeast, sourdough bread lost its attraction as yeast made production faster. Yet the tedious, expensive and rather messy process of sourdough production experienced a revival thanks to urban hipsters, young food-conscious men, and eco friendlies in big cities all over the western world. The complexity of sourdough worked to its favor; clubs, books and courses popped up and fueled this fast growing specialized market. Even a sourdough hotel was started, in Stockholm, charging about 30 euros a week for babysitting dough.[87] Sourdough is remarkably resilient; dried-up residue left in a bowl forgotten in the back of your kitchen can be revived after years of neglect, and somehow that symbolizes how jobs evolve, transform, disappear and emerge again in unpredictable ways.

The economic history of the West since the industrial revolution is that average performance has constantly improved. 70 percent of the American workforces in 1840 were farmers but less than 2 percent have that profession today. A typical life story from contemporary centenarians (this one is from the grandfather of one of the authors) started, after six years of education, on the family farm. He then became an errand boy for a shopkeeper, moved into light-technology milk and cheese production – and retired as president for a company with ten hydro electric plants. Other life stories are different, but the vast majority of labor has for centuries moved with technology and adjusted to new structures of cost, productivity, and competition.

Innovation famine rather than innovation feast

Prophets of the New Machine Age are getting the economy wrong – on many different levels. In a way, that is unfortunate news. The world economy is not on the threshold of a fast-and-furious technological shift when "all that is solid melts into air," to quote from the *Communist Manifesto*.[88] It is not technology we should worry about, but economic behavior determined or aided by regulatory uncertainty and corporate leaders whose lives are too focused on renter returns. If you consider what they are up to, the world economy is not preparing for a revolution. And that is the essence of the problem of western economies today. While the Western cognoscenti increasingly blame technological change for squeezing the middle class into stagnant incomes, unemployment, and the tattooed frustration of the xenophobic right, the real problem is that the past forty years have witnessed far too little innovation and technological change to carry large groups of people into higher incomes.

Without fresh ideas and new technologies that are generated at the same rate as in the past, markets become rigid and companies saturated, with the effect that the rate of economic development slows down. Work evolves in a perpetual process as our wants change. In the US, every quarter about 12-14 million jobs in the private sector usually get destroyed and created.[89] Ideally, the figure should be higher, across the Western world, because it would imply greater economic dynamism. Yet declining dynamism – in the general economy as well as in the business sector – has subdued the turnover rate of jobs and firms and, as a consequence, made markets less penetrable for innovation.

Young companies find it increasingly difficult to compete and expand when coming up against gatekeepers in the form of planning machine and ageing frontier firms who have more to protect.[90] Their ageing, suggests the OECD, "may foreshadow a slowdown in the arrival of radical innovations and productivity growth."[91] That is a rather worrying conclusion, particularly in light of the role played by frontier firms for channeling much of non-innovation productivity growth in the West in the past decades. Yet it is hardly surprising. Incumbents often find that they do not have to innovate to contest their own markets and that they can choose to either acquire new technology from upcoming new companies or protect their market positions by generating other forms of change. Far too often, they also have the power to convince legislators to slow down market intruders. Importantly, their incumbency advantage means they can afford to wait for a market to develop before they invest. Time is on the side of the incumbents, not the young firms that want to contest markets.

However, incumbents are not lazy or slow on their feet. They are very efficient in what they do. Growing corporate specialization has made them not only more efficient but alert to events and changes that threaten their core assets. It does not matter in which sector this takes place, big firms up their game protecting their firm boundaries. This is partly because these boundaries have narrowed to core ownership advantages and control over the end customer. There is still space for competition, but contestable competition through innovation has become far harder than in the past. Proponents of the New Machine Age predict that new technology will flood the economy. But the simple fact is that innovation require widespread adaptation if it is to have a discernable effect on business and the wider economy, and for most of the new technologies at the center of the current hype, that will not happen until incumbents begin to change their behavior. So far, incumbent companies and their owners have not been forced to step away from slow and incremental innovation. They continue to innovate, but not in a game-changing way.

That takes us to the heart of the West's "innovation problem." It is an illusion that the West has already stepped into the New Machine Age and that fast-and-furious innovation will destroy jobs on a mass scale. The thesis is not easily married with the current state of economics. The transformative power of the Internet petered out a decade ago and while the economy has far from exhausted the capacity of the Internet and digitalization to improve productivity and growth, it is not inevitable that their future will be far different from today. Assuming that the power of new digital technologies is on par with the hype, they still need entrepreneurs, massive investment, and a dynamic economy to be turned into innovation with significant economic payoff. The capitalist economy is increasingly dominated by planning machines with little appetite to contest markets or step back into an era of radical innovation. The instinct of managers – in corporate as well as political life – rather errs on the defensive side. Big and global firms, the towering characters of the business sector, have market positions and sunk capital to defend. They have owners that do not cherish the unpredictability of innovation competition, and substantial investment into building such businesses. Western economies, as we will discuss more in the next chapter of the book, should worry about innovation famine rather than innovation feast.

9

THE FUTURE AND HOW TO PREVENT IT

The future ain't what it used to be.

Yogi Berra, baseball legend

Civilizations die by suicide, not by murder.

Arnold Toynbee

Western economies should not worry about an innovation blitz. Its concern should rather be that innovation and fast technological change no longer powers their economies as much as they should and could. Gray capitalism, excessive corporate managerialism, second-generation globalization, and complex regulations have changed Western capitalism. Over the past decades, these Four Horsemen of capitalist decline have made Western economies far less dynamic and prone to experimentation. The current version of capitalism rather resembles rentier societies of the past. It is addicted to predictability and, therefore, unwelcoming of creative destruction.

Unfortunately, capitalism's future does not look brighter. The factors that shielded it to new ideas in the past four decades or so will not disappear. They will of course change but, without substantial reform, they will not change in a way that charts a new direction for Western economies. And beyond them, the West confronts strong economic headwinds in the form of ageing populations and greater inequalities. No doubt debt will weigh down dynamism, too. Countries like Italy and the United States have public debts that exceed 100 percent of GDP. Spain and France will soon pass that three-digit threshold, and many other countries are not far away from it. Add all private and non-financial corporate debt (standing at 196 per cent of GDP in advanced economies in 2013) and it is obvious that Western economies have a debt problem[1]. Future growth, therefore, cannot be financed by new debt in the same way it was from the 1980s onwards, and there is not much space for public investment that could spur growth. With little appetite for structural economic reforms, the growth potential of Western economies rather looks fixed on its continued voyage south.

Yet it is human growth, and not economic growth, that is the main casualty of hidebound capitalism. Falling creation of new prosperity is naturally unsettling, but it shrinks in comparison with the human aspect. Economies that cannot encourage and emancipate greater aspiration, or liberate imagination about life and work in the future, inevitably shrink the universe for people. Westerners have already lowered their expectations of the future. That is true even in the United States, otherwise known for its sunny optimism. Pessimism is a self-fulfilling prophecy, and the gradual degeneration of optimism about the future has invited fear of technological change and political reactions responding to people who are closing their mind.

"We are in short totally screwed," say economists Lawrence Kotlikoff and Scott Burns about the Western scenario in their *The Clash of Generations*.[2] That is not true. The forces that have made capitalism hidebound are accelerating but no economy is ever predestined for perdition. Now, however, is the time to panic.

From corporate globalism to global corporatism

Globalization is changing. The base scenario is that economic integration spawned in the past decades will remain – and perhaps increase a bit as emerging economies expand trade with each other. Trade and foreign investment will continue to grow outside emerging nations, too. People will also continue to cross borders – either as tourists or as individuals seeking a better life somewhere else. Western opinions on immigration are getting shrill, but a good part of its economies will be in desperate need of foreign labor to come and work as native populations are getting older.

However, even in an optimistic scenario, the future of economic globalization will be far less exciting than its recent past, especially for Western economies. Two trends explain why. *First*, there are shrinking payoffs for Western companies and economies from the rise of emerging markets, which powered much of globalization in the two decades up to the financial crisis. And, *second*, the global agenda for greater trade openness has stalled and new forms of protectionism, embodied especially by market and social regulations, increasingly cut the potential for more trade.

The slowdown of emerging market growth, to start with the first trend, has direct consequences for Western economies and firms. The rise of the BRICs (Brazil, Russia, India, and China) and other economies was central to globalization. With billions of people stepping into the global economy for real, sluggish economies in the West that had lost past economic strengths could again be ignited. A new "global division of labor" emerged—with raw materials from Brazil and Russia, service and back-office operations in India, the factory floor in China, and high-skilled labor and technology from advanced economies. By putting Adam Smith's economy of specialization art work, every economy could accelerate growth.

That period is now a distant memory. The fantasy that enveloped the BRIC economies, the notion of perennially fast and almost infinite growth, has quietly moved away from the world's economic psychology. For a decade or more, the BRICs fantasy charmed a lot of people. They got engrossed by the notion that political minions in state-directed economies could control their complex economies like you control the temperature of a house. Goldman Sachs economists, in a paper that defined the BRICs era, predicted how these economies would out-distance other countries in league tables of income and wealth up to 2050.[3]

The fantasy of infinitely high economic growth in emerging markets has now fizzled. It was a move rich on symbolism when Goldman Sachs in 2015 closed its special BRIC fund. Having declined by 88 percent since its peak in 2010, it seemed to confirm those who had derided BRIC as a Bloody Ridiculous Investment Concept.[4] The continental economic awakening in Asia is no doubt real, but the BRIC fantasy neglected a simple lesson of economic history: high-growth eras always come to an end. It is much easier to play economic catch-up than to compete at the frontier of innovation and productivity.

Contrast the image of roaring BRICs with current economic realities. Brazil and Russia were hardly inspiring growth examples once the super-commodity cycle petered out. Both countries have had periods of sustained negative growth in recent years, impoverishing the population. In the case of Russia, geopolitics, nostalgia, and delusions of grandeur have taken primacy over economic policy and invited severe economic mismanagement. So there is no longer a B and an R in the BRIC chimera, if there ever were.

What about the I and the C? India and China are either trapped in reform resistance or on the course of a great economic deceleration. India has good levels of economic growth, but its growth potential is reduced by intrusive and inept governments at federal and state levels still imbued with the "Licence Raj." India, says economist Gurcharan Das, "only grows at night," when bureaucrats are asleep.[5] The cause célèbre of protectionism, India's high border barriers are nothing but corrosive for its ambition to spur economic growth on the back of trade and external demand. Expectations about new economic reforms after the landslide 2014 victory for reformist Indian Prime Minister Narendra Modi have weakened. Just like the previous government, reform promises have been honored in the breach rather than the observance.

China has entered a structural economic slowdown intimately linked to its exhausted model for economic growth and its high levels of debt. China was critically important for global growth in the past ten years, but expectations for the next ten years are far less promising, to say the least. Its economy remains unbalanced; its growth still mirrors high levels of investments in the economy and its careless efforts to support investment through sudden and unpredictable stop-go monetary and fiscal operations.

Expansion of domestic consumption cannot cover for continued reductions of investment growth.[6] The sums simply do not add up. Productivity growth has decelerated for several years. Manufacturing employment has reached levels where it is difficult to grow by adding more labor to the economy, and the service economy remains ossified. The dependency ratio between the working population and the retired has climbed after decades with a one-child policy that skewed the country's demographics. The rural-urban labor transfer is largely an exhausted force for rapid growth. And, importantly, there is strong resistance from vested interests to the root-and-branch reforms essential for China's growth to remain at decent levels.

The mixed, or poor, status of the BRICS is bad news for Western companies: a big source of their expansion and profits from the past decades is running dry. While there is still a big potential from increased globalization, especially in the service sector, those opportunities look distant as demand is shifting to sectors that politicians are less willing to liberalize. Add to this the growing regionalization of Asia's trade growth, which Western multinationals have greater difficulties to benefit from.

The second trend is how stalling trade and market liberalization have made globalization a passive rather than active force of market change. New economic integration through trade and investment is now largely cyclical and not a reflection of structural shifts of global production patterns, which defined globalization in the past decades. Clearly, the economic liberalism that guided global-economy reforms after the end of the Cold War has given way to greater passion for government intervention. While there is not resurging protectionism, mercantilism is again a popular economic strategy for growth. Moreover, governments are increasingly innovative in using subsidies and their regulatory power to benefit domestic companies.

In this new version of the global economy, crony ties between business and government become more important. The age of corporate globalism is moving into a new era of global corporatism. Political controversy around trade, investment, tax, and M&As has already gone up, and there is nothing that sharpens political elbows as much as a low-growth environment where everyone fights to maintain market shares. Globalization's new personality is likely to manifest itself in levels of trade and investment growth that are far below the levels from the early 1980s up to the financial crisis. Between 1997 and 2006, world trade grew annually by 6.8 percent; in recent years that growth has been less than a half of previous rates.[7]

The power of big and global companies remains strong – but to prosper in the new era of global corporatism they find themselves pressured of having to consolidate their market positions and defend them with greater urge. They will double down on the protection of firm boundaries and defending their markets against intruders that could spark greater competition. With far less market growth, sustaining margins on current stock becomes even more essential – and Western corporateville has already set the terms for how margins can be maintained: greater market concentration through mergers and acquisitions, and more managerialism. It is a form of globalization that will create less economic opportunity.

The continued rise of regulatory uncertainty

Regulation increasingly clogs the arteries of innovation. Unfortunately, Western governments are likely to continue the current trend of raising market restrictions and reducing the space for more and contestable competition. Worryingly, they are also prone to create more regulatory complexity and bring even more uncertainty for those innovators that aspire to bring something radically new to the market. The trends are likely to remain unchanged because they connect with broader developments in the Western polity undermining the quality of regulation and eroding the capacity of political leaders to accept uncertainty and the consequences of greater experimentation in the economy. Regulations choking innovation are not by-products or unintended consequences of political action; they are designed to that effect.

In our view, the growth of regulatory uncertainty has three main sources, and they are far from exhausted. The first source is, for want of a better

term, the new sociology of politics and how it has changed the way policy
evolves. Political parties, governments, and other organizations of the
Western polity that used to carry trust and authority have steadily devalued
those currencies. For a long time, constituents have long ago voted with
their feet – away from those entities that organized democratic politics in
the past. Parties, politicians and governments are now receptive to changing
opinions in a way they were not before, and sometimes those opinions
change very fast. Political leaders have become a very anxious specie –
occupied as much with the Twitter reaction to policy as with the quality of
it. The increasingly noisy political climate makes politicians reactive and
there is always a crisis that demands a political or regulatory response. In
today's speed of politics and, some say, with falling probity of those that are
elected to political office, laws and regulations all too often get poorly
constructed, partly because they respond to a limited and selective view of
an issue. Fast politics make for poor policy.

Today's politicians may sound confrontational, but the paradox is that
they are less ideological. It does not seem that way. Like an alchemist trying
to make gold out of sand, modern politicians have the strange habit of trying
to make ideology out of matters that are technical or practical, like the size of
the debt limit for the US federal government. While that habit often pushes
Western politics into gridlock, it also drives complex regulation. Such regulations are a consequence of insecure and confused political leadership
responding to events. Regulatory complexity and uncertainty is not the
favored outcome of conservatism, liberalism, socialism or any other coherent
ideology; nor does it accompany political leadership acting on thoughtful
ideological principle. It is the consequence of politics blowing in the wind.

The second source of growing political uncertainty is the structure of
regulation. Regulation has largely become more prescriptive and less
proscriptive. It is increasingly specific, detailed and instructive about what
companies and people should do – and, therefore, less concerned with
universal rules for just conduct. In short, regulation is positive, not negative.
This trend started many decades ago and reflects an age-old instinct in
public administrative law. As every society has become more complex
and heterogeneous, positive regulation had to follow in the same steps.
New layers to regulation was added, and every layer became ever more
granular – targeting actors with a high degree of specificity, sometimes
down to one single firm.

Politicians and regulators recognize, however, that far too detailed and
specific regulations can suppress initiative and entrepreneurship, and turn
markets into command economies. They admit real-world complexity and

know that ludicrously detailed regulations can make them look ridiculous. Faced with conflicting constraints the result of political action has too often been that regulation has become complex and ambiguous. Regulations often detail what companies should do but are vague and inconclusive about what they exactly mean and what companies need to do in order to be on the right side of regulations. In that way, regulatory uncertainty is consequence of a prescriptive regulatory culture.

There is a third source behind the rise of regulatory uncertainty that follows on a prescriptive regulatory culture. Legislators are outsourcing rule making, and sometimes law making, to regulatory authorities. It is a consequence of prescriptive but ambiguous regulation because someone has to interpret and make sense of them. Regulatory bodies are increasingly seen as the right instance of not just interpretation, but also the implementing regulations and the formulation of adaptions of regulation, because they have better knowledge about those that are regulated. But there are, in the first place, limits to what unelected regulators can do. In the second place, regulatory authorities have their own motivations and they are driven by other sentiments than flawlessly upholding the laws and promoting regulations that are effective. The fault is not necessarily that they impose too many or too strict regulations on business. Sometimes it is the reverse, especially when regulatory bodies have been captured or co-opted by the industries they are regulating. The problem is rather rulemaking by regulators often adds new layers of vagueness and complexity, and that regulators do not really know how to act.

Take the wave of financial regulations since the financial crisis. No doubt past regulations needed to change. At the same time, many of the new regulations did not bring more clarity but created a higher degree of complexity in both the concept and compliance of regulation. Again, the result is uncertainty for everyone. The new bank regulations that followed on the so-called Basel III rules, for instance, allow for unhealthy levels of discretion for regulatory authorities, partly because they are so complex and ambiguous. Thomas Hoenig, the Director of America's Federal Deposit Insurance Corporation, claimed basic capital rules are "more complicated than simple, more confusing than clear and more easily gamed than not."[8] Other regulators have made the point that to police these confusing rules, financial authorities are demanding so many submissions from banks about their operations that no one really knows what to do with all the information they receive.

Complex regulations are toxic when combined with a good amount of compliance discretion for regulators and lack of transparency of how authorities work. Financial authorities regularly stress tests banks, for example, but the assumptions and scenarios of the future they work with – and that determines whether a bank passes or fails a test – are often hidden from the outside world, including the banks that fail. Systemically important financial institutions, so called SIFIs, get an additional embrace of financial regulators, but there is still a good amount of confusion exactly what constitutes a SIFI or why some receives that distinction. MetLife, the insurer, had to take the American Financial Stability Oversight Council to court to get the information about why it became classified as a SIFI, something it desisted.

Worse, there is an evolving method in the madness. "The best way to regulate is to line up the banks occasionally and shoot one of them," confessed a former financial regulator.[9] True to form, in all the secretive deals between banks and regulators that have been made since the crisis, it is just impossible for an outsider to know how decisions were taken, if justice has been made, and what they mean for future rule making. Only in the United States, banks and other financial institutions were fined close to 139 billion US dollars between 2012 and 2014 because they violated regulations.[10] Perhaps they deserved harder or weaker punishment; perhaps some of them were innocent. No one outside the rooms where decisions were made can tell.

Regulatory uncertainty keeps growing and will undoubtedly play a significant role for markets and innovation in the foreseeable future. The factors behind it are getting stronger rather than weaker. Many companies are already making these assumptions about the future. The International Federation of Accountants (IFAC) discovered in 2015 that 85 percent of the surveyed professionals expected the "impact of regulation to be more or much more significant" for innovation and growth in the next five years. Revealingly, four out of five thought regulations affecting companies were either complex or very complex.[11]

The "silver tsunami" for cash

Just like globalization and regulation, gray capitalism is changing but in a way that makes capitalism grayer. Several factors conspire to that end. Ageing drives more Westerners toward retirement and a greater part of global savings will be held for people close to or in retirement. While savings and capital allocation broadly follows the lifecycle hypothesis, and retired people draw down savings for the purpose of consumption, it is unlikely that there will be a surge in consumption growth in Western economies with ageing populations. For the retired individual, there is such an effect – what economists call the intertemporal choice or allocation. However, there is a mixed picture for societies. Both public and private pension plans have funding gaps. Combined with mean-reverting corporate profit levels (reducing the return on equity), it means that more money will have to go into the plans to cover the difference between pensions promises and available resources. The paradox of savings will rather become more present: the world saves too much and too little at the same time.

The retirement of boomers is therefore reinforcing current patterns of capital allocation. With ageing, corporate funding is likely to depend more on debt and less on equity. Just as in the past decade, increasing average age urges savers to move to financial services with a reasonable and predictable return. Households in Europe, for instance, allocate 48 percent of total financial assets to cash and deposits, and 35 percent to equities, when they are between 35-65 years old. But for those older than 65, cash and deposits are up to 55 percent and equities down to 20 percent. The effect is similar in the US, where cash and deposits go from 24 to 37 percent, and equities from 47 to 27 percent.[12] Equities also need to be considered in their different parts. A large share of private retirement savings or savings by those close to retirement is invested in mutual funds, which is the preferred equity-based product for those close to or in retirement. Naturally, a greater role for mutual funds, institutions, and asset managers drains economies of capitalist owners.

It does not stop there. With underfunded public pension systems and private savings products based on defined benefits, there will be a greater hunt for capital to finance pensions. The liability gap is depressingly big. For countries in the Eurozone, fiscal expenditures will need to increase by around nine percent of GDP up to 2050 in order to cover for a graying population.[13] And that concerns only the public pension system. In a stress test of about 200 insurance and occupational pension plans, a European authority found significant gaps between assets and liabilities, amounting to about 750 billion euros missing under a scenario of low interest rates that are similar to current market conditions.[14] In the United Kingdom, over 5000 companies are facing pension deficits.[15]

It is not better in the United States. For pension plans to hold together, returns have to improve. One estimate of US public pensions, erring on the extreme side, suggests the return on capital is going to drop to such low rates that up to 85 percent of US pension plans risk failure within 30 years.[16] More moderately, Moody's estimate that there is a two trillion US dollar missing in the 25 largest public US pension plans.[17]

Perhaps that estimate over or undershoots the real size pf the problem, but it is easy to see why they and others are worried about a growing pensions crisis. Estimates for the return on investment on pension savings rely on historic financial performances. With historically low interest rates, it becomes necessary for savers and investment funds to increase risks to reach expected returns. A deflationary economy with low nominal growth lowers the possible returns on safe savings. Even if Western economies would improve on current trend in the next two decades, they will still be in a low-growth economy. Therefore, the return on savings and most standard financial products will remain low. Bridgewater, the asset manager, has estimated that it would take a nine percent average return to make up for future liabilities in pension plans.[18] In a low-growth and low-yield economy, great risks have to be accepted to achieve such returns. Regulators in both America and Europe, however, want investment funds and others to moderate their risk levels.

Governments are better positioned than private companies to manage the growing quest for cash. In the extreme case, governments have the privilege to raise fiscal deficits, print money and create inflation, or cut the actual pensions. More moderately, they can set the rules for its own borrowing. Providers of private retirement savings, especially with defined benefits, do not have the same luxury. They cannot always cut pensions or invent their own rules of finance. Private providers can change their products away from defined benefits, but generally not retroactive. Naturally, private pension providers will push the risk-return profile when they invest, but when the regulatory environment is pulling in the opposite direction, investment gets ever more complex.

And this is where gray capitalism gets grayer, or changes color. Gray capital has in fact another option to manage the quest for cash. Given their ownership role in the economy, investment institutions representing retirement savers can turn to their cash-strong investees and demand that they return more capital to shareholders. Many investment institutions owning public companies have similar problems of liability gaps and suffer from a low-return economy. The temptation to draw down the capital balances of their investees in order to release resources, can become irresistible. Taking capital out of companies mute future corporate growth. Nor is it good for the economy. But companies with very strong or extremely dispersed ownership have one thing in common. Owners can connect themselves to the cash flow, influence the size of the balance sheet, and the way companies fund themselves.

Some might argue that this is already happening. In the past years, many institutional investors have been pushing companies to transfer capital to them. There are multiple reasons why companies have been hoarding cash, driving up their debt and returning an increasing amount of capital to shareholders through dividends and share buybacks. However, paranoia is not required to argue that one of them is that companies have owners with growing demand for predictable returns (capital is needed to cover for falling profitability), higher returns, or both. No doubt many investment institutions have been pressuring companies to improve their short-term earnings in order to push up yields, and companies seem to preparing for a future where such pressures will only grow. If putting capital to work in companies cannot generate expected earnings, and even if it does pay off in the long run, the fastest way to cash for shareholders is that companies gradually age their capital base.

Those who think this interpretation of capital market trends is paranoid should at least be reminded that we are in good company. Consider the view of Laurence Fink, the Chief Executive Officer of Blackrock, the world's largest asset manager, and others in similar position that have hit the alarm button in recent years. In early 2015, just after corporate America was closing their books for 2014 with record levels of dividends and share buybacks, Fink sent a letter to S&P 500 bosses with a simple message: stop sending capital back to us! If captains of corporate America do not invest for the long term the economic system is going to contract. True, that was not his exact words, but it was the essence. The effects of high dividends and share buybacks, Fink said, "are troubling both to those seeking to save for long-term goals such as retirement and for our broader economy."[19]

Fink is right. Corporate funding is not structured for long-term business growth. An even grayer version of capitalism is not a distant scenario, and the de facto raiding of corporate balance sheets of capital will likely accelerate. There are countervailing forces, but the consequence to capitalism of the silver tsunami for cash in Western economies seems to be about colorimetry: add gray color on gray and it loses light. Add more and the shade of the color subtly shifts; the complexion first gets sombre, then murky. Add yet more gray, and the color becomes – black.

Future imperfect

Pain, said writer C.S. Lewis, is bearable if it has a purpose or a deeper meaning. It is a decade now since the start of the Great Recession and, people should ask, is there a purpose behind the Western economy remaining troubled. The consequences of economic decline are visible almost everywhere, but more so in social psychology than economic data. It does not seem to get better. Capitalism, if we are right, is about to become grayer – if not turning black altogether – and in many parts of the Western society, people are weighing down their expectations about life, income and wellbeing.

Everyone is not unfortunate. As our economies increasingly behave as retirees, the gray-haired and retired seem to be doing rather well. A striking evidence of how capitalism is metamorphosing into a rentier-like economy is that the average income of pensioners is now higher than that of the working population in the United Kingdom.[20] Pensioners can allow themselves a vastly better standard of life because most do not have to worry about mortgages eating up their income. In 2010-14, shows the Economist, "spending by the over-75s on dining in restaurants rose twice as fast as similar spending by the under-30s." For cinema and theatre tickets, it rose five times as fast.[21]

Younger generations will not catch up, if you believe the general opinion. In countries like Germany, the United Kingdom and the United States, shows a YouGov poll, the dominating opinion is that the next generation will be worse off – neither richer nor safer or healthier.[22] In Western families, bambinos all too often stay bambinos, and then become what Italians call bamboccioni (big baby), as they cannot afford to leave the nest. The job market is getting worse for youths in many Western countries. Entry salaries have been going down for quite some time in many countries. The only thing that seems to grow is the class of pauperized graduates that jumps from one low or non-paying internship to another. A standard complaint in Western societies today is that older people and their experience are not respected enough, especially on the labor market. That is true. But that problem dwarfs in comparison to the standard recipe for the young to get a foothold on the labor market: make their labor so cheap that it almost becomes free.

Paradoxically, older generations are also feeling entrapped, especially at work. Job creation and destruction have for decades been on a slowing trend, and those unhappy at work have greater problems finding a new job. The bureaucratic mind-set will continue to spread inside organizations and increasingly define their ethos. Internal politics dominates much of the rhythm of work. Systems are designed to play defense or to hide in a culture of managerialism. Everyone is guarded, preferring the cuddly protection of bureaucracy rather than jumping into the cold water of uncertainty. Fewer possess the power to rebel against the culture. People are stressed but have developed a sixth sense for the bureaucratic lingo and hierarchical life. Unfortunately, it is a cognition that also benumbs organizations.

Working will continue to be spent in meetings, or preparing for them. Meetings, like committees, have their own way of life. Many in the private sector will know that meetings have to be prepared, often in a pre-meeting, and that before the pre-meeting is called, some of those that will attend the actual meeting have to be consulted about who should be invited to the meeting and the pre-meeting. The pre-meeting drafts the agenda of the meeting, and the draft is then re-drafted after the pre-meeting has discussed the draft. Then it can be released to people attending the meeting. The meeting takes place, invariably running for longer time than necessary. A meeting report is then written. The draft report is sent around for consultation, and is then re-drafted before a final draft, with operative conclusions added, is done. Then it gets approved and is sent higher up in the hierarchy. Sometimes it goes faster, but many times it is even more complicated.

For entrepreneurs, such an environment is just like entering Franz Kafka's novel *The Castle* as character K. It is a struggle against surreal bureaucracy and hierarchy. Creators lose their bearings inside the managerial labyrinths. They do not understand how the machine works – its rhythm, language and purpose. And now, when the managerialist culture has spread into such a big part of the private sector, it is difficult to build a career without conforming to that mentality, or – worse – capitulating to it.

That culture wears human dignity thin. It slowly entwines the vices of bureaucracy and gradually corrodes aspiration, imagination and other virtues of a flourishing society. It is hard to define the spirit of bureaucracy, or register when it has taken power over people and organization. But you know it when you see it. The Organization Man work incredible hard. Office hours are long and holidays from the constant information flow are almost impossible. They read countless for-your-information emails every day just to know whether they should be informed about something or not. They get nervous when they do not read them and they plan, plan, and plan. And then it suddenly happens. Planning and information management become their professional lifeblood. Their instinctive reaction is caution. Their approach to change, renewal and innovation is to organize it in their own structured bureaucracy.

Capitalism is an economic organization and a good part of the capitalist practice is to organize economic behavior. But organization does not equal managerialism or technostructure. Nor is the ethos of capitalism defined by organization, whatever form it takes. The culture and psychology of capitalism are intimate with the growth of talent and character – and the view that both labor and capital, or work and investment, are part of a larger culture encouraging the pursuit of human and economic growth.

Philosopher Hannah Arendt once observed about economic thinkers that they reduced the essence of labor, or *animal laborans,* to only instrumental outcomes, even if they anchored that creature in a larger cultural context. John Locke defined labor as the source of property, Adam Smith as the root of wealth, and Karl Marx treated it as the essence of man.[23]

Yet very few work only to put food on the table – or invest in capitalist enterprise just because they want to amass wealth. The desire for good material outcome is part of human psychology and embedded in most forms of economic organization through history. The weakness of socialism or mercantilism was not that individuals laboring under those systems never desired material outcomes as much as individuals in capitalist societies. Capitalism's exclusive attribute is the space it allows for what Arendt called "the human condition." It is an economic organization that builds not just on labor but, more importantly, on work. Labor is central for the sustenance of life. Work, however, is what people do to practice values that cannot be transacted on markets. Capitalism is therefore encouraging the moral imagination of individuals and societies; it espouses a notion about life, people, work, and their future as attendant to larger desires than just money.

The chief worry, therefore, is not that the Four Horsemen of capitalist decline will lower economic growth. Falling aspiration should be the main concern. Just like "iron rust from disuse," wrote Leonardo da Vinci, "inaction saps the vigor of the mind."[24] Societies that do not inspire people to greater imagination about their future inevitably decay. The way they die is by suicide, not murder, to paraphrase Alfred Toynbee. In decaying societies, people resign in front of seemingly merciless and unreceptive forces like technological change. The preference, at least for some, is to resist. They get suspicious of the unknown and embrace politicians that promise to veto change. Economic renewal becomes a threat, not an opportunity for human growth. As Western societies are voyaging in that direction, getting farther away from the ethos of capitalism, it should be an economic and moral obligation for all to prevent this darker future.

Preventing the future

The good news is that stagnation, like progress, is neither inevitable nor automatic. It is the consequence of choices made by elected officials, corporate leaders, and individuals. Moreover, what is done – for good or bad – can always be undone. The rise of modern capitalism a quarter century ago was the result of great political and institutional changes that allowed competition to old economic habits. If all the lessons of economic history have to be reduced into one basic proposition, it is surely that economies can change, and that they regularly do.

The last quarter century offers many examples of how people can release themselves from oppressing or taxing economic regimes, and how economies can begin to thrive after decades, if not centuries, of stasis or stagnation. For example, many countries that were satellites of the Soviet Union a little more than 25 years ago now belong to the top-25 ranked countries in the world in matters of competitiveness, economic freedom, and business friendliness. A quarter century ago, China's GDP per capita stood at 500 US dollar; now it is almost eight times higher.[25]

Such impressive change happens because of deep and wide regulatory reforms, and radical overhauls of economic institutions. Eventually political institutions need to change too in order to give people the freedoms and rights that are necessary for a culture in which people challenge the prevailing order and wisdom. However, that is only the start for a society that aspires to thrive on capitalism. For economies to chart new courses, people also have to change their habits of the hearts – their cultural and psychological disposition for experimentation and renewal. That is at least equally difficult. Many people in former authoritarian regimes have managed to capture new economic opportunities that emerged after economic reforms. Yet for sustained growth – of economies and individuals – the culture and psychology of capitalism also needs to be nursed. Unfortunately, all too often it is not – and, just like people in the West, some people liberated from authoritarian systems have found the comfort of bureaucracy and the culture of managerialism to be irresistible.

Unquestionably, today's Western economies can be, if you like, "fixed," even if it will take a generation or so to change the culture. However, it will not happen if the focus is on the standard, off-the-rack, generic reform programs that economist usually advice. To spark new life into capitalism, attention must be given to, first, severing the link between gray capital and corporate ownership. Secondly, competition needs to get a real boost, and thirdly, a culture of dissent and eccentricity.

A. Sever the link between gray capital and corporate ownership

The greatest danger to Western capitalism is gray capital stampeding it beyond recognition. Capitalism simply cannot recover its health unless the silent takeover of companies by institutions and anonymous owners is halted, and its future will remain bleak unless actions are taken with the effect of boosting distinct and capitalist ownership of companies. Two things are urgent.

First, an emergency operation is needed to prevent current investment institutions from draining companies of capital. That is easier said than done, and in reality there is only one way plausible way forward: reform private and public pensions plans with the view of plugging their liability gaps. If the demand for plundering companies of capital does not go away, there will always be a supply. While several countries have reformed their pension systems in the past two decades, few Western countries have improved them to such a degree that they are financially stable, also in light of a prolonged period of low growth and poor yields. It is difficult to see how farther reforms could be achieved without reducing the direct income of current retirees and demanding larger contributions from pending pensioners, perhaps by substantially extending the retirement age. But that is also easier said than done. Governments can extend working life when it comes to access to the public system. Many countries, however, have organized pensions around institutions that manage occupational retirement plans and a good part of them are still based on defined benefit schemes or hybrid systems with defined benefits as critical parts. Moreover, many countries directly relies on fairly substantial private retirement savings, usually in investment funds. Changing such systems is more controversial than cutting state pensions, directly or indirectly by raising the retirement age.

Second, and more forward looking, gray capital must be stopped from taking complete hold of corporate ownership. Gray capital already represents a significant share of corporate ownership and no company with size or aspiration to grow can neglect its role. It is also programmed from taking a significantly bigger ownership role in Western capitalism. On current trends, gray capital will overrun those capitalist owners that remain, and its formula or portfolio approach to investment will accelerate the dispersion of ownership and create larger agency problems. Preventing gray capital from eroding capitalist ownership is therefore urgent.

Ideally, reforms should aim to push gray investors to link arms with capitalist owners, even if reforms imply a loss of influence for gray capital. Badly designed reforms can damage access to corporate funding or accelerate the transfer from equity to debt funding. With the current structure of savings in the Western world, companies find it almost impossible to avoid gray investors and their capital, and reduced access to their resources can make capitalism lose a key input. Hence, cleaning house of gray asset managers cannot be the purpose of reforms. Actions have rather to be focused on differentiation between forms of ownership.

One way to sever the link is to grant companies greater freedoms to discriminate between owners by expanding the usage of dual class stock structures. Active ownership is premiered by different rules for dividends and voting rights. With growing size and numbers of owners, maintaining entrepreneurial leadership becomes increasingly challenging, and when entrepreneurial leadership is weak, company development slows down. A successful company builder like Warren Buffet's Berkshire Hathaway, for example, exercises ownership differentiation between A and B classes of shares.[26] Both Google and Facebook have dual share structures, something that arguably has helped to maintain a culture of innovation in those firms. A few days after Facebook's initial public offering, founder Mark Zuckerberg, owned 18 percent of Facebook, but controlled fifty-seven percent of the share-votes.[27] The reason is obvious: maintaining entrepreneurial grit.

Ownership differentiation is a red blanket for many in corporate finance. Regulators do not like it either and tend to root for ownership democracy. In Europe, authorities have made efforts to remove ownership discrimination, and less than a decade ago there was a political campaign to rule out dual class stocks entirely. A key argument has been that discriminating share structures pacify ownership, and with references to investor and ownership behavior from earlier decades, that argument has not been difficult to prove.

However, the world is different now. Ownership has already become pacified (or gray) and the big challenge is no longer old ownership and or the corporatist cultures in companies that were previously run by founding families. It is true that ownership competition was stifled, but the main threat to such competition now comes from gray capital. Dual shares, rightly executed, can therefore help safeguard entrepreneurial capital and habits that are still present in companies, and thus help to defend and promote entrepreneurship more widely.

Another way to reform ownership structures is to ward state-owned gray capital, such as Sovereign Wealth Funds, from investing in publicly listed companies, or at least investing in stocks that give high voting power. Most business observers would agree that governments should not own companies. Few, however, appreciates the scale of corporate socialization that has taken place over the past decades through government investment vehicles and state pension funds. While past fears of government owners were that they wanted to be active owners, the main problem now is rather that governments are passive owners that are chasing yield just like every other money manager. There are still practices of government-owners intervening in business planning, and there are certainly remaining risks thereof, but the specific problem facing the West now is that governments just add to the pile of gray capital.

A third approach to severe the link between gray capital and corporate ownership is to reform tax systems, especially with the intention of levelling the playing field between debt-versus-equity financing of companies. Current approaches are rigged to favor debt financing. In most Western countries, big company owners are faced with a simple choice: if they borrow money, the interest is a deductible cost, whereas the returns on equity financing are taxed. In other words, a company that prefers to get funded by real owners through equity faces a completely different metric of capital costs. The capital advantages of debt financed companies, combined with the erosion of entrepreneurial corporate ownership, has diffused and confused corporate decision-making, chiefly by reducing the ownership role. What really makes debt-financing gray is the migration of influence away from equity owners to capital markets and bureaucratic credit committees. If the influence of such institutions, distant in mind and matter from real entrepreneurship, should be limited, the role of equity has to be promoted.

B. Boost contestable competition

Boosting competition in Western markets requires changes in regulation. Regulation has grown beyond control, leading to what political scientist Steven Teles calls a "kludgeocracy," a patchwork of badly constructed regulations that work with no common organizing principle. The cost and complexity of the Western regulatory system has become alarmingly high and, just like the German government, it is justified to introduce a "bureaucracy brake" that requires the government to take away a regulation every time it introduces a new one. Even better would be if governments made radical cuts in the amount of regulation and greatly improved the standards for transparency in and evaluation of them.

What should take primacy now, however, are reforms to spur contestable competition – competition that forces market actors to change. Business leaders now view overregulation as the dominant threat to business growth.[28] That is a bad consequence of regulation. Even worse is that many regulations, intentionally or not, preserve markets and hierarchies of markets, often by raising entry barriers to such a degree that few even bother to contest them.

A first approach to reform is to cut the influence of classic economic regulation on contestable competition. Zoning laws are one example. Or think about occupational licenses and the effect they have on the contestability of markets. Undoubtedly, there are instances where occupational licensing is important, but evidence clearly suggests that the practice of licensing has spiralled out of control and that far too many professions have become guilds shielding themselves from competition.

Greater competition should also help to speed up the exit of low-productivity firms in order to make space for higher-productivity firms. With the falling exit rates of firms, there has been an increasing variety in productivity between firms in the same sector, especially those sectors that have incumbency advantages. That also influences income inequality. In the US, for instance, there is greater variety in pay between firms than within firms, suggesting that a factor of rising inequality is that people work at the wrong firms.[29] Moving a person from a low-productivity to a high-productivity firm will raise his or her income. Like Europe and advanced economies in Asia, low rates of labor market flexibility are now a problem also in the United States as they keep people in companies that are not performing well enough.[30]

Related to that, market regulation has generally skewed the relative relation between old and new firms, leading to more consolidation of markets and higher entry barriers for new entrants that can offer contestable competition. To address the asymmetric competition between old and new firms will require a general cut in red tape and a different approach to regulation that limits the exposure to regulation while firms are small and young. Some regulations need to apply to all economic actors, but quite many can be differentiated.

Rising economic regulations of markets is generally a growing problem again in Western economies as they affect the contestability of markets. Economic regulations reallocate capital and labor between different parts of the economy, and for economies that are exposed to forces of natural market change – e.g. the "servicification" or digitization of the economy – that re-allocation can subdue the power of unfolding structural change to lift productivity and growth.

Take the example of Europe's digital economy. Its size, growth and contribution to GDP have been far less impressive than in other comparable economic regions like the United States. While Europe has a problem with fragmented markets in the field of digital services, a far bigger hinder to growth is the highly regulated services sector that disables the diffusion of new digital technology to ripple through economies.[31] Investors and labor adjust to the pattern of regulation, and channel their digital focus into those sectors where regulation is less of a hindrance to business expansion. The result is a misallocation of capital in the economy. Reducing the distorting effects of economic and complex regulations are therefore important for getting more economic vitality.

Another approach is to re-think the use of competition policy, especially anti-trust laws. Competition authorities should put greater attention to the dynamic aspects of market competition and hence value companies that contest markets, even if they are big and dominant. In a good part of Western economies, the trend now is rather to protect incumbents from the competitive effects of invaders that operate through technological platforms. In Europe, for instance, technological platforms are threatened with specific regulation, and its competition authorities have been advancing that regulatory ambition by going after big platform companies like Google and Amazon. Past lessons of dynamic competition, especially in sectors where technology drives competition, rather suggests that temporarily high market shares for some companies are beneficial to the general degree of competition on the market and fast change in other sectors. Competition authorities, however, fails to act in sectors where company or regulatory behavior saturate markets and reduce the space for competition. In Europe, there are several sectors such as energy that are ripe for an antitrust shake up.

A third approach is to progress global trade reforms, but focus them on sectors that are comparably protected and that have not been exposed that much to new competition. Such reforms would accelerate competition in many ossified markets, especially in the services sector, and help revive market experimentation as well as economic growth. Moreover, it would help to rebalance the world economy in a way that gives more incentives to invest and innovate in sectors that have recorded far less productivity growth than the average sector.

C. A culture of dissent and eccentricity

There is a last point to be made, but because it is more about culture than policy, it does not lend itself to a program of reforms. It concerns eccentricity or the space a society allows to those innovators and entrepreneurs that do not conform to the norm. And it is about dissent and the freedom people enjoy articulating and pursuing their ideas. A culture of dissent and eccentricity is of great importance to innovation – and not just to invention or technology creation. For economies to be innovative, there has to be tolerance of the unknown and acceptance of experimentation.

These qualities have been important advantages of Western economies for a long time. They are connected to great cultural and institutional changes around the time of the enlightenment, if not earlier – changes that fostered a liberal tradition of knowledge and individual freedom. Gradually, however, the modern West is eroding these advantages through regulation and a censorious culture that reduce the freedom to dissent, experiment and generally behave in ways that do not follow established formula. Conformism is a sure way to stagnation and few trends can undermine the long-term ability of Western society to prosper through innovation as much as growing intolerance.

One point of policy should be made, and it is to radically reduce the restrictive effect of precautionary regulation. What is needed is a new regulatory culture based on permissionless innovation[32] that promotes, as Joel Mokyr puts it, "tolerance toward the unfamiliar and the eccentric."[33] A hospitable policy climate for innovation requires a broad set of basic institutions and policies that conform to the commercialization of new technologies. Permissionless innovation, however, is more specific and attacks much of the cultural hostility to risk and uncertainty that have guided a good part of social regulation in the past decades and that is on the rise today. Innovation requires solid regulations, and a culture of permissionless innovation is therefore not equal to an economy free from regulations. A culture of permissionless innovation is rather based on clear proscriptive regulations that do not require innovators to ask for permission or apply for special licenses in order to put new products on the market.

Europe's precautionary principle is a case in point. It is an open-ended principle, enshrined in European law, and that gives every opportunity to charlatans and frauds with little regard for facts and science to block innovation and economic experimentation. Moreover, it gives incumbents, defending their product stock, opportunities to shield contestable competition. It is true that the precautionary principle is an extreme form of regulation because it causes widespread or systemic uncertainty, but similar approaches to new inventions also guide less extreme regulations. Western economies have developed a borderline obsession with precaution that simply cannot marry a culture of experimentation, and the addiction to regulate away various forms of risk have eroded the role of innovation in their economy and effectively neutralized entrepreneurship. That obsession needs to be cured, not nursed.

The precautionary habit permeates other areas than government policy and has even become a common feature in the academic republic – the one territory that should be the bastion for dissent, eccentricity and experimentation. Numerous universities in the West have gradually been reducing the space for free speech. Students even seem to be asking for more restrictions. Half of America's college students, studies show, favor speech codes on campuses to regulate both faculty and scholars from stepping over the line, however that is defined. An even larger proportion of them believe professors should be obliged to warn their students before showing "discomfiting" material, whatever that is.[34] There are ever growing demands of "safe spaces" where students should be allowed to shield themselves from academic teaching and thinking they do not like. Highly regarded universities allow for students to skip class if they find a subject offensive.[35]

This development at Western universities might seem innocent, but it is both a symbol of a greater societal erosion of the Western culture of dissent and a harbinger of what may come. An innovation culture requires people that are curious of new knowledge and willing to expose their own ideas to opposition. It is a soft institution that defines much of an individual's actual freedom to be something else than mainstream – and the chances of an economy to grow. Reduce the space for eccentricity and our economies will stagnate. Encourage the same habit – and we will prosper.

NOTES

1 Introduction

1. Mill, *On Liberty*, ch. 3.
2. This book concerns Western capitalism. While the problems we cover also can be found in other countries, it is not our purpose to analyze them. Several chapters will discuss developments in other economies than those in the West, but only when it is relevant for our discussion about Western capitalism. In this book, references to the Western world, Western economies, the West, or similar expressions mean North America and Western and Central Europe.
3. Cheng et al., "Job Satisfaction."
4. Blanchflower and Oswald, "Well-Being, Insecurity, and the Decline of American Job Satisfaction."
5. Crabtree, "Worldwide, 13% of Employees Are Engaged at Work."
6. Dreyer and Hindley, "Trade in Information Technology Goods."
7. The Economist, "Planet of the Phones."
8. Bogost, "The Secret History of the Robot Car."
9. The "second half of the chessboard" is an expression by Ray Kurzweil to explain the power of exponential growth. Legend has it that when the inventor of chess presented the game to the emperor of India and was offered to choose a reward, he asked for one grain of rice on the first square, two on the second, four on the third, and so one. The emperor found the request modest but accepted it. It was not until they got to the second half of the chessboard that the emperor realised where it would end. At the sixty-fourth square, the pile of rise equaled the size of Mount Everest.
10. Nietzsche, *Thus Spoke Zarathustra*, 41.
11. Levy, *Love and Sex with Robots*.
12. Holley, "Apple Co-founder on Artificial Intelligence."
13. Romm, "Americans Are More Afraid of Robots Than Death."
14. Smith and Anderson, "AI, Robotics, and the Future of Jobs."
15. This section on Stafford Beer and Project Cybersyn builds on Medina, *Cybernetic Revolutionaries*.
16. Medina, *Cybernetic Revolutionaries*, 25.
17. Morozov, "The Planning Machine."
18. Huebner, "A Possible Declining Trend for Worldwide Innovation," 985.
19. Taleb, *Antifragile*.
20. Kelly, "The New Socialism."
21. Mason, *Postcapitalism*.

22. The Economist, "Caught in the Net."
23. Gilder, *Microcosm*.
24. Carswell, *The End of Politics and the Birth of iDemocracy*.
25. Fukuyama, *The End of History*, 98–108.
26. Kaminsky, "Iran's Twitter Revolution."
27. Nixon, "Lack of Innovation Leaves EU Trailing."
28. OECD, "Territorial Review: Stockholm, Sweden 2006."
29. Legrain, *European Spring*, 367.
30. Gordon, "Secular Stagnation."
31. Gage, "The Venture Capital Secret."
32. Marmer et al., "Start-up Genome Report Extra," 10.
33. Schumpeter's vision of capitalism is explained in Schumpeter, *The Theory of Economic Development* and, in a different way, in Schumpeter, *Capitalism, Socialism, and Democracy*.
34. For a discerning analysis of the similarities between Marx and Schumpeter, see Elliott, "Marx and Schumpeter on Capitalism's Creative Destruction."
35. Schumpeter, *Capitalism, Socialism, and Democracy*, 61.
36. To avoid repetition in the book we will use terms like contestable innovation, big innovation, radical innovation, or game-changing innovation to describe the same phenomenon: innovation that contests markets. Similarly, we will often talk about contestable competition. As will be discussed in Chapter 5, there are various forms of competition. What we are interested in is the extent to which innovation leads to "contestable competition" – not a synonym for, but with a reference to, William Baumol's thesis of "contestable markets." By contestable competition we mean competition that defines a market and goes beyond aspects of competition that relate to variations in price and quality. It creates new markets or changes old markets to such an extent that competitors will have to fundamentally adapt in order to survive.
37. Mokyr, "Long-Term Economic Growth and the History of Technology," 4.
38. Broadberry et al., *British Economic Growth*.
39. Clark, *A Farewell to Alms*, 1.
40. Phelps, *Mass Flourishing*.
41. Our version of modern capitalism and its birth draws on several scholars such as Gregory Clark, David Landes, Joel Mokyr, and Edmund Phelps. There are differences between them but all anchor modern capitalism in a new structure of economic, political, social, and legal institutions that allowed a different type of behavior than in the past.
42. Gerschenkron, "The Modernization of Entrepreneurship."
43. McCloskey, *The Bourgeois Virtues: Ethics for an Age of Commerce*, presents a fascinating story of capitalism, its history, and its relation to beliefs and habits of the heart. It is similar to the intellectual history of capitalism in Hirschmann, *The Passions and the Interests*. Despite coming from a different end of the ideological spectrum, Hirschman portrays the intellectual foundation of capitalism as an offspring of philosophy and humanism, and describes its virtues of bringing calm, moderation, and humility to human behavior.
44. Rainey, "Britons are 'Lazy.'"
45. Mahbubani, "The Case Against the West."
46. McGregor, "China's Drive for 'Indigenous Innovation'"; Coase and Wang, *How China Became Capitalist*.
47. Schmitz, "Why Can't China Make a Good Ballpoint Pen?"; McGregor, "China's Drive for 'Indigenous Innovation.'"
48. Jonquières, "Who Is Afraid of China's High-Tech Challenge?"
49. For good analyses of the difficulties for China because of its heavy state influence in the economy, see McGregor, *No Ancient Wisdom, No Followers*; Bergsten et al., *China's Rise*; Pettis, *Avoiding the Fall*.
50. U.S. President, "Economic Report of the President."
51. Data retrieved from the Bureau of Economic Analysis, National Income and Product Account tables.

52. Federal Reserve, Financial Accounts of the United States, Household Debt Service Payments as a Percent of Disposable Personal Income.
53. Federal Reserve, Financial Account of the United States, Nonfinancial Corporate Business; Credit Market Debt as a Percentage of the Market Value of Corporate Equities.
54. Autor, Dorn, and Hanson, "The China Syndrome."
55. Dettmer et al., "The Dynamics of Structural Change."
56. Summers, "U.S. Economic Prospects."
57. Caballero, Farhi, and Hammour, "Speculative Growth."
58. Kahneman, *Thinking, Fast and Slow.*
59. Haldane, "Growing, Fast and Slow," 18.
60. Moore, *The Conduct of the Corporation*, 227.
61. Mitchell, "Financialism."
62. Wilson, *The Man in the Gray Flannel Suit.*
63. Whyte, *The Organization Man.*
64. Galbraith, *The New Industrial State*, 40.
65. Marris, *The Economic Theory of Managerial Capitalism*, 232.

2 When Capitalism Became Middle-Aged

1. Kaplan and Zingales, "Investment Cash Flow Sensitivities" gives an overview of the debate.
2. Ozbas and Scharfstein, "Evidence of the Dark Side of Internal Capital Markets."
3. Calculations based on data from Angus Maddison's updated file in 2010 on real GDP per capita in the world, at http://www.ggdc.net/MADDISON/oriindex.htm.
4. Van Ark, "How Unique Are Current Times?" 15.
5. OECD, *OECD Economic Outlook* (2014), 224.
6. Maddison, "Confessions of a Chiffrephile," 27.
7. Krugman, *The Age of Diminishing Expectations.*
8. See, for instance, Hall and Jones, "Why Do Some Countries Produce So Much More."
9. See, for instance, Comin, Hobijn and Rovito, "Five Facts You Need to Know."
10. In Chapter 8 we will discuss the issue of mismeasurement of productivity and other economic indicators.
11. For the United States, the postrecovery spurt in TFP growth is due to a sharp increase in 2009 that turned the moving trend upward for later years. The actual rates of TFP growth in 2010–13 are smaller.
12. Gordon, "Is U.S. Economic Growth Over?" offers a condensed version of Gordon's productivity analysis. The full analysis of U.S. living standards is in Gordon, *The Rise and Fall of American Growth.*
13. Gill and Raiser, *Golden Growth*, 12, fig. 5.
14. Cowen, *The Great Stagnation.*
15. OECD, "The Future of Productivity."
16. Pellegrino and Zingales, "Diagnosing the Italian Disease."
17. Altomonte et al., "Assessing Competitiveness."
18. Navaretti et al., "The Global Operations of European Firms."
19. Zingales, *A Capitalism for the People*, 5.
20. Leung and Rispoli, "The Distribution of Gross Domestic Product."
21. Cardarelli and Lusinyan, "U.S. Total Factor Productivity Slowdown."
22. van der Marel, "The Importance of Complementary Policy."
23. Cette, Fernald, and Mojon, "The Pre-Global-Financial-Crisis Slowdown."
24. OECD, *Skills Outlook 2013.*
25. Base and Svioska, "Productivity Growth."
26. McGowan and Andrews, "Labour Market Mismatch and Labour Productivity."
27. Browne, "S&P 500 Firms Hoard Cash as CAPEX Declines."
28. Krantz, "$194B! Apple's Cash Pile Hits Record."
29. Williams, "Cash, Caution, and Capex."

30. Sánchez and Yurdagul, "Why Are Corporations Holding So Much Cash?"
31. Chen and Chang, "Peer Effects on Corporate Cash Holdings."
32. Hodrick, "Are US Firms Really Holding Too Much Cash?"
33. OECD, "Corporate Saving and Investment."
34. Armenter, "The Rise of Corporate Savings."
35. In this chapter we are presenting several figures to show the amount of corporate spending on investment and the capital stock. To track a development over time, the amount of spending on one area should be set in relation to total corporate spending. For the sake of simplicity and to make figures both more understandable and comparable, we present them with GDP as the denominator. Like every other choice of presentation, it does not show all the nuances. As business investments also reflect the price of investment goods, which have fallen over time, business investments can decline while output remains unchanged. However, as the depreciation rate of invested capital also has increased, the net results still show falling shares of business investment.
36. With reference to the previous note on different ways of measuring business investments, U.S. statistical authorities present data on net business investments. The relevant data can be retrieved from the St. Louis Fed, "Net Domestic Investment: Private: Domestic Business."
37. Using data from the U.S. Bureau of Economic Analysis, "Fixed Assets Accounts Tables," tables 4.1 and 4.4.
38. While there can be some measurement problems leading to an understatement of recent business investment, the long-term trend is still disappointing. See Byrne and Pinto, "The Recent Slowdown in High-Tech Equipment Price Declines."
39. Another way of looking at it is to consider the level of capital expenditures in the economy, and the amount companies spend on physical capital. For the United States, the data show a similar trend as for business investments. Starting in the late 1970s or early 1980s, capital expenditure, or capex, as part of the general economy as well as part of corporate debt has been on the decline. Data show an uptick in the 1990s; the second half of that decade was a period when companies rapidly increased their stock of assets, primarily because of the ICT revolution that pushed companies to build up their stock of fixed assets. Public data sources for European countries are not as rich in historic data as for the United States. Yet data starting from the mid-1990s show a similar development as in the U.S., a slowly declining capex/GDP ratio.
40. See Chapter 8 on "Capitalism and Robots" for a longer discussion of expenditure on ICT software.
41. Buiter, Rahbari, and Seydl, "The Long-Run Decline in Advanced-Economy Investment."
42. Cowen and Zingales, "A Conversation with Luigi Zingales."
43. Jaruzelski, Staack, and Goehle, "Proven Paths to Innovation Success."
44. Paul et al., "How to Improve R&D Productivity."
45. OECD, "Prospects for Growth."
46. However, as will be discussed later in this chapter, companies have probably raised productivity through their foreign operations, but not to the degree that most people would believe. While, for instance, the growth in net worth of U.S. nonfinancial company holdings in foreign subsidiaries accelerated from the late 1980s up to the late 1990s, a trend decline followed and its trend growth in the past ten years has been lower than from the late 1950s to the early 1980s.
47. PR Newswire, "Dealogic Data."
48. M&A activity is generally higher in periods of high stock market valuation.
49. Doidge, Karolyi, and Stulz, "The U.S. Listing Gap."
50. Litan, "Among Ingredients Needed for Faster Growth?"
51. The Economist, "Corporate Cocaine."

3 The Color of Capitalism Is Gray

1. Team, "Harley-Davidson's Success."

2. Gross et al., "The Turnaround at Harley-Davidson."
3. Piketty, *Capital in the Twenty-First Century*.
4. Kohn and Yip-Williams, "The Separation of Ownership from Ownership."
5. Beetsma and Vos, "Stabilisers or Amplifiers."
6. Vitali, Glattfelder, and Battiston, "The Network of Global Corporate Control."
7. Minsky, "Uncertainty and the Institutional Structure of Capitalist Economies," sec. 4.
8. Kay, *Other People's Money*, 1–2.
9. Greenwood and Scharfstein, "The Growth of Modern Finance"; Weissmann, "How Wall Street Devoured Corporate America."
10. Federal Reserve, "Assets and Liabilities."
11. Harris, Schwedel, and Kim, "A World Awash in Money."
12. Greenwood and Scharfstein, "The Growth of Modern Finance."
13. Roxburgh et al., "The Emerging Equity Gap."
14. Awford, "Room for a (Souped-up) Ford Fiesta?"
15. OECD, "Pension Markets in Focus, 2014," 9–10.
16. Çelik and Isaksson, "Institutional Investors and Ownership Engagement"; Kohn and Yip-Williams. "The Separation of Ownership from Ownership."
17. PwC, "Asset Management 2020."
18. EFAMA, "Asset Management in Europe."
19. Pinkowitz and Williamson, "Bank Power and Cash Holdings."
20. Aoyagi and Ganelli, "Unstash the Cash! Corporate Governance Reform in Japan."
21. TEA, "Texas Permanent School Fund: Comprehensive Annual Financial Report," 2014.
22. SWF Institute, "Fund Rankings," 2015.
23. SWF Institute, "Fund Rankings," 2015.
24. Karaian, "Norway's Gargantuan Sovereign Wealth Fund"; NBIM, "The Fund's Market Value," 2015.
25. PwC, "Asset Management 2020," 17.
26. SWF Institute, "Fund Rankings," 2015.
27. SWF Institute, "The Public Investor 100 – 2014 Rankings," 44.
28. Johnson, "Gulf States Redirect SWF Cash."
29. Couturier, Sola, and Stonham, "Are Sovereign Funds 'White Knights'?"
30. Blundell-Wignall, Hu, and Yermo, "Sovereign Wealth and Pension Fund Issues," 4.
31. NBIM, "The Fund's Market Value," 2015.
32. OECD, "Ageing and Employment Policies."
33. Cournède, "The Political Economy of Delaying Fiscal Consolidation."
34. Cournède, "The Political Economy of Delaying Fiscal Consolidation," 10.
35. Magnus, *The Age of Aging* provides a thorough analysis of retirement savings and their relation to the broader economy.
36. United Nations, *World Population Prospects: The 2012 Revision*.
37. Cournède, "The Political Economy of Delaying Fiscal Consolidation."
38. Iwamoto, "Abandoned Homes Haunt Japanese Neighbourhoods."
39. Galbraith, *The New Industrial State*.
40. Smith, *The Wealth of Nations*.
41. Isaksson and Çelik. "Who Cares?" 42.
42. Goldstein, "The State of Engagement between U.S. Corporations and Shareholders."
43. Van der Elst, " Revisiting Shareholder Activism at AGMs"; Van der Elst and Aslan, "The Economic Consequences of Large Shareholder Activism."
44. Berle and Means, *The Modern Corporation and Private Property*.
45. Drucker, *The Unseen Revolution*, 1.
46. Markowitz, "Portfolio Selection."
47. Bhide, "The Hidden Costs of Stock Market Liquidity," 31.
48. Pfleiderer, "Is Modern Portfolio Theory Dead?"
49. Haldane, "Patience and Finance."
50. Zweig, "Why Hair-Trigger Traders Lose the Race."
51. NYSE, "Fact Book Online: Interactive Viewer."

52. MoneyBeat, "Why Hair-Trigger Traders Lose the Race" and NYSEData.com Factbook, "Interactive Viewer."
53. Philippon and Reshef, "Wages and Human Capital in the U.S. Financial Industry."
54. Greenwood and Scharfstein, "The Growth of Modern Finance."
55. Cecchetti and Kharroubi, "Why Growth in Finance Is a Drag on the Real Economy."
56. Arcand, Berkes, and Panizza, "Too Much Finance?"; Cecchetti and Kharroubi, "Reassessing the Impact of Finance on Growth."
57. Swagel, "The Financial Crisis."
58. Cecchetti and Kharroubi, "Why Growth in Finance Is a Drag on the Real Economy."
59. Christensen, Kaufman, and Shih, "Innovation Killers," 1–2.
60. Piketty, *Capital in the Twenty-First Century*, 264–81.

4 The Rise and Rise Again of Corporate Managerialism

1. Martti, *Nokia: The Inside Story*.
2. Steinbock, *The Nokia Revolution*.
3. Ahmad, *Nokia's Smartphone Problem*.
4. Kuittinen, "Nokia Sells Handset Business to Microsoft."
5. Lomas, "Nokia's $7.2BN Devices & Services Exit."
6. Cheng, "It's Official: Motorola Mobility Now Belongs to Lenovo."
7. Bass, "Microsoft's Concept Videos."
8. Jenkins, "Jenkins: Only Bill Gates Can Change Microsoft."
9. Yarow, "Here's What Steve Ballmer Thought about the iPhone."
10. A good survey of companies failing at exits is McGrath, *The End of Competitive Advantage*.
11. Steinberg, "Among the First to Fall at I.B.M."
12. Crainer, "'Saving Big Blue.'"
13. Clinch, "How Apple Prompted This Country's Downgrade."
14. Schumpeter, *Capitalism, Socialism and Democracy*, 132.
15. Coase, "The Nature of the Firm," 388.
16. Oliver Williamson, who received the Nobel Prize in economics for his work on economic governance, developed the idea of firm boundaries and put the emphasis on the internal or endogenous capacity of the firm to generate output that is more competitive than the market.
17. Santos and Eisenhardt, "Organizational Boundaries and Theories of Organization," 491.
18. Coase, "The Nature of the Firm," 390.
19. Coase, "The Nature of the Firm," 404–5.
20. Zenger, Felin, and Bigelow, "Theories of the Firm–Market Boundary."
21. Tett, *The Silo Effect*.
22. Morieux, "How Too Many Rules at Work Keep You from Getting Things Done."
23. See, for instance, Caliendo and Rossi-Hansberg, "The Impact of Trade on Organization and Productivity."
24. Zhou, "Coordination Costs, Organization Structure and Firm Growth"
25. Langlois and Everett, "Complexity, Genuine Uncertainty, and the Economics of Organization"; Joskow, "Vertical Integration."
26. Strom, "Big Companies Pay Later."
27. Rajan and Zingales, "The Firm as a Dedicated Hierarchy."
28. Bhide, *The Origin and Evolution of New Business*, 94.
29. Rajan and Zingales, "The Firm as a Dedicated Hierarchy," 7.
30. Teece, "Profiting from Technological Innovation."
31. Jensen, "Agency Cost of Free Cash Flow, Corporate Finance, and Takeovers."
32. Stein, "Agency, Information and Corporate Investment"; Matvos and Seru, "Resource Allocation within Firms."
33. See Berger and Ofek, "Diversification's Effect on Firm Value"; Rajan, Servaes, and Zingales, "The Cost of Diversity."

34. Scharfstein and Stein, "The Dark Side of Internal Capital Markets."
35. Scharfstein and Stein. "The Dark Side of Internal Capital Markets."
36. Büthe and Mattli, *The New Global Rulers*.
37. Kelly, "The Majority of iPhone Users Admit to 'Blind Loyalty.'"
38. Kelly, "The Majority of iPhone Users Admit to 'Blind Loyalty.'"
39. Johnson, *De Lyfte Landet*, 21.
40. All quotes are from Galbraith, *The New Industrial State*, 19.
41. Morieux, "Smart Rules."
42. Bain & Co., "Busy CEOs"
43. Langlois and Cosgel, "Frank Knight on Risk."
44. Decker et al., "The Role of Entrepreneurship," 10.
45. Harvard Business Review, *Harvard Business Review on Strategies for Growth*, 25–6.
46. Byrne, "The Man Who Invented Management."
47. Porter, "How Competitive Forces Shape Strategy."
48. Stephenson, "What Causes Top Management Teams to Make Poor Strategic Decisions?" 22.
49. Rogers and Blenko "The High-Performance Organization."
50. Morieux, "Smart Rules."
51. Morieux, "Smart Rules," 3.
52. Buchanan, "You Stab My Back, I'll Stab Yours," 58–9.
53. The Economist, "Guru: Igor Ansoff."
54. Mintzberg and Lampel, "Reflecting on the Strategy Process."
55. Perhaps Henry Ford did not put it exactly like that, but it is an indicative view of innovation. See Vlaskovits, "Henry Ford, Innovation, and That 'Faster Horse' Quote."
56. Kim and Mauborgne, *Blue Ocean Strategy*.
57. Thiel with Masters, *Zero to One*.
58. Millman and Rubenfeld, "Compliance Officer: Dream Career?"
59. Taibbi, "Why Isn't Wall Street in Jail?"
60. European Commission, "Progress of Financial Reforms."
61. Hayek, "The Use of Knowledge in Society."
62. Millman and Rubenfeld, "Compliance Officer: Dream Career?"
63. Browning, "Why Chief Compliance Officers Are More Important Than Ever."
64. Fleming, "The Age of the Compliance Officer Arrives."
65. Härle et al., "Basel III and European Banking."
66. Financial Services Committee, "One Year Later: The Consequences of the Dodd-Frank Act," 13.
67. PwC, "Staffing and Budgets Are Rising."
68. Hill, Sears, and Melanson, "4000 Clicks."
69. Christensen, Kaufman, and Shih, "Innovation Killers," 1–2.
70. Christensen, Kaufman, and Shih, "Innovation Killers," 4–5.
71. Graham, Harvey, and Rajgopal, "The Economic Implications of Corporate Financial Reporting."

5 The Two Faces (and Phases) of Globalization

1. Hicks, "Annual Survey of Economic Theory: The Theory of Monopoly."
2. Montgomerie, "What the World Thinks of Capitalism."
3. Emmott, "Everybody's Favourite Monsters: A Survey of Multinationals."
4. See books like Klein, *No Logo*; Lasch, *The Revolt of the Elites*; Luttwak, *Turbocapitalism*.
5. Bernard, Jensen, and Schott, "Importers, Exporters and Multinationals"
6. Galbraith, *The New Industrial State*.
7. Micklethwait and Wooldridge, *A Future Perfect* describes elegantly the tone and substance of triumphalist globalization.
8. Woodward, *Maestro: Greenspan's Fed and the American Boom*.
9. Time Magazine, "The Committee to Save the World."

10. Rubin and Weisberg, *In an Uncertain World.*
11. Ruggie, "International Regimes, Transactions, and Change."
12. Smith, *The Theory of Moral Sentiments.*
13. Levinson, *The Box.*
14. Bernhofen, El-Sahli, and Kneller, "Estimating the Effects of the Container Revolution," 9–10.
15. Authors' calculation based on World Trade Organization, Statistics Database, at http://stat.wto.org/Home/WSDBHome.aspx?Language=E.
16. Authors' calculation based on World Trade Organization, Statistics Database, at http://stat.wto.org/Home/WSDBHome.aspx?Language=E.
17. Authors' calculation based on World Bank, World Development Indicators, at http://databank.worldbank.org/data/reports.aspx?source=world-development-indicators#.
18. Johnston, "Globalise or Fossilise!"
19. Smithers, *The Road to Recovery*, appendix 2.
20. For a comparison, see Lebrun and Pérez Ruiz, "Demand Patterns in France, Germany, and Belgium," 5.
21. The Economist, "The Sick Man of the Euro."
22. Sinn, "The Pathological Export Boom and the Bazaar Effect."
23. Aichele, Felbermayr, and Heiland, "Neues von der Basarökonomie."
24. Sally, *States and Firms.*
25. Servan-Schreiber, *The American Challenge.*
26. Safarian, *Multinational Enterprise and Public Policy.*
27. Dunning, *The Globalization of Business.*
28. IMD, *IMD World Competitiveness Yearbook.*
29. Hansakul and Levinger, "China-EU Relations," 2.
30. Galbraith, *The New Industrial State,* 38.
31. Bernard, Jensen, and Schott, "Importers, Exporters and Multinationals."
32. UNCTAD, "World Investment Report 2013."
33. Altomonte et al., "Global Value Chains during the Great Trade Collapse."
34. Baldwin, "Trade and Industrialisation after Globalisation's 2nd Unbundling."
35. Manyika et al., "Digital Globalization."
36. Baldwin, "Globalisation."
37. Desai, "The Decentering of the Global Firm."
38. Baldwin and Robert-Nicoud, "Trade-in-Goods and Trade-in-Tasks."
39. Krugman, "Growing World Trade." For documentation of literature and trade patterns, see also WTO, "World Trade Report 2008."
40. Escaith and Inomata, "Trade Patterns and Global Value Chains in East Asia."
41. Hummels, Rapoport, and Yi, "Vertical Specialization."
42. Lanz and Miroudot, "Intra-firm Trade."
43. Bernard et al., "Intra-firm Trade and Product Contractibility."
44. Timmer et al., "Slicing up Global Value Chains," 104.
45. Dedrick, Kraemer, and Linden, "Who Profits from Innovation in Global Value Chains?"
46. Athukorala, "Production Networks and Trade Patterns in East Asia."
47. IMF, "German-Central European Supply Chain – Cluster Report."
48. For data on the foreign value-added content of exports in Europe, see Amador, Cappariello, and Stehrer, "Global Value Chains: A View from the Euro Area."
49. Stehrer and Stöllinger, "The Central European Manufacturing Core."
50. Nordås, Pinali, and Grosso, " Logistics and Time as a Trade Barrier."
51. Boddin and Henze, "International Trade and the Servitization of Manufacturing"; Lodefalk, "The Role of Services for Manufacturing Firm Exports."
52. National Board of Trade (Sweden), "Everybody Is in Services," 9.
53. Grossman and Hart, "The Costs and Benefits of Ownership."
54. This view draws on Baumol, Panzar, and Willig, *Contestable Markets and the Theory of Industry Structure.*
55. Marx, *Capital,* ch. 32.
56. Shields, "Consolidation and Concentration in the U.S. Dairy Industry"

57. Corbae and D'Erasmo, "A Quantitative Model of Banking Industry Dynamics."
58. FCC, "18th Mobile Wireless Competition Report."
59. Murray, "5 Things You Didn't Know about the Fortune 500."
60. Freund, *Rich People Poor Countries*, 55.
61. Hillerud, "Ericsson var före Apple med paddan."
62. OECD, "The Future of Productivity."
63. Antràs and Yeaple, "Multinational Firms and the Structure of International Trade."
64. However, a note of caution is warranted. There are some differences between multinationals and home-market firms. The former is more typical in the manufacturing sector while the latter has a greater share of service-oriented firms, and they are usually more local. Furthermore, multinationals tend to be more active in sectors typically characterized by a higher R&D profile, which means there is a greater flow of skills in those firms than in home-market firms. See e.g. Barefoot and Mataloni "Operations of U.S. Multinational Companies"; Mayer and Ottaviano, "The Happy Few."
65. See e.g. comparisons between various European country groups in Van Ark et al., "Recent Changes in Europe's Competitive Landscape."
66. OECD, *Measuring Globalisation*; Hummels, Ishii, and Yi, "The Nature and Growth of Vertical Specialization."
67. Antràs and Yeaple, "Multinational Firms and the Structure of International Trade."
68. Cantwell, "Blurred Boundaries between Firms."
69. Kelly, "Sunk Costs, Rationality, and Acting for the Sake of the Past."
70. Economist William Baumol makes this case forcefully. Somewhat surprisingly, he does so by arguing the case of bureaucratic and routinized innovation. Baumol, *The Free-Market Innovation Machine*.
71. Simons, "Is the Cost of Innovation Falling?"
72. See, for instance, Rajan, Servaes, and Zingales, "The Cost of Diversity."
73. Seru, "Firm Boundaries Matter"; Scharfstein and Stein, "The Dark Side of Internal Capital Markets."
74. Hayek, "The Use of Knowledge in Society."
75. Dunning, "Location and the Multinational Enterprise."
76. Baumol, *The Free-Market Innovation Machine*.

6 The Return of the Regulators

1. Reagan, "The President's News Conference."
2. Frum, "Paris Taxi Shortage." OECD, "Taxi Services" suggests that the number of taxis in Paris actually went down between the early 1930s and the late 1960s, and that the number of taxi licenses only increased by 1,000 in the 40 years between 1967 and 2007.
3. OECD, "Taxi Services," 110.
4. Mawad and Fouquet, " Paris Police 'Boers' Pursuing Uber Drivers."
5. Drozdiak, "Uber Launches Petition over Brussels UberPop Ban."
6. Sheftalovich, "'Scrooge' Brussels Mayor Dampens Uber's Christmas Spirit."
7. BBC, "Uber Banned in Germany."
8. New York City capped the number of yellow cab medallions to 16,900 in 1937. Now, however, there are only about 13,500 such licenses issued.
9. Zingales, *A Capitalism for the People*, 4.
10. Thomas, *Investment Incentives and the Global Competition for Capital*.
11. Dervis, "Is Uber a Threat to Democracy?"
12. OECD, *Businesses' Views on Red Tape*.
13. Olson, *The Logic of Collective Action*.
14. Sellar and Yateman, *1066 and All That*.
15. This anecdote is from Diamandis and Kotler, *Abundance*.
16. Acemoglu and Robinson, *Why Nations Fail*.
17. Downes, "Fewer, Faster, Smarter."
18. Goodwin, "The History of Mobile Phones."
19. Rogers and Ramsey, "Tesla to Stop Selling Electric Cars in New Jersey."

20. Lepore, " How Santa Monica Will Enforce Its Airbnb Ban."
21. Coldwell, "Airbnb's Legal Troubles."
22. Tabarrok, "Book Review: 'Innovation Breakdown.'"
23. Gulfo, *Innovation Breakdown.*
24. Kay, "Miracles of Productivity Hidden in the Modern Home."
25. Erixon, "EU Policies on Online Entrepreneurship."
26. Tabarrok, "Book Review: 'Innovation Breakdown.'"
27. CSDD, "Cost of Drug Development."
28. Grabowski and Hansen, "Cost of Developing a New Drug."
29. Herper, " The Truly Staggering Cost of Inventing New Drugs."
30. Roy, "Stifling New Cures."
31. CSDD, "Cost of Drug Development."
32. Basu and Hassenplug, "Patient Access to Medical Devices."
33. That figure is for 2010 when one of the authors was given a guided tour of the FedEx hub.
34. Button and Christensen, "Unleashing Innovation."
35. Comin and Hobijn, "Technology Diffusion and Postwar Growth."
36. Agarwal and Gort, "First Mover Advantage."
37. Jaffe and Trajtenberg, *Patents, Citations and Innovations.*
38. Mansfield, "How Rapidly Does New Industrial Technology Leak Out?"
39. Lanjouw, "Patent Protection in the Shadow of Infringement."
40. Baumol, *The Free Market Innovation Machine.*
41. Comin and Hobijn, "An Exploration of Technology Diffusion."
42. Arnold, Nicoletti, and Scarpetta, "Regulation, Resource Reallocation and Productivity Growth."
43. Thiel with Masters, *Zero to One.*
44. Frey and Osborne, "Technology at Work: The Future of Innovation and Employment."
45. Anders, "WhatsApp's Growth Exceeds Christianity's First 19 Centuries."
46. Gerschenkron, *Economic Backwardness in Historical Perspective.*
47. Brown, " Nowhere in the World Uses Mobile Banking as Much as Africa."
48. Aeppel, "50 Million Users."
49. Hannemyr, "The Internet as Hyperbole."
50. These examples are from the Institute for Justice, a US "National Law Firm for Liberty," at http://www.ij.org/pillar/economic-liberty/?post_type=case#all.
51. The figure comes from the Global Trade Alert's database, http://www.globaltradealert.org.
52. Vetter, "The Single European Market 20 Years On," 14.
53. European Commission, "Upgrading the Single Market," note 19.
54. These examples are from The Economist, "Rules for Fools" and the Institute for Justice website.
55. Kleiner, "Reforming Occupational Licensing Policies."
56. Almeida, Campello, and Weisbach, "Corporate Financial and Investment Policies."
57. Kelly, Lustig, and Van Nieuwerburgh, "Too-Systemic-to-Fail."
58. Ernst & Young, " The World of Financial Instruments Is More Complex."
59. See the analysis in Kay, "The Kay Review."
60. Haldane and Davies, "The Short Long."
61. Budish, Roin, and Williams, "Do Firms Underinvest in Long-Term Research?"

7 Killing Frontier Innovation with Regulatory Complexity and Uncertainty

1. European Parliament, "Resolution of 20 May 2015."
2. Gensch et al., "Assistance to the Commission."
3. CSES, "Interim Evaluation."
4. Dekkers, "Why Europe Lags on Innovation."
5. Sunstein, "Beyond the Precautionary Principle."
6. Bailey, "Precautionary Tale."

7. European Commission, "Nanomaterials."
8. Rabesandratana, "E.U. Court Annuls GM Potato Approval."
9. Dunmore, "Monsantoo Withdraw EU Approval Requests."
10. Moynihan, "What Are Quantum Dots."
11. Ahmed, "Quantum dots."
12. NASA, " High Efficiency Quantum Dot III-V Thermophotovoltaic Cell."
13. Stern, "Innovation under Regulatory Uncertainty."
14. Mandel and Carew, " Regulatory Improvement Commission."
15. Carnegy and Foy, "French Ban on Mercedes Cars."
16. McLaughlin and Williams, "The Consequences of Regulatory Accumulation."
17. Al-Ubaydli and McLaughlin, "RegData: A Numerical Database on Industry-Specific Regulations."
18. Anderson et al, *Autonomous Vehicle Technology*.
19. Thierer and Hagemann, "Removing Roadblocks to Intelligent Vehicles."
20. Winston and Mannering, "Implementing Technology to Improve Public Highway Performance," 7.
21. Rodrik, "Policy Uncertainty and Private Investment"; Hassett and Metcalf, "Investment with Uncertain Tax Policy."
22. Gulen and Ion, "Policy Uncertainty and Corporate Investment."
23. Baker, Bloom, and Davis, "Has Economic Policy Uncertainty Hampered the Recovery?"
24. See, for example, Bartelsman, Haltiwanger, and Scarpetta, "Cross-Country Differences in Productivity."
25. Greenstone, List, and Syverson, "The Effects of Environmental Regulation."
26. Golec, Hegde, and Vernon, "Pharmaceutical R&D Spending and Threats of Price Regulation" shows how R&D spending in a highly innovative sector such as pharmaceuticals gets distorted by price regulations.
27. See, for example, Atkinson and Garner, "Regulation as Industrial Policy"; Gerard and Lave, "Implementing Technology-Forcing Policies."
28. See, for example, Prieger, "Regulatory Delay and the Timing of Product Innovation."
29. This section draws on Erixon, "Biofuels Reform in the European Union"; Erixon, "The Rising Trend."
30. Dabla-Norris et al., "The New Normal."
31. Acemoglu, Aghion, and Zilibotti, "Distance to Frontier, Selection, and Economic Growth."
32. Ranasinghe, "Impact of Policy Distortions"; Gabler and Poschke, "Experimentation by Firms, Distortions, and Aggregate Productivity"; Da-Rocha, Mendes Tavares, and Restuccia, "Policy Distortions and Aggregate Productivity with Endogenous Establishment-Level Productivity"; Bhattacharya, Guner, and Ventura, "Distortions, Endogenous Managerial Skills and Productivity Differences"; Gabler and Poschke, "Experimentation by Firms, Distortions, and Aggregate Productivity"; Bartelsman, Haltiwanger, and Scarpetta, "Cross-Country Differences in Productivity"; Restuccia and Rogerson, "Policy Distortions and Aggregate Productivity."
33. Gabler and Poschke, "Experimentation by Firms, Distortions, and Aggregate Productivity."
34. See for example Bhattacharya, Guner, and Ventura, "Distortions, Endogenous Managerial Skills and Productivity Differences."

8 Capitalism and Robots

1. The Economist, "Coming to an Office Near You."
2. Gapper and Waters, "Google Chief Warns of IT Threat."
3. Matulka, "Timeline: The History of the Electric Car."
4. Deffree, "Karl Benz Drives the First Automobile."
5. Krugman, "The Big Meh."
6. ATA, "New ATA Report Shows Growing Shortage of Qualified Truck Drivers."
7. Akst, "What Can We Learn from Past Anxiety over Automation?"

8. Keynes, "Economic Possibilities for our Grandchildren."
9. LIFE Magazine, "Parking Consultants and Surfboarding Instructors May Keep the Economy Going."
10. Williams, *The Year 2000*.
11. Akst, "What Can We Learn from past Anxiety over Automation?"
12. Ad Hoc Committee on the Triple Revolution, "The Triple Revolution."
13. Tracy, "Why Some of Google's Coolest Projects Flop Badly."
14. Tracy, "Why Some of Google's Coolest Projects Flop Badly."
15. E-money Blog, The History of Electronic Payments.
16. MIT Technology Review, "Technology Repaints the Payment Landscape," 66.
17. Mainelli and Milne, "The Impact and Potential of Blockchain on the Securities Transaction Lifecycle," 4.
18. Mainelli and Milne, "The Impact and Potential of Blockchain on the Securities Transaction Lifecycle," 5.
19. Simmons, "George Foster: Are Startups Really Job Engines?"
20. AlixPartners, Press release on "C.A.S.E. – Car of the Future."
21. Phelps, *Mass Flourishing*, 19.
22. Hathaway and Litan, "Declining Business Dynamism in the United States."
23. Sahin and Pugsley, *Grown-up Business Cycles*.
24. Sahin and Pugsley, *Grown-up Business Cycles*.
25. Sahin and Pugsley, *Grown-up Business Cycles*. Startup employment went from 4 to 2 percent.
26. Buchanan, "American Entrepreneurship Is Actually Vanishing."
27. Simon and Barr, "Endangered Species."
28. Litan, "Start-Up Slowdown."
29. OECD, "The Future of Productivity."
30. Gordon, "The Demise of U.S. Economic Growth," figs. 9 and 10.
31. Haltiwanger, Hathaway, and Miranda, "Declining Business Dynamism in the U.S. High-Technology Sector," 9.
32. Hatzius and Dawsey, "Doing the Sums on Productivity Paradox v2.0."
33. Fernald and Wang, "Why Has the Cyclicality of Productivity Changed?"
34. Brynjolfsson and McAfee, *The Second Machine Age*, 105.
35. Brynjolfsson and McAfee, *The Second Machine Age*, 105.
36. Fernald, "Productivity and Potential Output."
37. Fernald and Wang, "The Recent Rise and Fall of Rapid Productivity Growth."
38. Frey and Osborne, "Technology at Work," 62.
39. Summers, "Making Sense of the Productivity Slowdown," 5.
40. Cardarelli and Lusinyan, "U.S. Total Factor Productivity Slowdown."
41. Syversen, "Challenges to Mismeasurement Explanations."
42. Syversen, "Challenges to Mismeasurement Explanations."
43. Copeland, "Seasonality, Consumer Heterogenity and Price Indexes."
44. The data reference is from the US Bureau of Economic Analysis's chained price index for IT software.
45. The data reference is from the US Bureau of Economic Analysis's chained price index for IT software.
46. Nakamura and Soloveichik. "Valuing 'Free' Media across Countries in GDP."
47. Braithwaite, "Unicorns Beware."
48. Robinson, "Ex-BOE Bean."
49. Marx's theory is not crystal clear and has been interpreted differently. See Blaug, *Economic Theory in Retrospect*.
50. Smithers, *The Road to Recovery*, 28–32.; Lebrun and Ruiz, "Demand Pattern in France, Germany and Belgium," 5.
51. Galston, "Closing the Productivity and Pay Gap."
52. Brynjolfsson and McAfee, *The Second Machine Age*, 132.
53. Mishel, Gould and Bivens, "Wage Stagnation in Nine Charts."
54. Blanchard, Solow, and Wilson, "Productivity and Unemployment."

55. For overview, see Tang, "Employment and Productivity."
56. Manyika et al., "Growth and Renewal in the United States," 28–9.
57. OECD, "Growing Income Inequality in OECD Countries."
58. Mui, "Companies Have Found Something to Give their Workers."
59. Mui, "Companies Have Found Something to Give their Workers."
60. Lawrence, "The Growing Gap between Real Wages and Labor Productivity."
61. Shapiro, "Income Growth and Decline."
62. Karabarbounis and Neiman, "The Global Decline of the Labor Share."
63. Benzell et al., "Robots Are Us."
64. Groemling, "Falling Labor Share in Germany," 1–20.
65. Feldstein, "Did Wages Reflect Growth in Productivity?"; Anderson, "Productivity Growth?"
66. Bridgam, "Is Labor's Loss Capital's Gain?"
67. Diewert and Fox. "The New Economy and an Old Problem."
68. Lawrence, "Recent Declines in Labor's Share in US Income."
69. Acemoglu and Robinson, "The Rise and Decline of General Laws of Capitalism."
70. Pessoa and Van Reenen, "Decoupling of Wage Growth and Productivity Growth?"
71. Roine and Waldenström, "On the Role of Capital Gains in Swedish Income Inequality."
72. Konjunktur Institutet, Lönebildningsrapporten, 30.
73. US President, "Economic Report," 34.
74. US President, Economic Report," 34.
75. Mokyr, "What Today's Economic Gloomsayers Are Missing."
76. Frey and Osborne, "The Future of Employment," 45.
77. Ford, *Rise of the Robots,* 284.
78. Kan, "Foxconn Expects Robots to Take over More Factory Work."
79. Kan, "Foxconn Expects Robots to Take over More Factory Work."
80. Kan, "Foxconn's CEO Backpedals on Robot Takeover at Factories."
81. IFR, "Robots Improve Manufacturing Success and Create Jobs."
82. Graetz and Michaels, "Robots at Work."
83. Fox Nation, "Obama Blames ATMs for High Unemployment."
84. Bessen, *Learning by Doing,* 108.
85. Approximately in 1745 in England, and one year later in France
86. Joyce, *Ulysses,* 82.
87. Rothschild, "The Sourdough Hotel."
88. Marx and Engels, The *Communist Manifesto,* 12.
89. Haltiwanger, Hathaway, and Miranda, "Declining Business Dynamism in the US High-Technology Sector," 1.
90. Andrews, Criscuolo, and Gal, "Frontier Firms, Technology Diffusion and Public Policy."
91. Andrews, Criscuolo, and Gal, "Frontier Firms, Technology Diffusion and Public Policy," 14–15.

9 The Future and How to Prevent It

1. Buiter, Rahbari, and Seydl, "The Long-Run Decline in Advanced-Economy Investment."
2. Kotlikoff and Burns, *The Clash of Generations,* 229.
3. Wilson and Purushothaman, "Dreaming with BRICs."
4. Xie, "Goldman's BRIC Era Ends."
5. Das, *India Grows at Night.*
6. Magnus, "Hitting a BRIC Wall."
7. IMF, "Adjusting to Lower Commodity Prices."
8. Hoenig, "Back to Basics."
9. The Economist, "One Regulator to Rule Them All."
10. Zingales, "Does Finance Benefit Society?" table 1.
11. IFAC, "Is Regulation Impacting Growth?"
12. Roxburgh et al., "The Emerging Equity Gap."

13. Cournède, "The Political Economy of Delaying Fiscal Consolidation."
14. EIOPA, "First EU Stress Test for Occupational Pensions."
15. Pension Protection Fund, "PPF 7800 Index."
16. Delevingne "Outlook for Pensions Is Pretty Awful."
17. Schoen, "$2 Trillion Deficit for Public Pension Funds."
18. Delevingne "Outlook for Pensions is Pretty Awful."
19. Sorkin, "BlackRock's Chief."
20. Stewart, "Scrap Triple Lock."
21. The Economist, "Shades of Grey."
22. Montgomerie, "What the World Thinks of Capitalism."
23. Arendt, *The Human Condition*, 101.
24. da Vinci, *The Notebooks of Leonardo da Vinci*, 88.
25. Data from the World Bank's *World Development Indicators*, GDP per capita at constant 2005 U.S. dollars.
26. See Nasdaq at http://www.nasdaq.com/symbol/brk.a and http://www.nasdaq.com/symbol/brk.b.
27. Surowiecki, "Unequal Shares."
28. PwC, "Redefining Business Success in a Changing World."
29. Barth et al., "It's Where You Work"; Song et al., "Firming Up Inequality.".
30. Davis and Haltiwanger, "Labour Market Fluidity and Economic Performance."
31. van der Marel, "The Importance of Complementary Policy."
32. Thierer "Embracing a Culture of Permissionless Innovation."
33. Mokyr, *Lever of Riches*, 182.
34. Bradley Foundation, "Survey by Buckley Program at Yale."
35. Ali, "Oxford University Law Students Being Issued with 'Trigger Warnings.'"